Classroom Management

T0083583

Hong Kong
Teacher Education

General Series Editor: Kerry J. Kennedy, The Hong Kong Institute of Education

The volumes in the series set out to provide contextualized reflections on issues that most teachers come across. Each volume will delve into discussions that will enhance and improve teaching skills. The series covers a wide range of topics including curriculum and assessment, understanding and managing diversity, guidance and counselling, and human development.

Classroom Management

Creating a Positive Learning Environment

Hue Ming-tak and Li Wai-shing

香港大學出版社

HONG KONG UNIVERSITY PRESS

Hong Kong University Press
14/F Hing Wai Centre
7 Tin Wan Praya Road
Aberdeen
Hong Kong

ISBN 978-962-209-888-6

Secure On-line Ordering
http://www.hkupress.org

British Library Cataloguing-in-Publication Data
A catalogue record for this book is available from the British Library.

Printed and bound by ColorPrint Production Co. Ltd. in Hong Kong, China

Contents

Foreword by Kerry J. Kennedy   vii

Preface   ix

1. Understanding Classroom Behaviour and Situations   1

2. The Influence of Chinese Culture on Hong Kong Classrooms   21

3. Effective Classroom Management   45

4. Managing Misbehaviour   63

5. Approaches to Students' Misbehaviour   85

6. Enhancing Communication and Strengthening Teacher-Student Relationships   109

7. Promoting Positive Peer Relationships   129

8. Collaboration with Colleagues to Improve Classroom Behaviour   149

9. Working with Parents to Create a Positive Classroom Environment   165

10. Learning from Classroom Experience: Reflection and Action Research   183

Index   203

Foreword

Teachers play a fundamental role in the social and economic development of any society. Their preparation as professionals to meet the challenges of post-modern living is a key priority for both governments and universities. Many changes have taken place in teacher education since the establishment of formal institutions of teaching training in Hong Kong over one hundred years ago. Today, the Hong Kong government is committed to an "all graduate, all trained" profession and university level institutions are now responsible for all teacher education across early childhood, primary and secondary education. It is against this background that the Hong Kong Teacher Education Series has been developed.

The incentive behind the series is simple: the need for resources that reflect local values, professional contexts and cultures. The market for resources is dominated by Western materials that are either embedded in non-local contexts or that assume there is a general context that is relevant across cultural boundaries. Such resources, of course, can be useful but they do not help Hong Kong's future teachers appreciate and understand the unique contexts that characterize Hong Kong's schools. Thus the Hong Kong Teacher Education Series will provide culturally relevant resources that embed both theory and practice in local classroom contexts.

Hong Kong's aspirations to be a bilingual triliterate society will be reflected in the Hong Kong Teacher Education Series. Dual-language versions of the resource material will be produced for use in either Chinese or English teacher education contexts. This is recognition of the centrality of language in the lives of Hong Kong people. It places value on both English and Chinese in the teaching/learning process and will ensure that the resources are accessible to all teacher education students in Hong Kong.

The initial titles that have been selected for this series reflect the needs of future teachers in Hong Kong's classroom: classroom management, assessment for learning, managing and understanding diversity. Subsequent titles will deal with curriculum, human development, and school guidance and counselling. These professional areas will introduce teacher education students directly to the concepts, ideas and practices they will need as young professionals in Hong Kong's classroom. Case studies of actual school practice will bring the text to life as students engage with the realities of actual teachers and classrooms. This will help to prepare them in a realistic and practical way so that they are well prepared for their own students and classrooms.

As important as the focus on practice is in this series, it does not mean that theory has been neglected. Concepts, ideas and issues are located in broader theoretical and cultural contexts but not in an abstract way. For teachers, classrooms and students provide the ultimate context against with theories can be tested and cultures can be better understood. In these challenging and demanding times, teachers need to be fully equipped with the latest thinking and ideas based on research and advances in understanding. Yet these must always be tested in the laboratory of practice so that teachers are not only knowledgeable but they also know how to translate this knowledge into action that can benefit students.

In developing this series, I have been grateful for the dedication of my colleagues at the Hong Kong Institute of Education. They have taken up the challenge of writing and shown great commitment in providing meaningful and relevant resources for their students. I am also grateful to Senior Management at the Hong Kong Institute of Education since they supported this endeavour from the very beginning. I have also been encouraged by Hong Kong University Press which has seen the value of the series and the need to support Hong Kong's future teachers. As is so often the case in educational matters, collaboration and cooperation can produce great outcomes, and I believe such has been the case in this instance.

Hong Kong's future is in no small way linked to the quality of its teachers and their capacity to support the learning of young people throughout this new century. Hopefully, the Hong Kong Teacher Education Series will contribute to this important objective.

Kerry J. Kennedy
General Series Editor
The Hong Kong Teacher Education Series

Preface

Teachers in Hong Kong, like those elsewhere, are concerned about classroom discipline. During the period we worked with them, they had expressed grave concern about how to handle students' misbehaviour positively and effectively. This is the case particularly for those who feel it necessary to defend their roles as teachers when facing difficult classes and spend most of the time on discipline rather than instruction. This book is based on listening to their inner voices and recognizing their needs. In it, we have attempted to provide practical ideas and theoretical frameworks for student teachers, in-service teachers and school managers to help them develop ways of creating and maintaining learning environments in which teaching is conducive to better learning, positive discipline is exercised, and helping relationships between teachers and students, and among students, are established.

By combining literature, research evidence and examples from everyday practice, we encourage teachers to develop their personal systems of classroom management and ways of engaging their students in learning. For this purpose, the book examines classroom management in both Chinese and Western societies, especially recent developments for managing discipline in non-confrontational and supportive ways. Other topics of concern to all teachers, such as managing challenging behaviour, establishing classroom rules, communicating authority and coping with bullying, are also dealt with. A broad perspective is taken to view issues in classroom discipline at the whole-school and cultural levels.

In this book, we invite teachers to consider what constitutes a positive learning environment and cover the following topics to help them in this endeavour:

- Classroom behaviour is examined from an interactionist perspective, and teachers are led in particular to look closely at the contexts in which incidents and problems arise (see Chapter 1).
- An effort is made to raise teachers' awareness of cultural influences on their beliefs and practices of discipline (see Chapter 2).
- The major components of effective classrooms which teachers must take into account in constructing an inviting environment for students are identified, and teachers' roles as good classroom managers are discussed (see Chapter 3).

- A continuum of strategies for managing student misbehaviour is examined, to facilitate personal planning (see Chapter 4).
- Various approaches and models for managing classrooms are introduced, and a framework with simple and practical strategies to help teachers in using them is outlined (see Chapter 5).
- The importance of good communication for productive teacher-pupil relationships is stressed, and ways of inviting communication and communication roadblocks are analysed (see Chapter 6).
- Various strategies are suggested for enhancing friendship among students to enrich their school lives and learning experience, including the teaching of some social and emotional skills which promote and maintain positive relationships among peers (see Chapter 7).
- The benefits of collaboration are emphasized and practical ideas are given to enable teachers to identify contexts in which they can work collaboratively and collegially to deal with issues of concern and develop action plans for implementing change (see Chapter 8).
- The potential contribution of parents to improving classroom behaviour and the quality of learning both inside and outside the classroom is highlighted, and teachers are advised to create contexts in which positive and creative partnerships with them can take place (see Chapter 9).
- Reflection and action research are promoted as effective means for examining and tackling problems in the classroom, and ways of establishing personal management plans are introduced (see Chapter 10).

Our schools are subject to increasing demands for particular sorts of performance in the current wave of educational reform and the overwhelming culture of auditing and accountability. This may narrow our attention, diverting it from those aspects which contribute to healthy behaviour, helping relationships, a positive learning environment and effective achievement. Classroom management is, after all, about creating an environment that is inviting and appealing, so that students are pleasantly engaged in their learning and teachers share their enjoyment of the learning process. Only when the efforts of management fail should teachers have to resort to controlling or intervention strategies.

It is hoped that this book will broaden the ways in which teachers examine classroom episodes and provide insights into how to create a positive environment where all school participants work together for the welfare of students and put effort into making things better.

1

Understanding Classroom Behaviour and Situations

Hue Ming-tak

A leader is best when people barely know that he exists; not so good when people obey and acclaim him; worst when they despise him. "Fail to honour people, they fail to honour you." But of a good leader, who talks little, when his work is done, his aim fulfilled, they will all say, "We did this ourselves."

(Lao Zi, 500 BC)

Synopsis

This chapter encourages teachers to continue to expand their repertoire of classroom management and discipline strategies. It offers a broad view of classroom management and stresses its positive functions in promoting students' academic, social and emotional growth. An interactionist perspective is adopted and its theoretical framework is explained, with the cycle of interaction being used to highlight the complexity of classroom behaviour. Some types of classroom situations are then described, and their implications for good classroom management strategies are outlined. The discussion then shifts from whole-class to individual behaviour, for explaining which a framework of "ten important questions" is introduced. Finally, the chapter focuses on the importance of identifying patterns of classroom behaviour for effective management.

Objectives

After reading this chapter, you should be able to:
* define the term "classroom management" and identify its purposes;
* take an interactionist perspective in examining classroom behaviour;
* identify features of classroom situations and their implications for behaviour management;

- explain classroom behaviour by examining the linkages between the situation, the person and the behaviour;
- use the framework of "ten important questions" for diagnosing classroom behaviour.

Pre-Reading Reflection and Discussion

- What factors contribute to the creation of an effective classroom?
- What do teachers and students do in an effective classroom?
- How can a classroom be managed in an effective manner?
- What kinds of student behaviour should be viewed as misbehaviour?
- What are the common causes of student misbehaviour?
- How may students explain their misbehaviour? How might this differ from teachers' explanations?
- What can be done to prevent student misbehaviour?
- What are the best ways for students to become disciplined?

Introduction

Teachers clearly wish to teach effectively and make learning meaningful for students. However, they are often frustrated in attaining their goals because of behavioural and academic problems of some students for whom they are responsible. Many teachers ask: "How can a good classroom be created and maintained?" Effective classroom management does not, of course, happen automatically, even with proper teacher and student attitudes and expectations in place. How a teacher manages the classroom will have an important influence on whether most of the time is spent on promoting learning or on confronting management and discipline problems. There is no single best way to manage classrooms; and no one model or theory can address the great variety of circumstances and difficulties teachers encounter.

In the following case, before Miss Yeung entered the classroom, the whole class was in chaos. Why did the students behave in this way? What do you think Miss Yeung could do to restore order and avoid this happening again?

Classroom scenario

After playtime, Miss Yueng was on her way to take class 3B for an English lesson. When she got close to the classroom, she heard a very loud noise, and she was surprised to find that the door was closed. When she opened it, she saw five students standing in front of the blackboard drawing graffiti, and four others throwing folded paper to each other. At the same time, a group of students was busy decorating the display boards at the back of the class. Also, three students were chasing a classmate and others were chatting and laughing.

Definition of Classroom Management

Different views

Effective management is a key factor contributing to a positive classroom environment. While considerable effort and attention has been directed to the development of teachers' instructional roles, less emphasis has been placed on the knowledge and skills required for management and discipline. This is partly related to teachers' varied conceptions of what "classroom management" means. Their first point of reference in defining the concept is their own experience of schooling and personal growth, and particularly the culture which nurtured them. The culture in which they grew up provides the foundation for their social and moral values which can be shared and communicated, and it contributes to the development of a common language related to management and discipline.

The term "classroom management" has been defined in many different ways, depending on which of its aspects one focuses on, the particular philosophical positions held, and the operational approaches adopted. Some examples of different views on classroom management are summarized below.

- It is a dimension of effective teaching, and a process through which an effective classroom environment is created (Good and Brophy, 1997).
- It focuses on student behaviour, especially discipline problems, and deals with issues of low learning motivation and poor self-esteem (Campbell, 1999).
- It refers broadly to all activities that teachers carry out in the classroom. It aims to promote student involvement and cooperation (Sanford et al., 1983, cited in Jones and Jones, 2001).
- It emphasizes the educational value of promoting the growth of students. Its focus is also on proactive and developmental classroom practices, rather than those with negative features of control and punishment (McCaslin and Good, 1992).

Although teachers make sense of classroom management in different ways, in general they have a common approach to promoting classroom discipline. It includes the following features (Hue, 2005) which are elaborated throughout this book:

- adopting effective approaches to teaching and learning;
- having plans for avoiding disruption;
- establishing a positive relationship with students;
- using knowledge of individual students and the class to develop appropriate strategies for discipline; and
- being sensitive to the influence on classroom management of factors such as the student seating plan, the arrangements for floating classes, and the examination schedule.

Definitions

While various views on classroom management are included in this book, in general it refers to teachers' actions which lead to the creation of a learning environment where positive interpersonal interaction is promoted and effective learning is facilitated. It aims to enhance the cognitive, personal and social growth of students, developing in particular their self-motivation, self-understanding, self-control, self-evaluation and self-management. Some other terms related to the concept of classroom management which are also used frequently in this text are defined below:

- **Classroom behaviour**: This refers to the actions or reactions of classroom participants. The behaviour of an individual is complex as it is controlled not just by the nervous system but also by the social context in which she/he participates. The actions of individual teachers and students form particular patterns of classroom behaviour.
- **Discipline**: This is the act of responding to misbehaving students in an effort to restore and maintain order, authority and control. It is also considered to be a form of training, aimed at influencing students' moral and mental development in ways which promote self-control, self-discipline and self-management.
- **Misbehaviour**: This refers to behaviour that interferes with teaching, violating the right of other students to learn, and sometimes makes them feel psychologically uncomfortable and physically unsafe.

❒ **Activity 1.1**

Your perceptions of classroom management

Answer the following questions which will help you to understand how you perceive the key concepts of classroom management.

- When you enter a classroom, in what ways can you tell if it is managed effectively or ineffectively?

- What can a teacher do to manage a classroom in an effective manner?
- To what extent do you think your understanding of "misbehaviour" and "discipline" differs from students' understandings?
- What kinds of off-task behaviour do students perform? Why do they do this?

General purposes

Classroom management is concerned not just with discipline and student behaviour but, in a wider sense, can be considered a means by which the broader purposes of classroom life can be achieved. Just as a manager in a company does not aim simply to manage, but to achieve pre-set targets, discipline is not an end in itself: rather, it is a means through which the wider aims of schooling can be fulfilled and students are socialized into moral, ethical and social values.

Two specific purposes of classroom management are highlighted below.

- First, it is a necessary condition for the creation of a supportive, respectful learning environment. Effective teaching and learning can take place only if there is good order and a positive learning climate in the classroom. The view that discipline is a crucial dimension of classroom management and is essentially a means to create the necessary conditions for learning has been endorsed by various educationalists (e.g. Ames, 1992; Corrie, 1997).

- Second, it is a proactive and developmental way to promote the growth of students, in terms of their personal, social and emotional selves. There is a commonly held perception that classroom management, particularly when it refers to discipline and punishment, is related to reactive control and sterile practices. However, classroom discipline should never be considered in isolation from the students' academic, personal and social growth. This is because positive classroom management has enormous potential for increasing students' motivation, learning and self-esteem and, more specifically, positive disciplinary practices can give students a sense of achievement and of control over their classroom behaviour (Gillborn et al., 1993).

☐ **Activity 1.2**

Your reflection on positive classroom management

As indicated above, classroom management has two basic purposes: creating and maintaining a positive learning environment, and promoting students' whole-person growth. Can you think of other purposes? What difficulties can you foresee when putting such purposes into practice? Would you expect to receive any support from the school to overcome these difficulties?

Making Sense of Classroom Behaviour

The classroom is a social setting where participants interact with each other in "classroom behaviour". As such behaviour takes many different forms, it is necessary to develop a theoretical framework to explain it and so gain a deeper understanding of those involved.

An interactionist perspective is taken here for understanding how classroom participants interact with each other as individuals and groups, as well as the relationships between individual and group behaviours. In the course of interpersonal interaction in the classroom — a context in which teachers and students spend much of the school day — meanings are constructed and shared with others. To clarify how interactionists view the classroom, the basic principles of interactionism (Ritzer, 1992: 348) and its implications for classroom management are summarized in the Table 1.1 below. Also highlighted is the ways in which G. H. Mead's ideas, which laid the foundation for symbolic interactionism, can enhance our understanding of classroom behaviour.

From the seven basic principles proposed by Mead, two points in particular need to be highlighted. First, to understand the social experience of teachers and students, priority has to be given to examining the social world of the classroom, rather than by looking first at the behaviour of individuals as separate participants.

The second important aspect is the dialectical feature of the interaction. As Mead explained, when individuals think about how to react to a stimulus, they not only consider the situation in which they are participating but also review their past experience and anticipate the results of their reactions. They do not simply respond immediately to external stimuli but rather think about and assess them through mental imagery.

In the following scenario in a Chinese language lesson, a student, Ah Wing, misbehaves by refusing to obey the teacher, Mr. Lee. The case is then analysed from an interactionist perspective.

Classroom scenario

In a Chinese lesson, a teacher, Mr. Lee, asked the class to copy answers for a test which he wrote on the blackboard. Occasionally, he asked some questions from the test paper. In response to a question, a boy, Ah Wing, called out without standing up as he was supposed to and gave a totally irrelevant and ridiculous answer. The class laughed. The teacher looked stern but simply told him that his answer was wrong. Ah Wing then turned his back and started chatting to the three students behind him. Mr. Lee said, "Shh! Ah Wing, stop chatting and making a noise!" He stopped for a while, but then chatted again. "Ah Wing, did you hear what I said — how many times do I have to tell you? You are meant to be copying the answer, but you just keep talking and talking. I won't give you another warning, You know very well how you were punished last week," Mr. Lee said, beginning to lose his temper and staring at Ah Wing with a severe look. Ah Wing made a face and responded in a rude manner, "You see. I have copied the answer. I haven't made any noise. I talked because I asked them (his classmates) about the answers you wrote on the blackboard!" Mr. Lee got very annoyed and ordered Ah Wing to see him after the class.

Table 1.1 The basic principles of interactionism and its implications for classroom management

Basic principles	Implications for classroom management
1. Human beings have the capacity for thought.	1. Teachers and students have their own thoughts and motives when participating in the classroom.
2. The capacity for thought is shaped by social interaction.	2. Teachers' and students' understanding of the classroom keeps changing in the course of interaction. They act and react in relation to the actions of other participants.
3. In social interaction, people learn the meanings and symbols that allow them to exercise this capacity.	3. Teachers and students have been socialized into the cultures of the classroom, the school and the society so that they can make sense of symbols which they use in the course of interaction.
4. Meaning and symbols allow people to carry out human actions and interactions.	4. In the classroom, the participants have a set of commonly shared symbols, such as verbal and non-verbal signs, which allow them to interpret the meaning of others' behaviour.
5. People are able to modify or change the meaning and symbols that they use in action and interaction on the basis of their interpretation of the situation.	5. New meaning and symbols may arise in a particular class which can only be interpreted by the participants in this class.
6. When interacting with others, people are able to examine possible courses of action, assess their relative advantages and disadvantages, and then choose one.	6. All behaviours are purposeful. There is always a reason for the occurrence of any classroom event.
7. The intertwined patterns of action and interaction make up groups and societies.	7. The patterns of interaction among classroom participants make up the classroom reality.

From an interactionist perspective, three points stand out in the behaviour of Mr. Lee and Ah Wing. First, the whole incident is composed of a cycle of interaction between them, as illustrated in Figure 1.1. Also, the class inevitably played a role in influencing how Mr. Lee reacted to Ah Wing: the fact that they laughed carried a symbolic meaning that Ah Wing was successfully taking over the classroom and getting the attention of the class and the teacher. This might be one of the reasons why Mr. Lee gave Ah Wing a stern look — if the class had not reacted in this way, Mr. Lee would probably not have become so angry and the outcome might have been different. Only by examining the series of actions and reactions by the two participants can one see the complexity of the incident: to view the situation simply as a case of a boy making a noise oversimplifies it.

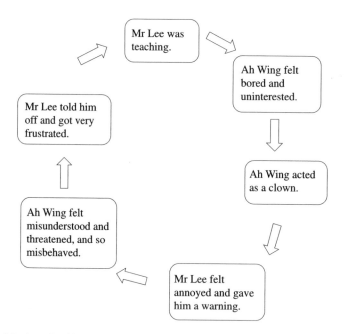

Figure 1.1 A cycle of interaction between the teacher, Mr. Lee, and the student Ah Wing

Second, many verbs carry various symbolic meanings which can be interpreted, shared and understood by the classroom participants. For example, the verb and gesture of "Shh" meant something more than just "keep quiet". It can be interpreted as a warning to those students who were engaged in chatting, which told them that the teacher was alert and was to be in control of the classroom.

Third, the interactions among the participants are determined by their previous classroom experience. In a sense, what is going on at present has a connection with "the past", which shapes the classroom reality and has an impact on how students make sense of everything happening there. For example, Mr. Lee threatened Ah Wing by referring to the punishment he had given him the week before. However, Ah Wing did not feel threatened as the teacher expected and continued to misbehave. Maybe he took this as an opportunity to get his revenge by fighting with the teacher for power.

☐ **Activity 1.3**

Using an interactionist perspective to explain classroom behaviour

Study the scenario below, and then try to: (1) draw a cycle of interaction to show the interpersonal relations between the teacher Miss Hung and the student Kwok King; and (2) explain the motives for their behaviour from an interactionist perspective.

When Miss Hung copied the answers to a listening exercise on Chinese language on the blackboard, she noticed that Kwok King did not write down anything for a long time. She urged him several times to do what he had been told. Kwok King gradually got annoyed, and then listlessly picked up a worksheet and attempted to show it to Miss Hung. The gesture was intended to pass the message to Miss Hung that he had already done it. Miss Hung then got close to him and, unsurprisingly, found that it was not his work. In fact, he had just taken it from Hui Ting, the student who sat next to him, and shown it to her. Miss Hung, who felt this showed lack of respect for her, was very irritated and scolded Kwok King severely. Without pausing for a second, Kwok King said loudly to her: "You need not be so harsh. You want to put me into 'a dead corner', don't you?"

Characteristics of Classroom Situations

Each classroom is unique in terms of the patterns of interpersonal interaction and the types of behaviour. One of the ways to identify the features of a classroom is to ask teachers what metaphors they use to describe it. The answers they give can be fascinating and diverse. Each metaphor tells a story and captures a particular type of classroom experience. For example, some say the classroom is like "a market", in which people are busy with their own business and talk loudly; others describe it as being "like Nathan Road", the most crowded and busy street in Hong Kong; and yet others compare it to "a prison", to capture the sense of boredom which prevails.

The characteristics of the classroom can be identified by summarizing all these metaphors. For example, Watkins and Wagner (2000: 54–58) list five common features of school classrooms, the key points of which are presented and elaborated in Table 1.2 on pp. 10–11. This analysis draws attention to the complexity of the classroom, which cannot be romantized as simply a place of teaching and learning. In relation to each of the characteristics, particular forms of interaction, interpersonal relationships and classroom dynamics are indicated and some related managerial skills are also suggested.

Table 1.2 The characteristics of classroom situations and various related classroom management skills

Characteristics of the classroom	Description of the classroom	Required managerial skills
1. Classrooms are busy places.	• Teachers and students engage in a large number of interactions every day. • Events happen fast. • As they are very "busy" places, aspects of classroom life need to be made routine. • Little attention is given to individual students. • Students have got used to being one of many.	• Manage through the timing and pacing of activities. • Learn to react quickly. • Make decisions rapidly. • Build up classroom rules and routines. • Care for the needs of individual students.
2. Classrooms are public places.	• The behaviour of each classroom participant is highly visible to others. • The teacher is expected by all school members to be the centre of the classroom. • A teacher's reaction to one student's behaviour affects others. • Students have learned to cope with the public evaluation of their work and behaviour. • Students have learned to be treated as members of a group.	• Play the role of a leader. • Blend public and personal interests. • Take care of the issue of "face", especially when managing students' behaviour in front of the whole class. • Help students to play their roles as members of a group.
3. Classroom events are multi-dimensional.	• A wide variety of purposes, interests and goals are represented by different participants. • Classroom life is affected by personal and social aspects of participants' lives. • There is a multiplicity of information sources, such as participants' verbal and non-verbal behaviour.	• Manage instruction and students' behaviour on a multiplicity of dimensions, such as knowing your subject and encouraging thinking. • Interpret classroom behaviour using various types of information from, for example, students' body language and social networks.
4. Classrooms events are simultaneous.	• Classroom events do not happen in a step-by-step fashion. • Many events happen at the same time. • Students have skills for avoiding teachers' monitoring.	• Manage numerous aspects of classroom life at the same time. • Monitor more than one aspect of classroom life at a time. • Choose which aspects to respond to and which to ignore. • Exercise the skill of selective ignoring.

(continued on p. 11)

(Table 1.2 continued)

5. Classrooms events are unpredictable.	• There are always internal and external interruptions in the course of teaching and learning. • Students develop strategies for dealing with unpredictability, such as searching for answers the teacher expects and requesting predictable and familiar tasks.	• Become skilled in recognizing and tolerating unpredictability. • Develop various plans for dealing with unpredictability. • Make classroom life routine and reduce its ambiguity. • Constantly review and re-establish classroom rules and routines. • Constantly examine classroom situations where difficult behaviour is exhibited.

❐ **Activity 1.4**

Identifying classroom situations and developing strategies for improvement

Study the following three classroom scenarios (you will recall reading the third scenario in an earlier section.) Identify the characteristics of the classroom, and then suggest strategies for managing students' behaviour.

1. When Miss Lee was writing some notes on the blackboard, she found two students involved in a game of throwing pieces of chalk to each other. She gave a serious warning to those involved. Less than a minute later, two other students joined in the game. Miss Lee asked the four students to stand up. They refused to do so and said to her disrespectfully: "Go back to your teaching. No one cares for what you teach."

2. In the course of teaching, Mr. Wong heard the beep-beep sound of an alarm clock. He asked the class who owned it, but nobody responded. With the beep-beep sound going round the classroom, he raised his voice and gave another warning in a very serious tone: "You all must know who brought in the alarm and where it is. Tell me, or the whole class will be punished." All the students sat still and the classroom was silent.

3. After playtime, Miss Yeung was on her way to take class 3B for an English lesson. When she got close to the classroom, she heard a very loud noise, and she was surprised to find that the door was closed. When she opened it, she saw five students standing in front of the blackboard drawing graffiti, and four others throwing folded paper to each other. At the same time, a group of students was busy decorating the display boards at the back of the class. Also, three students were chasing a classmate and others were chatting and laughing.

Explaining Classroom Behaviour

As each classroom is unique, the same behaviour performed in different situations can carry different meanings; and even if the situation is the same, the participants may react differently. Watkins and Wagner (2000) attempted to illustrate the complexity of classroom behaviour by using the formula, $B=f(P.S)$, which was suggested by Lewin (1946), a social psychologist. This formula indicates that behaviour varies in relation to the two variables of person and situation. For instance, a student who misbehaves in a lesson on a particular subject may not do so in another. Similarly, a teacher who reacts to a particular kind of student behaviour in class X may not do so in class Y.

You can probably think of many examples of the operation of this principle. In most cases, teachers tend to react in relation to not only students' behaviour but also the context in which they are participating. For example, when a student breaks a rule in the last few minutes of a lesson, most teachers tend to tolerate this as the lesson is coming to an end, whereas they would probably have taken action had it occurred earlier.

In the light of this, for a better understanding of students' behaviour, it is useful to examine the context in which it occurs (Dolye, 1986; Geiger and Turiel, 1983; Hargreaves, 1980; Watkins and Wagner, 2000). This involves teachers in analysing teacher-student interactions and the circumstances at particular moments, to help them see the uniqueness of each classroom incident. More important, such an analysis gives them a more comprehensive picture of the behaviour and eventually leads to the development of a more reflective explanation and a wider range of possibilities for action.

To achieve this, Watkins (1999) and Watkins and Wagner (2000) have suggested a set of ten questions which were selected from the work of Hamblin (1984) (see Table 1.3). By asking these questions when managing students' behaviour, a teacher will have a better understanding of classroom behaviour in terms of the context, the interactions between the participants involved, and the situation in which the behaviour problems arise. According to research carried out on teachers who used this approach when managing students' behaviour (Watkins and Wagner, 2000: 100), it is effective in:

- broadening their thinking;
- facilitating discussion with other school members involved;
- enhancing exploration with students;
- improving the system for collecting information on misbehaving students.

Table 1.3 Ten important questions

1. What is the cause for concern?
2. In what situation does the concern arise?
3. In what situations does the concern not occur?
4. What happens before the events of concern?
5. What follows the events of concern?
6. What skills does the person apparently not demonstrate?
7. What view does the person have of the events of concern?
8. What view does the person have of him/herself?
9. What view do others have of the person?
10. Who is most concerned by this behaviour? (Watkins, 1999: 17)

Using the ten important questions to explain student behaviour

For a better understanding of how teachers can use the framework of "ten important questions" to explain student behaviour, two cases of classroom incidents are reported below — one from a secondary school and the other from a primary school — and the interaction between the participants is explained by using this framework.

Classroom scenario from a secondary school

This scenario is about a boy named Siu Keung who is in his second year in a secondary school. In the course of a Chinese lesson, the teacher, Mr. Tse, wrote the answers for a test on the blackboard, and everyone copied them as instructed except Siu Keung, who just sat without attempting to copy a single word. Mr. Tse urged him to do as he had been told and Siu Keung immediately showed him a piece of written work and said he had completed it already. However, from the handwriting, Mr. Tse could tell immediately that this was the work of another student, Fei Yin. Mr. Tse got very angry and scolded both of them. Siu Keung then said very impolitely, "Don't be so harsh!" and Mr. Tse asked him what he meant. At this point, another student, Ah Ping — who had already been punished for being late for class — interrupted and said loudly: "Siu Keung doesn't intend to make you feel threatened, but just wants to teach you something." Mr. Tse scolded him as well and sent the three students to the team of discipline teachers.

In this scenario, it can be seen that what made the teacher most concerned kept shifting away from teaching and learning to the management of students' social behaviour. This can be shown clearly when the case is examined by asking the four participants the ten important questions listed earlier, as shown in Table 1.4 on pp. 14–15.

Table 1.4 The interactions between the teacher and the three students

Diagnosis of the case	The teacher	Siu Keung	Fei Yin	Ah Ping
1. What is the cause for concern?	Feels disrespected and cheated	Refuses to copy answers; takes another student's work and claims it is his own	Works well and shares her work with Siu Keung	Interrupts when the teacher talks to Siu Keung, and makes a loud comment
2. In what situation does the concern arise?	Copying the test answers on the blackboard	Feels bored with copying	Gets involved when her neighbour Siu Keung refuses to work	Intends to support Siu Keung, and uses this occasion to express his discontent with the teacher's actions
3. In what situations does the concern not occur?	When students behave as instructed	When he finds the class interesting	When she is not disturbed by the classmates near her	When the teacher shows him some respect
4. What happens before the events of concern?	Asks students to copy answers	Feels bored with the class and realizes that he is labelled as a difficult student	Completes the copying as instructed	Punished by having to stand for being late for class
5. What follows the events of concern?	Feels angry, and stops teaching	Talked to and scolded directly by the teacher	Scolded by the teacher	Scolded by the teacher
6. What skills does the person apparently not demonstrate?	Keeps her emotion in calamity when managing students' misbehaviour	Deals with authority; gets attention from proper ways	Refuses Siu Keung's in-appropriate request	Supports Siu Keung in positive ways
7. What view does the person have of the events of concern?	Students have failed to behave as instructed	Behaved as other classmates expected, as they expect him to respond to the teacher in a hostile way occasionally.	Did a favour for another classmate in need	Used this as an occasion for expressing his anger
8. What view does the person have of him/herself?	Feels cheated, disrespected, and losing face as the the students are hostile	Feels that he was being picked on, labelled and loses face	Feels strongly that she is innocent	Feels very angry

(continued on p. 15)

(Table 1.4 continued)

9. What view do others have of the person?	Much time was spent on managing the students' behaviour	Admired by certain members of the class and gains a reputation for being tough	Viewed as innocent	Viewed as an opportunist
10. Who is most concerned by this behaviour?	Acts to defend her teaching and leading roles and protect her authority from being undermined			

Classroom scenario from a primary school

Mei Lai is a 10-year-old girl who refuses to engage in learning tasks and is unable to get on well with other students. On many occasions, she has attacked other students verbally in the classroom. Her teacher, Miss Fung, has tried various strategies to change Mei Lai's behaviour, such as putting her in a remedial group, using different assessment tools and involving her mother. However there has been little change in the way Mei Lai behaves.

Miss Fung tried to diagnose Mei Lai's case, and listed the features shown in Table 1.5.

Table 1.5 A diagnosis of the behaviour of Mei Lai

What is the current concern?	• Mei Lai has difficulty in concentrating on her work. • She likes to attack others verbally and snatch implements from them. • Many classmates are upset when trying to relate to her. • She is a loner. • Teaching is sometimes interrupted by Mei Lai.
Expectation of others	• Many girls feel they suffer from Mei Lai's behaviour, but apparently the boys do not share this view. • Many girls tolerate her, but some have started to complain. • The boys have started to ignore her. • Most members of the class expect her to act in this way.
When does she behave in this way?	• When engaged in learning tasks, she takes much more time to complete them as she cannot concentrate on them. • When others are getting on with a task she has difficulty in doing, she snatches things from them. • When she is frustrated by, for example, getting a poor result in a test, she verbally abuses others.

(continued on p. 16)

(Table 1.5 continued)

When does she not behave in this way?	• When she finds a learning activity interesting. • When she knows what she is doing. • When her best friend Mui Kuen works with her. • When a teacher works with her, prompting her through the task.
What does she seem to gain?	• She seems to gain nothing. Although she grabs things from other she just keeps them for a short time and returns them to the owners when asked. • She wants to be the one in control by verbally attacking others, but all this does is to upset them.
What strategies do you find are helpful?	• The behaviour of Mei Lai is getting worse. Some teachers have found that she works well in small groups, particularly when a teaching assistant, as her personal tutor, helps her to go through tasks by frequently asking her brainstorming questions. • She concentrates better when she is encouraged frequently by the teacher. • Time out does not help; it just makes her more and more upset. • Things got worse when her mother was informed about what she had done in the classroom.
Is there any other relevant information?	• Her father works in mainland China. When he arrives home two or three time a week, Mei Lai is already in bed. • Mei Lai does not have any brothers and sisters, and gets excessive affection from her parents. • Her mother seemed hesitant when contacted by the school and may not want to bear the responsibility for Mei Lai's behaviour.

◻ **Activity 1.5**

Study the above information, and try to think about what could be done in the classroom context to improve Mei Lai's behaviour. Use the ten questions to help you in this task.

Summary

This chapter introduces commonly used terms such as "classroom management", "classroom behaviour", "discipline" and "misbehaviour". It aims to help teachers take a broad view of classroom management, focusing not merely on preventing and eliminating student misbehaviour, but also on its proactive and positive functions in promoting student growth academically, socially and emotionally. The chapter stresses that effective classroom management is an inseparable part of the process of teaching and learning which helps students to develop self-control in a way that allows both teachers and students to feel good about themselves.

Two intellectual frameworks are provided as a theoretical basis for understanding classroom behaviour. First, an interactionist perspective is adopted for explaining the interaction among classroom participants and illustrating the complexity of classroom behaviour — with the idea of a cycle of interaction being introduced as a practical way for behaviour analysis. The second perspective involves looking closely at the classroom situation in which the misbehaviour takes place, and taking situational factors into account when explaining student behaviour. For this purpose, "ten important questions" are introduced to collect more relevant information about the events and broaden views on the participants' behaviour.

Also, five characteristics of classroom situations are summarized, and the events which take place there are described as being "busy", public, multidimensional, simultaneous and unpredictable. Finally, teachers are encouraged to manage classroom situations with appropriate managerial strategies for improving whole-class behaviour.

Questions for Discussion

1. State your goal for classroom management and then compare your view with those of others to see to what extent they differ.
2. How could this goal be put into practice? What difficulties do you think you are likely to encounter?
3. Are there any differences in managing higher-form and lower-form classrooms?
4. What differences are there between the causes of classroom misbehaviour in lower and higher forms?
5. Can you think of any student behaviours which would be considered "misbehaviours" in one classroom but not in another? If so, why is this the case?
6. To what extent is students' classroom behaviour related to their academic ability and achievement? Do you agree that disruptive students tend to be of lower academic ability, and that those of higher ability do not exhibit such problems?

Useful Resources

Websites

1. Classroom Management Site:
   http://www.ez2bsaved.com/class_manage.htm
2. Education World:
   http://www.education-world.com/a_curr/archives/classmanagement.shtml
3. Kimskorner for Teacher Talk:
   http://www.kimskorner4teachertalk.com/classmanagement/menu.html

4.   Teachnet.com: http://www.teachnet.com/how-to/manage/
5.   The Association for Supervision and Curriculum Development (ASCD):
     http://www.ascd.org/portal/site/ascd/menuitem.8835d3e3fbb1b0cddeb3ffdb62108a0c/

Further Reading

Burden, P. R. (2003). *Classroom management: Creating a successful learning community.* New York: Wiley.

Iverson, A. M. and Froyen, L. A. (2003). *Building competence in classroom management and discipline* (4th edn). Upper Saddle River, NJ: Merrill.

Landau, B. M. (2004). *The art of classroom management: Building equitable learning communities* (2nd edn). Upper Saddle River, NJ: Merrill.

Levin, J. and Nolan, J. F. (2004). *Principles of classroom management: A professional decision-making model* (4th edn). Boston, MA: Pearson.

Petty, R. (2001). *Classroom management: A resource manual for frontline teachers.* Lanham, MD: Scarecrow Press.

Stone, R. (2005). *Best classroom management practices for reaching all learners: What award-winning classroom teachers do.* Thousand Oaks, CA: Corwin Press.

References

Ames, C. (1992). Classrooms: Goals, structures, and student motivation. *Journal of Educational Psychology,* 84(3): 261–271.

Campbell, J. (1999). *Student discipline and classroom management: Preventing and managing discipline problems in the classroom.* Springfield, IL: Charles C. Thomas.

Corrie, L. (1997). The interaction between teachers' knowledge and skills when managing a troublesome classroom behaviour, *Cambridge Journal of Education,* 27(1): 93–105.

Doyle, W. (1986). Classroom organization and management. In M.C. Wittrock (ed.), *Handbook of research on teaching* (3rd edn). New York: Macmillan.

Geiger, K.M. and Turiel, E. (1983). Disruptive school behaviour and concepts of social convention in early adolescence. *Journal of Educational Psychology,* 75(5): 677–685.

Gillborn, D., Nixon, J. and Rudduck, J. (1993). *Dimensions of discipline: Rethinking practice in secondary schools.* London: HMSO.

Good, T. and Brophy, J. (1997). *Looking in classrooms* (7th edn). New York: Harper and Row.

Hamblin, D. (1983). *Guidance: 16–19.* Oxford: Blackwell.

Hargreaves, D.H. (1980). Teachers' knowledge of behaviour problems. In G. Upton and A. Gobell (eds.), *Behaviuor problems in the comprehensive school.* Cardiff: University College Cardiff Faculty of Education.

Hue, M.T. (2005). *Preliminary findings: The social construction of classroom discipline in Hong Kong secondary schools.* Funded by an Internal Research Grant, the Hong Kong Institute of Education.

Jones, V. and Jones, L. S. (2001). *Comprehensive classroom management: Creating communities of support and solving problems* (6th edn). Boston: Allyn & Bacon.

Lewin, K. (1946). Behaviour and development as a function of the total situation. In L. Carmichael (ed.), *Manual of child psychology*. New York: Wiley.

McCaslin, M. and Good, T. (1992). Compliant cognition: The misalliance of management and instructional goals in current school reform. *Educational Researcher*, 21: 4–17.

Ritzer, G. (1992). Sociological theory (3rd edn). USA: McGraw-Hill, Inc..

Watkins, C. (1999). *Managing classroom behaviour: From research to diagnosis*. London: Institute of Education, University of London and Association of Teachers and Lecturers.

Watkins, C. and Wagner, P. (2000). *Improving school behaviour*. London: Paul Chapman Publishing Ltd.

2

The Influence of Chinese Culture on Hong Kong Classrooms

Hue Ming-tak

Only the soft overcomes the hard, by yielding, bringing it to peace. Even where there is no space, that which has no substance enters in. Through these things are shown the value of the natural way. The wise man understands full well that wordless teaching can take place, and that actions should occur without the wish for self-advancement.

Lao Zi (500 BC)

Synopsis

This chapter looks at the influence of Chinese culture on the Hong Kong classroom. It begins by describing the three schools of Chinese philosophy: Legalism, Daoism and Confucianism. Their effects on how teachers develop their strategies for classroom management are discussed. Also, four cultural features of the interpersonal relationships in the Hong Kong classroom are summarized as (1) hierarchical human relationships; (2) collectivism and conformity; (3) Chinese practices of childhood socialization; and (4) the social game of "face". Lastly, the yin and yang doctrine is adopted for understanding the complexity of the classroom and the teaching roles of teachers.

Objectives

After reading this chapter, you should be able to:

- identify the four aspects of classroom management — physical, cognitive, social and affective;
- understand the different approaches to classroom management;
- show awareness of the influence of Chinese culture in interacting with students;
- use the doctrine of yin and yang to explain the dynamics of classroom behaviour;
- identify the teacher's role as a classroom manager.

Pre-Reading Reflection and Discussion

- How would you define the term "culture"?
- What does Chinese culture mean to you?
- How familiar are you with the key beliefs of Legalism, Daoism and Confucianism?
- In the ongoing process of modernization, how sharply does Chinese culture differ from Western culture?
- To what extent do you think the classroom life of teachers and students has been influenced by Chinese culture?
- Are there any current disciplinary practices which can be explained by the Chinese philosophies of Legalism, Daoism and/or Confucianism?

Introduction

Culture is a complex and elusive concept. It is embedded within almost all elements of daily life such as language, ideals, beliefs, customs, gestures and ceremonies. In using all these elements, individuals can make sense of their social world and interact with others. Culture also helps people to connect and integrate various parts of their lives as a meaningful whole. Because of its monolithic nature, culture can be inherited from one generation to another and can be shared in common by all members of a society. Despite this, one should note that it has some flexible and varying characteristics: it has a life of its own which evolves and transforms through time, in the course of which some new dimensions of meaning are added to people's preconceptions of the social world to which they belong.

What is going on in the classroom is related to the wider context in which the school is located, and cannot exclude itself from the influence of the culture to which it belongs. In Hong Kong society, Chinese culture has a significant influence on the social behaviour of most people, even though Western culture and trends in globalization have produced some profound and extensive changes in the society. In education, we can still trace back some influences to their roots in Chinese culture. The scenario below is seen in most classrooms in Hong Kong schools. Can you identify any influence of Chinese culture on the behaviour of the teacher and students? Can this be explained by any Chinese philosophy with which you are familiar?

Classroom scenario

When the teacher, Miss Lam, entered the classroom for an English language lesson, all the students became alert. The monitor reacted immediately to announce loudly, "Stand up!", and the students stopped whatever they were doing and stood up politely without pausing for a second. Miss Lam kept her back straight and stood in front of the whole class, with an obvious sense of authority, and constantly glanced round to make sure everyone was paying attention to her presence and was standing in an orderly fashion. As the classroom became very quiet at this point, she felt satisfied with their behaviour and said to the class in a serious tone, "Good morning class!" In doing so, she kept looking around the classroom and made eye-contact with as many students as she could. This was done as a way of informing the students of the importance of conformity, orderliness and politeness in her classroom. Mechanically, the whole class greeted Miss Lam in return: "Good morning Miss Lam!" However, Miss Lam regarded their voices as being too soft. "Louder please!", she announced in a raised voice, with an unpleasant facial expression. The whole class greeted her again in a louder, but still modest way. This time Miss Lam gave an almost unnoticeable smile. Obviously, she felt satisfied with the greeting and announced in a serious tone, "Sit down!", and the whole class did as instructed.

Chinese Approaches to Classroom Management: The Three Schools of Legalism, Daoism and Confucianism

Hong Kong teachers are used to borrowing ideas from the three schools of Chinese philosophy — Legalism, Daoism and Confucianism — and using many sayings from their classic texts to describe how they manage their classrooms (Hue, 2001, 2005a, 2005b, 2007). They are also used as references for how students should be cultivated as "educated citizens", in terms of their moral, social, emotional and personal selves. For example, the common saying, "teaching all diverse students" (*you jiao wu lei*) is rooted in Confucianism, while some teachers may apply the Daoist principle of "dealing with changing things with the strategy of doing nothing" (*yi bu bian yin wan bian*) for managing a very difficult class. Other principles of this kind include "harsh rules should be enforced during chaotic and unsettled times" (*zi luan shi, yong zhong dian*) which can be traced back to the principles of Legalism. The key thinking of the three schools, and their implications for classroom management strategies, are described in the following sections.

The Legalist approach

Legalism was one of the three main philosophic schools at the end of the Zhou dynasty (256 BC), its representatives including Han Feizi (韓非子) (233 BC) and Li Si (李斯)

(280 BC). Legalism became the central governing idea in the Qin dynasty and since then has had a very considerable impact on the political, social and business domains of Chinese society. As modern observers of Chinese politics and society have argued, Legalist ideas have merged with mainstream Confucianism and still play a role in Chinese society. This phenomenon is mirrored in the common saying, "on the bright (*yang*) side it is Confucianism; on the dark (*yin*) side it is Legalism" (*yang yu yin fa*). The influence of Legalism on Chinese society can be considered to be as strong as that of Confucianism.

Legalists believed that a ruler has absolute power and authority, whereas his subjects hold junior positions in society and are considered inferiors. Within the relationships dominated by such a concept of power, there is little room for morality and humanity. To maintain his position, a ruler has to ensure that he is in control of his subjects through the three strategies of *fa* (法), *shu* (術) and *shi* (勢).

Fa literally means "the law", and the legal code must be written clearly and made public. All people under the ruler were equal before the law; and those who obeyed the laws should be rewarded, while those who broke them should be punished severely. This ensured that all actions taken were explicit and predictable.

Shu refers to the methods of control. Special methods and "secrets" were employed by a ruler to ensure that his control was not taken over by someone else. It was especially important that no one should be able to fathom the ruler's motivations, and thus know what might help them get ahead, other than following the *fa*/laws.

Shi is concerned with legitimacy, power and charisma. It is the position of the ruler and his image of leadership, not the ruler himself, that holds power. To maintain this situation, the ruler should determine the subjects' behaviour and their impression of his leadership through impression management, distancing himself from them, and behaviour manipulation.

As regards classroom management, the school of Legalism provides teachers with many ideas about how the social setting of the classroom can be managed, and it can be seen in how they construe their roles and classroom incidents (Hue, 2005a). Teachers associate their roles with the rulers while their students are defined as the subjects. According to this perspective, students' behaviour and conduct should be controlled by using their *fa*, *shu*, and *shi* to establish and maintain rules, give orders and commands, build up a punishment-and-reward system and use the skills of impression management. Each of these aspects is elaborated below.

- *Establishing and enforcing* fa : Teachers establish clear expectations, limits and consequences, and insist on acceptable behaviour from their students. During this process, students are told precisely what is expected of them, and why.
- *Using the managerial skills of* shu: Teachers use commands as one of their controlling strategies for telling students what they are supposed to do. In most cases, they issue them without using force to compel students to obey, and students submit to them as a way of respecting teachers' leadership and authority.

- *Building a punishment-and-reward system of* shu: Another strategy adopted from Legalism follows the behaviourist use of reinforcement through rewards and punishment. Rewards cause the desired behaviour to increase in frequency, and the undesirable behaviour to decrease; while punishment is a way of discouraging undesirable behaviour. Also, the removal of the punishment serves to strengthen behaviour and increase the tendency for it to be repeated. It is assumed that these consequences influence student behaviour in line with the established behavioural principles of *fa*.

- *Using* shi *for impression management:* Impression management is a managerial strategy for manipulating students' impressions of teachers and their behaviour. It is a goal-directed, conscious or unconscious, attempt to influence and maintain the students' perceptions of the leadership and authority of teachers. As Shakespeare said, "All the world's a stage, and all the men and women merely players", which means that everyone has a role to play in the social world. Putting this saying into the context of the classroom, it can be rewritten as "The classroom is a stage, and all the teachers and students merely players." From a Legalist perspective, the images of teachers as leaders and authority figures in the classroom should be enhanced and maintained, for both the teachers and the students to function effectively. To ensure this, any behaviour which may harm a teacher's image should be avoided and, in some cases, punishment should be administered.

❐ **Activity 2.1**

The tensions between Legalism and Confucianism

The ideologies of Confucianism and Legalism appear to conflict with each other. Can teachers blend them together effectively in managing a classroom? Can you identify classroom situations in which this could happen?

The Daoist approach

Daoism was founded by Lao Zi (老子) (400 BC) and one of the most brilliant representatives of this school is Zhuangzi (莊子) (400 BC). Many aspects of Chinese culture have been influenced deeply by Daoist philosophic thought, such as the concepts of action through inaction, the power of emptiness, detachment, receptiveness, spontaneity, the strength of softness, the relativism of human values, and the search for a long life. Daoism offered a breeding ground for the development of the yin-yang philosophy which has been widely adopted by the Chinese for explaining the complexities of the social, political and natural worlds, and for building up knowledge of sciences, medicine and astronomy. More details of yin-yang philosophy are introduced later in this chapter.

One of the key thoughts in Daoism is *wu wei,* which literally means "action through inaction". It is regarded as the "Dao" (道) (the Way, nature or principle) for accomplishing things. This does not mean that one should simply do nothing, but that one should avoid explicit intentions and strong will: one should follow the principles of Nature to reach real efficiency by acting according to one's capabilities and desires.

Actions taken in accordance with the Dao (Nature) are easier and more productive than actively attempting to counter it. For example, Lao Zi believed that violence and conflict should be avoided, and that victory was an occasion for mourning the necessity of using force against others, rather than an occasion for triumphant celebrations. If we follow this thinking, it can be inferred that classroom practices involving codified laws, rules, rewards and punishments may make management difficult. In Foucault's terms, they merely symbolize the failure of power.

Daoism places emphasis upon spontaneity and teaches that individuals should follow natural ways appropriate to themselves. This implies that, in the classroom the natural potential of students should be released and kept flowing like a running river, rather than being bounded by any artificial institutional arrangements. In essence, most Daoists feel that teachers should appreciate the lives of students and respect each individual's capabilities, rather than lead them to desire a life predicated on the demands of institutions, or other external forces, that is always beyond their reach. The teachings of Daoism are frequently adopted by teachers in the following ways:

- *Valuing the individual differences of students*: The uniqueness of students should be recognized as each of them has different potential and abilities. It is like the hot air rising up to the sky and the river running from high to low land. Even a student who is regarded as "useless" (*wu yong*) from one perspective can always be considered as extremely "useful" (*da yong*) from the point of view of Nature. With this understanding in mind, students' individual differences should be respected and valued, and teachers have a crucial role in releasing students' potential and making them grow naturally.
- *Looking at the classroom relatively*: Everything in the classroom should be understood in a relative sense. There are always two sides — for example, good and undisciplined behaviour, orderly and disorderly classrooms, and being in and out of control. Superficially, they are different things, but in fact they are one thing being viewed from two sides.
- *Complementary roles of teachers and students*: The roles and importance of the teacher and student are complementary to each other. For successful learning and teaching, both parties have to play their roles effectively without one dominating the other. Ideally, students should be barely aware of teachers' authority and perceive them as their friends or peers. Students should not always be asked to

conform and submit to their teachers' wishes, and so perceive them as powerful authority figures whom they may even come to despise.

- *"Action through inaction" (wu wei er wei)*: There is an order for everything in Nature, and "Action through inaction" means taking action in accordance with the order or principles of Nature. Teachers who behave in this way will be effective in resolving the issues or problems concerned; but if they take many measures to manage student behaviour, this may upset the balance of Nature, especially if the actions are unnecessary.

- *Replacing the "hard" strategies with the "soft" ones*: It has been said that "using softness to control hardness" (*yi you ji gang*) is an effective approach. This is so particularly when a class is very disruptive, as using harsh punishments and rules in such cases is likely to provoke anger and more rebellious behaviour. Being "soft" does not mean that one is "weak" — it is like water which is soft when it is still, but which can cut through a valley when it runs. From this viewpoint, teachers should try to adopt some "soft" strategies to manage difficult classes by, for example, attempting to avoid imposing their authority, remaining calm and ensuring they communicate well with their students, using skills such as active listening and empathy.

The Confucian approach

Confucianism, which was founded by Confucius (孔夫子) (551–479 BC) — addressed as "The First Teacher" (先師), "The Sage" (至聖), and "The Former Teacher who Reached Sainthood" (至聖先師) — is credited with shaping much of Chinese thought. It was the official philosophy throughout most of Imperial China's history, and mastery of Confucian texts was the primary criterion for entry into the imperial bureaucracy.

In Chinese society, Confucius is commonly depicted as "The Model Teacher of a Myriad Ages" (萬世師表). In his teaching, Confucius emphasized personal morality, correctness in social behaviour, harmony in interpersonal relationships, justice and sincerity. In his view, human beings and their relationships were more important than the laws themselves as the function of the laws is to serve people. From a Western perspective, his teaching is normally viewed as a variant of humanism.

The ethical values of Confucianism are grounded upon the three concepts of *li* (禮), *yi* (義) and *ren* (仁), and its ultimate principle for human behaviour is captured in the saying, "What one does not wish for oneself, one ought not do to any one else; what one recognizes as desirable for oneself, one ought to be willing to grant to others". The concepts of *li*, *yi* and *ren* are as follows:

- *Li* was a form of social norm, providing guidelines on the social behaviour people should follow to build the ideal society. It referred to all aspects of an individual's social life, and Confucius insisted that should flow from humanity.

- *Yi* literally meant "righteousness". One was advised not to pursue one's own personal interests but to do what was right for others and considered moral by society. By basing your life on *li*, rather than self-interest, you would be a better, more righteous person.
- *Ren* can be translated as "human-heartedness". Confucius's moral system was based upon empathy and understanding others, rather than on divinely ordained rules. To live by *rén* was even better than living by the rules of *yi*, as *ren* involved another Confucian version of the Golden Rule: he argued that you must always treat your inferiors just as you would want your superiors to treat you.

In relation to classroom management, Confucianism still serves as a major reference for the social behaviour of teachers and students and how their roles should be played out (Hue, 2005a, 2005b). Noted below are some related thoughts on teachers' classroom behaviour.

- *No one is unchangeable*: Teachers should take a positive view of human beings and believe that their nature is originally good. The individual differences between students are recognized, with teachers acknowledging that they need to accommodate such diversity in managing their classrooms. Teachers should never give up in supporting any student, and if something goes wrong in the classroom, they should consider the potential of the students involved and develop appropriate strategies to help them change.
- *Showing students the loving heart of ren*: *Ren* is the way to promote the growth of students and help them to learn. The interpersonal relationships between teachers and students, and among students, should be based on the basic principles of *ren*. In their practice, teachers have to relate to their students with genuineness, empathy and caring — the key qualities of interpersonal relationships; and when they behave in this way, they expect students to obey them.
- *Promoting students' personal and social development in the classroom*: Teachers are not just concerned with academic achievement: indeed, in many circumstances their role in students' individual development should be given a higher priority. Teachers must therefore ensure that, in their interpersonal relationships with them, students' personal and social growth are promoted.
- *Being socialized as "perfect gentlemen"* (君子): Teachers have an important role in helping students to understand the Way, or the principles of life, so that they can be socialized as the "perfect gentleman". They can act as role models who cultivate humaneness, act politely in accordance with *li*, and show loyalty to the social groups to which they belong.

In brief, the three schools of Chinese philosophy — Legalism, Daoism and Confucianism — offer many ideas for teachers to develop in their strategies for classroom management; and they also serve as a basic reference for the social and moral behaviour of classroom participants. Although the Hong Kong education system often imports Western ideas, theories and practices, teachers and students, consciously or unconsciously, inherit some of these Chinese teachings and incorporate them into their personal systems for classroom behaviour and management.

> ❑ **Activity 2.2**
> **The cultural responsibilities of a teacher**
>
> According to Confucianism, the teacher has three key responsibilities: transmitting the Way (傳道) to students, developing their career lives (授業), and helping them to resolve their difficulties (解惑). How do you interpret these three responsibilities? Do you think they are still crucial for teachers and, if so, how can they be fulfilled in the classroom?

To help in considering the influence of Chinese culture on classroom behaviour, the key thoughts of the three schools and their implications for classroom management are summarized in Table 2.1 on p. 30.

The Influence of Chinese Culture on Classroom Behaviour

Although the three schools of Chinese philosophy which have been described originated over 2,000 years ago, they still have a profound effect on society and on the classroom lives of teachers and students. This section focuses on how Chinese culture affects the behaviour of classroom participants and the extent to which this can be explained from the literature on Chinese social behaviour, drawing on the work of Hue (2005a, 2005b, 2007).

First, the hierarchical relationships between the senior and junior members in a social group are highlighted and then the emphasis in Chinese society on collectivism and conformity, and its association with Confucianism, is examined. Next, how far Chinese practices of childhood socialization are applied in the process of establishing classroom discipline is explored; and, finally, the discussion shifts to a more dynamic dimension of social behaviour — how the issue of "face" is of concern to Hong Kong teachers and students when they interact in the classroom.

Hierarchical human relationships

In Chinese culture, teaching has been based on a tradition which emerged from a hierarchically organized society. In such a society, one group of individuals is regarded

Table 2.1 Chinese approaches to classroom management (Hue, 2004, 2005a)

Chinese philosophy	Basic ideas	Links to classroom management
Legalism	• Consolidate one's ruling status with power and authority. • Establish legal codes and a system of control and manipulation. • Emphasize legitimacy, power and charisma. • Use the strategies of *fa*, *shu* and *shi*.	• Establish and enforce classroom rules. • Build a classroom system based on reward and punishment. • Manipulate students' impressions of teachers and their behaviour. • Make a distinct division between the roles of teacher and students.
Daoism	• Connect oneself to Nature. • Follow Nature to reach real efficiency.	• Respect the uniqueness of each person. • Act according to individual students' capabilities and desires. • Adopt the principle of "action through inaction". • Teachers and students have supplementary roles and relations. • Release the potential of students and keep it flowing like a river. • Avoid imposing explicit intentions and a strong will on students. • Avoid harsh rules, rewards and punishments as they make effective classroom management impossible.
Confucianism	• Emphasize humanism. • Socialize individuals as moral and responsible members of groups and society. • Promote harmonious interpersonal relationships.	• Everyone is changeable. • Show students the loving heart of *ren*. • Show students genuineness, empathy and care. • Promote students' personal and social development. • Teach students how to behave properly according to norms and rituals. • Socialize students to be "perfect gentlemen".

as being superior to another, and this superior-inferior continuum is applied not only to the relations between husband-wife, old-young, upper and lower generations and parent-child, but also to teacher-student relationships (Bond and Hwang, 1986; King, 1981; King and Bond, 1985; Wright, 1962). Teachers who hold senior positions tend to dominate students who hold junior positions: they have the authority to define the legitimacy of subject knowledge and have the right to decide on students' standards in various aspects of life, such as dress, deportment, language, manners, social conduct and interpersonal relationships. In most cases, students are expected to show conformity and obedience.

This hierarchical relationship between teachers and students can be seen in a Chinese proverb very often heard in school: "the seniors and juniors have their ranking" (*zhang you you xu*). When students fail to conform, for instance by challenging teachers' judgments, teachers might condemn them by saying, "no order of seniors and juniors" (*wu shang wu xia*), and in some severe cases the political term "subversion" (*zuo fan*) might be used instead. All these sayings carry the message that any misbehaviour which appears to be intended to overturn the hierarchical relationship between teachers and students is socially, culturally and politically unacceptable in all schooling contexts.

Other examples which illustrate this point can be seen from how two teachers talked about their classroom roles in interviews. One teacher affirmed "in my classroom, I tell my students that I am the Queen, the classroom is my territory and you're all my people"; and the other said, "I think I am a teacher whereas they are the students. If I meet them outside the classroom, they are supposed to come up and greet me first." Traditionally, students should always be respectful to their teachers, in the same way as they are to their parents, which is reflected in a Chinese saying, "teacher for a day, parent for life" (Ho, 2001: 103).

Collectivism and conformity

Collectivism and conformity are strongly emphasized in Chinese society (Hofstede, 1980, 1983; Yang, 1981). At one level, this phenomenon can never be separated from the hierarchical human relationships of the *wu lun*, as noted earlier, in which juniors are expected to show conformity and subordination to seniors. At another level, the social norm of *ren*, *yi* and *li*, some writers argue (Hsu, 1971; Hsu et al., 1961), is the root of Chinese collectivism and conformity.

As explained in the previous section, *ren* refers to benevolent acts and conduct, *yi* represents the righteousness and appropriateness of individuals' behaviour, and *li* refers to a set of norms and rituals for social behaviour (Hsu, 1953; Ip, 1996). The *ren-yi-li* system provides individuals with a set of social and moral obligations, through which Chinese people know how to play their roles and define their social relationships with others within the hierarchy of the *wu lun* (Bond and Hwang,1986; Bond and Lee, 1988; Gabrenya and Hwang, 1996; Ip, 1996; Solomon, 1971; Wilson, 1981; Yu, 1996).

Brought up within the *wu lun* and the *ren-yi-li* systems, Chinese individuals become strongly aware of the image of their social selves, and feel an obligation to show their conformity to the social group to which they belong. Hence, many writers have argued that Chinese society is characterized by "group-orientedness" (Wilson, 1981), or "collectivism" (Ip, 1996). As Wilson (1981: 11) states,

> In modern Chinese society, school training, the media, and associational pressures generally emphasise identification with larger groups such as brigades and communes and, of course, with society as a whole. The emphasis in training is on shifting identification to these larger secondary groups . . .

It can be inferred that Chinese students are generally encouraged to prioritize collective over individual interests, and submit themselves to the organization of the classroom and the school: any individual's interests should be suppressed so as to pursue the group interests and achieve the notion of harmony within the hierarchy (Ip, 1996). Ip (1996: 51) elaborates on this idea by saying:

> Indeed, the harmony thus espoused helped generate a kind of holism which in turn gave greater significance to the whole than to the parts . . . The manifestations of this holistic collectivism within an institutional setting were the family and the state, which took precedence over the individual in terms of values and importance.

Such studies show the impact of collectivism on individual social behaviour in Hong Kong classrooms. When students thought of themselves, there was a clear tendency to use more group-related concepts, such as being attentive to others, and being respectful and polite to them. Also, when talking about their classroom lives, students liked to use the pronoun "we" more often than "I". In addition, they were socialized to show conformity to rules even when they found them unreasonable, as a way of pursuing the group interests by ignoring and suppressing their own individual interests. The fact that teachers warned students that they would be punished if they spoke to a very talkative student was further evidence that group pressure was commonly used as a strategy for managing students' misbehaviour in classrooms.

To ensure that students are socialized into the values of collectivism and conformity, teachers were supposed to be "strict" — as a Chinese aphorism indicated, "Rearing without education is the fault of the father; teaching without strictness is the negligence of the teacher" (Yuan, 1984: 57). Teachers were to carry out the important task of supervising students' behaviour with constant reminders and intensive help to ensure they met the moral standards of proper behaviour and obeyed their instructions.

To a great extent, Hong Kong classrooms are still characterized by group-orientedness and collectivism, which is reflected in the endorsement given to group-related traits and roles, and the close involvement of ideal selves in social relationships. The dimensions used to perceive themselves and others are likewise focused on interpersonal concerns, not on mastery of the external world or absorption with narrowly personal processes.

Classroom scenario

Collectivism in the Chinese classroom

After playing basketball during the playtime, a boy's white school shirt was soaking with sweat and stuck tightly to his body. Just before he entered the classroom, he was stopped by the teacher who said in a serious tone: "How did you wet your shirt like this? Don't you know how smelly you are? All your classmates will suffer from the bad smell." Throughout the whole conversation between the teacher and this student, the focus was on the impact of this behaviour on the feelings of others rather than on the welfare of the student.

Chinese practices of childhood socialization

Chinese people have generally used practices such as control, punishment, and discipline for socializing children into the social value of conformity and collectivism (Bond, 1991; Ho, 1986; Wilson, 1981; Yang, 1986). The same phenomenon can be seen in Hong Kong classrooms where students are expected to show obedience to the senior members of the school (Hue, 2005a, 2005b).

As Chinese parents normally do, teachers in Hong Kong tend to restrict and control their children's behaviour from a very young age, often using harsh disciplinary practices, such as ridicule and shaming, to ensure conformity and compliance (Ho, 1981), and affective manipulation such as threatening, scolding and punishment (Ho, 1986).

The close relationship between Chinese practices for childhood socialization and the methods employed for classroom management can be seen in the fact that the words used for the former are often transferred to the latter. For instance, parents often use the word *shek,* which in Cantonese literally means "kiss", to express their concern, love and care for their children, and this same word is frequently used in talking about classroom management. Also, other Cantonese words from parental disciplinary practice, such as *da* (beating), *cou* (shame), *ma* (scolding) and *yan* (strictness) are commonly employed by teachers and students to depict classroom life. Furthermore, the parents of some difficult students plead with teachers to exercise more severe discipline by saying something like: "I give you the right to beat and scold him if my child is bad in class" as they have found such practices to be effective in changing their children's behaviour. Many teachers share this view and believe that the practice can be transferred from the home to the classroom.

Many social psychologists are, however, concerned about the effects of using such harsh disciplinary practices on students' development. For example, these practices make students develop a very strong sense of "social self" rather than "individual self" (Wilson, 1981) as well as dependency, and a moral orientation with a high internalization of conformity to standards of behaviour, and to parental examples (Wilson, 1974, 1981).

The social game of "face"

Chinese people are used to playing the social game of "face" (*mianzi*) (Bond and Hwang, 1986; Ho, 1976; Stover, 1974) which has special meanings in interpersonal interaction. There are many expressions and proverbs about "face" which are regarded by Chinese as guidelines for one's social behaviour. For example, there is the common Chinese expression "A man needs face as a tree needs its bark". Obviously a tree without bark cannot grow and, similarly, a person without "face" cannot function successfully in a social group. In any social setting, people have to master the skills of saving and enhancing their "face". Understanding this social game can help in making sense of how teachers and students interact with each other in Hong Kong classrooms.

In general, "face" refers to how an individual's self-image is perceived by others and also how each responds to other group members' expectations of them. However, its meaning has to be interpreted in the context in which the term is used. For example, when one says that "face" is maintained, this means that individuals are able to define situations, their roles and others' roles in line with the group's expectations and so establish their social self-image among group members as they wish (Hu, 1944). However, "losing face" refers to situations in which individuals cannot perform the roles expected in a social group, and this is likely to have a negative effect on their social self-images and their ability to function properly in a group.

In addition, "enhancing one's face" is used when individuals are assertive enough to know the behaviours and attitudes which are most praised by others in their social network, and act accordingly (Hu, 1944); and in doing so, they manage others' impressions of their social self-images in the ways they want to. The junior members in a hierarchical structure tend to play the role of enhancing the "face" of the seniors. Reciprocally, the seniors may give more "face" to the juniors in an effort to increase subordinates' prestige in front of other group members, so that both the seniors and juniors have "face" and maintain harmonious relationships.

In contrast, in "losing face", individuals fail to play the social roles that are expected (Hu, 1994). Such failure may cause them to feel deeply ashamed and embarrassed, and finally to lose confidence in interacting with others in the social group to which they belong (Bond and Hwang, 1986; Hu, 1944).

Since "losing face" has such undesirable effects, normally people try to save everyone's face in such situations (Hu, 1944). Various patterns of emotional arousal, consisting of anger, embarrassment, shame, anxiety and self-blame, are closely related to different types of face-saving behaviours (Chu, 1983). The termination of face-losing behaviour, the reinterpretation of situations in which they lose face, or seeking an apology from others, are examples of face-saving behaviour. In some extreme cases, people may even react in aggressive and rebellious ways to express their dissatisfaction with the unpleasant feelings caused by the face-losing behaviour.

In the classroom, teachers and students are deeply concerned with their own and others' social self-image and "face". Since losing "face" has such negative effects, there is considerable potential for this issue to create a tense relationship between teachers and students, particularly when most students have not yet been well socialized into playing this game properly or when they, wittingly or unwittingly, make teachers lose "face" publicly. It can also have an effect on school staff when they interact with each other in the process of guidance and discipline.

So far, this section has shown how the classroom life of teachers and students is linked to some aspects of Chinese culture: hierarchical human relationships, insistence on collectivism and conformity, Chinese parental practices for childhood socialization and the social game of "face" (*mianzi*). However, it needs to be stressed that the focus has been on examining the monolithic entity of Chinese culture, not on its evolving nature and on finding out how it affects the behaviour of classroom participants.

❐ **Activity 2.3**

When West meets East in Hong Kong schools

Since Hong Kong was ceded to Britain by China in 1842 under the Treaty of Nanking, the society has been undergoing a process of modernization. Many Western influences have changed every aspect of society and people's lives but, despite this, society and, in particular, Hong Kong schools are still influenced to some degree by Confucianism.

- What Western influences can you identify in schools?
- How has Chinese culture reacted to such influences?
- What Chinese cultural traditions of schooling have been lost?
- Are there any cultural practices in schools which can never be changed?

From the Yin-Yang Perspective: Making Sense of the Chinese Classroom

According to Hue's study (2005a), classroom participants in Hong Kong schools are strongly influenced by yin-yang philosophy which leads them to delineate their roles and behaviour in these two opposing dimensions. This point is further elaborated below and is followed by a description of the basic principles of yin-yang philosophy and its links to classroom management.

The duality of teachers' roles

The adoption of the yin-yang philosophy can be seen in the way teachers talk about their classroom roles. A classroom teacher has to play two roles which are very different in nature and apparently in opposition to each other — such as punishing and caring, being both reactive and proactive, disciplining and providing guidance, stopping misbehaviour and promoting good behaviour, and controlling and facilitating students' learning. One side of this duality leads teachers to be "more active" in managing the classroom by acting in "hard" and "negative" ways, but the other appears to relate to behaviour which is "less active", "positive" and "soft".

Further evidence can be found in the ways teachers describe their strategies for classroom management, which include, for example, "being hard at the beginning and being soft at the end", "being strict outside and being kind inside", "scolding students verbally and caring for them with the heart" and "looking frustrated outside but keeping calm inside". Some other sayings which illustrate the same point include: a basket of 'sugar' (reward and caring) and "a basket of 'shit' (punishment)"; "the complementary of softness and hardness" (*gang you bin ji*); "beating one up (scolding or being stern to others) means love" (*da zhe ai ye*); "using *jin* (calmness and inactiveness) to control *dong* (movement and activeness)" (*yi jin ji dong*); "dealing with changing things with the strategy of doing nothing" (*yi bu bian yin wan bian*). Yet more examples of the dual nature of teachers' talk about their classrooms are summarized in Table 2.2 on p. 37.

The duality of teachers' roles, as illustrated in the way they talk about their classroom management, can be explained by the yin-yang philosophy. Teachers are used to taking it as a frame of reference for their roles and behaviour in the classroom (Hue, 2005a). Teachers who cannot balance these dual roles are likely to experience difficulties and conflicts in managing their classes, whereas those who harmonize them feel confident in managing their classroom in an efficient manner.

Table 2.2 The yin-yang perspective: teachers talking about their classrooms (Hue, 2005a)

	The yin side of the classroom	The yang side of the classroom
What the classroom is like	• It is humanistic and flexible. • It is depicted as involving living things which grow and has the function of metabolism.	• It is bureaucratic and inflexible. • It is depicted as a factory and a royal court.
What the classroom is for	• Enhancing the welfare of students and their personal growth • Promoting students' self esteem	• Achieving the targets set previously • Guaranteeing the quality of "output" • Socializing students into showing respect for authority and conformity to social rules
How teachers may make sense of students' roles	• As human beings who have free will and whose individual needs should be respected and fulfilled	• As a subject and a subordinate • As a candidate for public examinations
How teachers may make sense of their own roles	• As a carer and a counsellor, offering guidance and pastoral care • Defining their roles in more proactive, humanistic and expanded ways	• As a controller, an authoritarian figure imposing strict discipline • Defining their roles in more reactive and hierarchical ways
Strategies that may be adopted for improving the classroom situation	• A Confucian approach • Adopting an intrinsic, proactive, developmental and "soft" approach • Adopting approaches which tend to be permissive and socio-emotional • Giving mutual respect, encouragement, praise, acceptance, empathy, trust, support, understanding and care • Promoting positive relationships	• A Legalist approach • Adopting an extrinsic, and "hard" approach • Adopting approaches which tend to be behavioural, authoritarian and intimidating • Setting limits and consequences, and clarifying expectations • Establishing classroom rules, issuing commands and using coercion, punishment and rewards

Basic principles of yin-yang philosophy

The yin-yang philosophy goes back to ancient agrarian religion. It existed in the school of neo-Confucianism developed in the fifteenth century, and figures prominently in Daoism. The two Chinese characters for yin-yang literally mean the "sunny side of the hill" (*yang*) and "shady side of the hill" (*ying*) and they refer to the day and more active functions, and the night and less active functions, respectively.

Figure 2.1 The symbol of yin-yang or Taijitu

The basic principles of yin-yang are well illustrated by the yin-yang symbol or Taijitu (太極圖), with black representing yin and white representing yang, as shown in Figure 2.1. This symbol reflects the inescapably intertwined duality of all things in Nature, a common theme in Daoism. No quality is independent of its opposite, nor so pure that it does not contain its opposite in a diminished form; and these concepts are depicted by the vague division between black and white, the flowing boundary between the two, and the smaller circles within the larger regions. It is suggested that Chinese teachers are used to adopting the philosophic framework of yin-yang for making sense of the classroom and their roles in its management. In what follows, the basic principles of yin-yang and the implications for classroom management are described.

1. *They are in opposition.*

    Everything has an opposite, but this is merely in a relative sense: everything carrying yin contains some elements of yang. Neither side is more important or better than the other. For example, water can be in the soft form of liquid and in the hard form of an iceberg; and in the same vein, a student who acts in a disruptive way in an English language lesson can behave reasonably well in other lessons. Also, a teacher may behave in an authoritarian manner when aiming to restore order on one occasion but on others the same teacher can play the role of carer.

2. *They are interdependent.*

    There is a dynamic relationship between yin and yang: they are interdependent and one cannot exist without the other as they are equal aspects of the oneness, or the seamless whole. For example, there is no happiness without sadness, and night cannot exist without day. In the classroom, everything is interdependent and constantly redefined as circumstances change. Good behaviour does not exist if there is no misbehaviour, and an orderly classroom does not exist without a disorderly one: they are not mutually exclusive.

3. *They support each other.*

    Yin and yang are interflowing dynamically at the same time: as one grows, the other diminishes. A "healthy" classroom, with a positive environment for learning, is one in which ying and yang are constantly kept in balance.

4. *They can transform into one another.*

    In particular conditions, or where some new factors trigger change, yin can be transformed into yang and vice versa. This can be seen as a process of transformation in which there are changes between phases of a cycle. Nothing is unchangeable and non-transformable, except "the change" itself, known as the Way or the Dao in Chinese philosophy. For example, heat changes to cool and rich changes to poor; and in the same way, a disorderly classroom can be transformed into an orderly one and vice versa, and a disruptive student can be changed into one who can behave in the ways teachers expect.

Keeping the balance of yin-yang

As highlighted above, teachers who can maintain a balance between yin and yang can be confident about managing their classrooms in an efficient and harmonious manner, while those who are unable to do so may encounter problems and conflict. As suggested earlier in Table 2.2, teachers have to play two roles in which they need to balance the opposing ways of yin and yang, according to the patterns of interpersonal relationships in the class and the context in which they participate.

The yin of the classroom

As shown in Table 2.2, classroom teachers have a role in pastoral care. They are responsible for students' feelings, needs and welfare in both an individual and collective sense and should build an ethos of caring and helping through using strategies such as mutual respect, encouraging, praising, building trust, empathy and acceptance — all of which aim to enhance students' self-esteem and personal growth and promote a positive classroom environment. Most strategies are proactive and developmental in nature which is reflected in the ways teachers normally react to classroom incidents before they arise. They have a belief that "something should be done before pupils do X" which is captured in the Chinese saying, "Get your raincoat ready before it rains, and never dig the well until you feel thirsty."

The yang of the classroom

On the yang side, teachers are responsible for controlling the quality of output of the classroom, such as students' learning and their academic performance. Generally, this can be achieved by using "Feedback" or ways of preventing or ending disturbances to teaching and learning. When teachers play this role, they focus more on the collective interests of the class than the interests of individual students.

Furthermore, the strategies adopted tend to be reactive. The teachers concentrate more on whatever does not work in the classroom and then react to difficulties. They are used to having to decide what they need to do when pupils act in particular ways, and this reactive approach can again be illustrated in a Chinese idiom: "When the enemy comes, we have soldiers to fight with them. When the flood comes, we have earth to stop it." As most teachers recognize, it is crucial to master and refine this skill for responding to any students who violate classroom rules and to resolve any problems with individuals or groups of students. Teachers who put more emphasis on this are inclined to have tight procedures and enforcement of rules, and a clear statement of rights, expectations and roles.

In some contexts, teachers exercise their power directly in managing classes, believing that administering punishment and scolding are the most appropriate ways to control students' misbehaviour and get respect for their authority; and students become used to being treated strictly and constantly disciplined. However, according to the yin and yang doctrine, such a classroom has excess yang. In Hong Kong's examination-dominated culture, there is a place for classrooms with excess yang since, as Hue (2002) argued, one of the teachers' roles is to ensure that students are familiar with all the skills which are helpful for managing examinations and entering a university.

Summary

This chapter attempts to explain how the Hong Kong classroom has been affected by Chinese culture. While Western influences have had a major effect on Hong Kong society, the influences of Confucianism, Daoism and Legalism can still be found in its classrooms. Consciously or otherwise, the thinking and social and moral behaviour of teachers and students are still affected by aspects of these philosophies.

The influence of Chinese culture on the social behaviour of classroom participants is reflected in the following four ways: (1) hierarchical human relationships; (2) collectivism and conformity; (3) Chinese practices of childhood socialization; and (4) the social game of "face". Nonetheless, it is necessary to note that their degree of influence may vary widely from classroom to classroom, which means that, although they are all influenced by Chinese culture, the patterns of social behaviour vary across schools.

It is also suggested that classroom participants in Hong Kong schools are affected by yin-yang philosophy which leads them to socially construct their roles, interpersonal relationships, social behaviour and classroom incidents in line with its two opposing dimensions. These principles are summarized as follows: yin and yang (1) are in opposition; (2) are interdependent; (3) consume and support each other; and (4) can transform into one another. Teachers who are unable to balance yin and yang may experience difficulties and conflicts, whereas those who can keep this balance can play their various roles in classroom management in a confident, harmonious and effective manner.

Questions for Discussion

1. How have teachers been influenced by Confucianism, Daoism and Legalism as regards their roles in the classroom? In relation to this, how can students react reciprocally?
2. Some teachers are used to adopting the Daoist principle of "action through inaction" (無為而為) for classroom management. What strategies can be regarded as "action" and "inaction"?
3. There is a Chinese saying, "Superficially it is Confucianism but underneath it is Legalism." (陽儒陰法). To what extent do you think this saying is applicable to Hong Kong classrooms?
4. What similarities and differences are there between teachers' and parents' common practices in childhood socialization? What cultural elements may a teacher use to promote effective classroom management?
5. What cultural elements may a teacher use for effective classroom management?

Useful Resources

Website

Chinese Literature Classics: http://www.chinapage.com/classic1.html

Further Reading

Biggs, J. B. (1994). What are effective schools? Lessons from East and West. *Australian Educational Researcher*, 21: 19–39.

Bond, M. H. (ed.) (1987). *The psychology of the Chinese people* (2nd edn). Hong Kong: Oxford University Press.

Stevenson, H. W. et al. (1987). Classroom behavior and achievement of Japanese, Chinese and American children. In R. Glaser (ed.) *Advances in instructional psychology* 3. Hillsdale, NJ: Lawrence Erlbaum Associates.

Tani, M. (2005). Quiet, but only in class: Reviewing the in-class participation of Asian student. Retrieved 6 October, 2005, from: w.itl.usyd.edu.au/herdsa2005/pdf/non_refereed/030.pdf" http://www.itl.usyd.edu.au/herdsa2005/pdf/non_refereed/030.pdf.
Watkins D. A. and Biggs, J. B. (2001) (eds.) *The Chinese learner: Cultural, psychological and contextual influences.* Hong Kong and Melbourne: Comparative Education Research Centre, University of Hong Kong, and Australian Council for Educational Research.
Wong, K. C. (2001). Chinese culture and leadership. *International Journal of Leadership in Education.* 4(4): 309–19.

References

Bond, M. H. (1991). Chinese values and health: A cultural level examination. *Psychology and Health,* 5: 137–152.
Bond, M. H. and Hwang, K. K. (1986). The social psychology of Chinese people. In M. H. Bond (ed.) *The psychology of the Chinese people.* Hong Kong: Oxford University Press.
Bond, M. H. and Lee, P. W. H. (1988). Face saving in Chinese culture: A discussion and experimental study of Hong Kong students. In A. Y. L. King and R. P. Lee *Social life and development in Hong Kong* (2nd edn). Hong Kong: The Chinese University Press.
Chu, R. L. (1983). *Empirical research on the psychology of face.* Unpublished doctoral thesis, Taiwan: National Taiwan University (in Chinese).
Gabrenya, W. K. and Hwang, K. K. (1996). Chinese social interaction: Harmony and hierarchy on the good earth. In M. H. Bond (ed.) *The handbook of Chinese psychology.* Hong Kong: Oxford University Press.
Ho, D. Y. F. (1976). On the concept of face. *American Journal of Sociology,* 81: 867–884.
———. (1981). Traditional pattern of socialization in Chinese society. *Acta Psychologica Taiwanica,* 23(2): 81–95.
———. (1986). Chinese patterns of socialisation: A critical review. In M. H. Bond (ed.) *The psychology of the Chinese people.* Hong Kong: Oxford University Press.
Ho, I. T. (2001). Are Chinese teachers authoritarian? In D. A. Watkins and J. B. Biggs (eds.) *Teaching the Chinese learner: Psychological and pedagogical perspectives.* Hong Kong and Melbourne: Comparative Education Research Centre, University of Hong Kong, and Australian Council for Educational Research.
Hofstede, G. (1980). *Culture's consequences: International differences in work-related values.* London and Beverly Hills: Sage.
———. (1983). Dimensions of national cultures in fifty countries and three regions. In J. B. Deregowski, S. Dziurawiec and R. C. Annis (eds.) *Expiscations in cross-cultural psychology.* Lisse, Netherlands: Swets and Zeitlinger.
Hsu, F. L. K. (1953). *Americans and Chinese:* Two ways of life. New York: Abelard-Schuman.
———. (1971). Psychological homeostasis and *jen*: Conceptual tools for advancing psychological anthropology. *American Anthropologist,* 73: 23–44.
Hsu, F. L. K., Watrous, B. G. and Lord, E. M. (1961). *Culture pattern and adolescent behaviour. International Journal of Social Psychiatry,* 7: 33–53.
Hu, H. C. (1944). The Chinese concept of face. *American Anthropologist,* 46: 45–64.

Hue, M. T. (2001). *The relationship between school guidance and discipline in Hong Kong secondary schools.* Unpublished PhD thesis. UK: Institute of Education, University of London.

———. (2005a). *Preliminary findings: The social construction of classroom discipline in Hong Kong secondary schools.* Funded by an Internal Research Grant, the Hong Kong Institute of Education.

———. (2005b). The influences of Chinese culture on teacher-student interaction in the classrooms of Hong Kong Schools. *Curriculum Perspectives, Australian Curriculum Studies Association* 25(3): 37–43.

———. (2007). The influence of classic Chinese philosophy of Confucianism, Taoism and Legalism on classroom discipline in Hong Kong junior secondary schools. *Pastoral Care in Education,* 25(2):38–45.

Ip, K. C. (1996). Confucian familial collectivism and the underdevelopment of the civic person. In W. N. K. Lo and S. W. Man (eds.) *Research and endeavours in moral and civic education.* Hong Kong Institute of Educational Research, Hong Kong: The Chinese University of Hong Kong.

King, A. Y. C. and Bond, M. H. (1985). The Confucian paradigm of man: A sociological view. In W. S. Tseng and D. Y. H. Wu (eds.) *Chinese culture and mental health.* New York: Academic Press.

Solomon, R. H. (1971). *Mao's revolution and the Chinese political culture.* Berkeley: University of California Press.

Stover, L. E. (1974). *The cultural ecology of Chinese civilization.* New York: New American Library.

Wilson, R. W. (1974). *The moral state: A study of the political socialisation of Chinese and American children.* New York: The Free Press.

———. (1981). Moral behaviour in Chinese society: A theoretical perspective. In R. W. Wilson, S. L. Greenblatt and A. A. Wilson (eds.) *Moral behavior in Chinese society.* New York: Praeger.

Wright, A. F. (1962). Values, roles and personalities. In A. F. Wright and D. Twitchett (eds.) *Confucian personalities.* Stanford: Stanford University Press.

Yang, K. S. (1981). Social orientation and individual modernity among Chinese students in Taiwan. *Journal of Social Psychology,* 113: 159–170.

———. (1986). Chinese personality and its change. In M. H. Bond (ed.) *The psychology of the Chinese people.* Hong Kong: Oxford University Press.

Yu, A. B. (1996). Ultimate life concerns, self and Chinese achievement motivation. In M. H. Bond (ed.) *The handbook of Chinese psychology.* Hong Kong: Oxford University Press.

Yuan, G. (1984). Six measures to ensure the success of key middle schools. *Chinese Education,* 17(2): 57–60.

3

Effective Classroom Management

Li Wai-shing

A good classroom manager carefully plans everything that occurs in the classroom from the seating arrangements to instructions for children who finish planned activities early.

American Federation of Teachers (1995–96)

Synopsis

Classroom management is a multi-faceted concept. This chapter describes and discusses four major components of effective classroom management: management of the physical environment, curriculum management, managing discipline and managing classroom procedures. The related concepts and strategies which are discussed include: the use and decoration of classroom space; principles for effective lesson planning and design; classroom rules and routines; and the use of punishment and rewards. Classroom management must go beyond just managing classroom behaviour — it is also about the management of learning. Classroom management as a whole is a complex task of designing an environment that facilitates better teaching and learning.

Objectives

After reading this chapter, you should be able to:
*   understand the nature of effective classroom management;
*   understand the concepts of classroom management and management of learning;
*   identify the major factors conducive to learning in managing the physical environment;
*   establish classroom routines and rules with pupils;

- apply principles for using rewards and punishment in the classroom;
- understand the teacher's authority in learning and teaching.

Pre-Reading Reflection and Discussion

- What is the ultimate purpose of effective classroom management?
- What kind of classroom environment do pupils prefer?
- How would you decorate your classroom to help your pupils learn better?
- On the basis of your experience as a student or teacher, are there any principles for developing useful classroom procedures that you wish to suggest to colleagues or peers?
- In your opinion, what differentiates good and bad classroom rules?
- Do you think teachers offer limited praise to their students because they often take it for granted that students ought to behave well in class?
- Where does a teacher's authority come from?

Introduction

Good classroom management is challenging. Traditionally, it was viewed as a matter of exerting control over the learners, but more recently classroom management has been perceived as the art of establishing a good climate and managing instruction effectively. It involves more than just implementing procedures for organizing the students or setting rules for a disciplined classroom — it is about how a teacher establishes his/her authority by offering interesting lessons. Teachers need to gain students' respect and confidence by showing concern for their needs, and this is reflected and realized in their preparation of lessons that actively engage the students. An effective manager of a classroom knows how to use praise to encourage good behaviour and apply appropriate measures to prevent misbehaviour. We start by examining the classroom management of Mr. Lam, a local teacher in a primary school. Are there any respects in which you consider he is a poor manager? If so, make a list of recommendations for improving his classroom management.

> **Classroom scenario**
>
> Mr. Lam entered the classroom and greeted the pupils. It was a dull room with only a few worn-out posters on the walls. He turned on the computer in order to run a DVD for his social studies lesson. It took him more than five minutes to

get the computer to produce the right images, and during that time Mr. Lam said nothing as he was focusing on what had happened to his computer. As a few pupils started talking and the noise began to get louder, Mr. Lam shouted, "Please keep quiet!", but none of the pupils paid any attention to him. All of a sudden, Mr. Lam banged his table and shouted to the pupils in an intimidating tone, "If you keep on making a noise, all of you will be punished." At that point, Qing-mei whispered to her neighbour Ni-hui, "I have not made any noise at all, so why does Mr. Lam have to punish me?"

The Reality of Classroom Management

Some non-teachers may view the teaching process as a simple "teach, listen and learn" activity: the teacher just stands in front of a number of pupils in a classroom, talks to them and orders them to complete pre-arranged tasks. However, this conception overlooks completely the multidimensional nature of the classroom environment in which things happen very quickly and publicly, and are sometimes unpredictable and spontaneous. In addition, teachers vary in their educational aims and objectives and the students differ in a wide variety of ways (Waterhouse, 1990: 1–2); and to make matters even more complicated, teachers' management styles generate different types of classroom climate which affect student learning and behaviour (and parents' reactions to the teacher's behaviour). So, overall, classroom management involves teachers steering and coordinating a complex environment for the purpose of effective learning and teaching.

Classroom management can be very taxing, especially for novice teachers. It is much easier to learn if you know how to break it down into smaller components. The four major components of classroom management are noted below and discussed in the rest of this chapter.

1. *Management of the physical environment:* Teachers need to create the best possible physical environment to ensure that their students have a comfortable and pleasant atmosphere in which to learn.

2. *Management of learning:* Teachers must prepare learning objectives, select content, prepare teaching and learning materials and design activities with the goal of devising a curriculum that meets their students' diverse needs.

3. *Classroom procedures and rules:* Teachers have to set guidelines for the smooth and efficient running of classrooms as these are important for conveying their expectations, for establishing classroom norms and for "house-keeping" purposes.

4. *Managing discipline:* Apart from such guidelines, teachers need to set up a discipline system to deal with difficult and bad behaviour.

Managing the Physical Environment of the Classroom

> ❐ **Activity 3.1**
>
> **Designing your own classroom seating arrangements**
>
> Prepare a floor plan of a classroom which you have observed or taught in. Try out various designs with different patterns of seat and furniture arrangements. As you experiment, examine and discuss the advantages and drawbacks of your designs with regard to direct teaching, group work, project work and various other kinds of activities. Keep a record of your designs for future reference.

As pupils spend most of their school learning time in the classroom, its design clearly has an impact on them. However, the management of the physical environment is often overlooked by both teachers and school administrators; and, unfortunately, most classrooms are designed or furnished in ways that make it difficult for pupils to stay motivated and work happily (Gordon, 1974: 156). This should be one of the top priorities of classroom management and needs to be handled at the start of the school year. Here are some preliminary questions:

- Do you feel comfortable with the planning of your classroom?
- Do you think your students find your classroom stimulating and pleasant?
- Have you considered not putting the teacher's desk at the front of the class and reorganizing the students' seats in various ways other than in rows?
- What message does your floor plan send to your students? Do you think it is consistent with your educational values?

Good use of space

Teachers have very little control over the size of their classrooms, but they are able to decide how to utilize the limited space within them. As a creative use of physical space has a significant effect on children's learning (Evans and Lovell, 1979), it is worth spending some time on making as good use of it as possible. According to Charles and Senter (2002), there are six facets of the physical environment of a classroom which teachers have to consider in providing a pleasant place for learning, viz. floor space, wall space, countertop space, shelf space, cupboard and closet space, and the general ambience.

Floor space: The most common seating arrangements include horizontal rows, vertical rows, circles and long tables, all of which serve different purposes. A good seating arrangement is one which facilitates specific learning tasks and activities and communicates a teacher's beliefs about learning and teaching. Leaving sufficient space for an "interior loop" or a passage to give teachers easy and efficient access for working with different groups of pupils is paramount (Jones, 2000). In addition, the routes for daily routine movement should be safe and free from congestion to avoid generating disruptive behaviour. Pupils need some "housekeeping" training on seating arrangements at the beginning of the school year.

Some more creative uses of classroom space may be of value. For example, some teachers like to set aside a special place for pupils to retreat from the general hubbub (Bredekamp, 1987); and similar spaces or corners can be set up for privacy and reflection, and as a reward for good student behaviour. Allowing a certain degree of mobility in the class can help to relieve student boredom and discomfort. Also, although the teacher's desk should be located in a good position for overseeing the whole class, it need not be placed in front of the pupils. Finally, teachers should monitor how well their arrangements work, including asking for pupils' views.

Wall space: Wall space is another area which needs special attention. Very often it is utilized merely for decorative purposes, and more effort could be given to its use for teaching, for example by posting large art prints or maps. Also, bulletin boards are useful for displaying students' work, newspaper clippings and issues for class debate and discussion.

Countertop space: As the countertop space is normally close to windows and has natural light, it is one of the best places for, for instance, plants and aquariums which can provide a beautiful and interesting spot for students.

Shelf, cupboard and closet space: A teacher needs to take care of a wide range of items, such as worksheets, teaching aids and supplies of paper or reference materials for the class. Shelves and cupboards, which are the best places for keeping such items, need to be kept clean and tidy.

General ambience: Charles and Senter (2002: 44) refer to the classroom ambience as "the totality of intangible impressions that pervade the physical classroom", and teachers should try to create as safe, pleasant and stimulating an atmosphere as possible so that learning is enjoyable and effective.

To summarize, in managing the physical environment of the classroom, teachers should aim to provide a secure, welcoming context for learning which facilitates social contact among teachers and pupils to increase pupils' knowledge, confidence and skills in human relationships. Also, the way in which the physical aspects of the classroom are arranged should reflect the goals and values the school wishes to promote.

A checklist for a better physical environment

√   The arrangement of the desks should facilitate the teaching strategies employed.
√   The desk arrangement should allow interaction between the teacher and pupils, and among the pupils themselves.

√ Appropriate decoration, heating and ventilation are conducive to effective teaching and learning.

√ Bulletin boards and display areas provide opportunities for the active participation of students.

√ Any aspects of the room arrangements which are potentially harmful to pupils when they move around should be avoided.

Management of Learning

Curriculum planning and the organization of teaching are major aspects of pedagogy which are often referred to as the "management of learning" (Tsui, 2002). The management of learning is not examined in detail here but, as it is inextricably linked with classroom management, some mention of the concept is necessary. The management of learning, which is concerned with the strategies teachers employ to manage their classes for improved learning, is a wider term than "classroom management"; and, for the purposes of this chapter, it is construed as effective planning, motivating students to become more engaged in learning, and making the classroom enjoyable and challenging, while being responsive to children's needs and the goals of education.

Principles of effective instruction

Some classrooms are more exciting and appealing to pupils than others. While the seating arrangements and decoration can make a significant difference, more important is what goes on in the classroom — how stimulating the subject matter, activities and teaching strategies are. Some key elements in effective teaching are noted below:

(a) *Effective planning:* Good preparation is vital for quality classroom instruction. In their research on planning, Rosenshine and Stevens (1986: 49) highlighted a number of basic principles for effective instruction and curriculum enactment: (i) well-organized lessons; (ii) systematic delivery; (iii) activities that can be applied in authentic situations; (iv) clear criteria for assessing student performance; and (v) constructive feedback. These guidelines show how teachers can improve the design of their lessons and provide appropriate activities for their students.

(b) *Meeting the needs of the students:* When students find lessons attractive, they are less likely to feel bored and misbehave. To be stimulating, lessons should be enjoyable and be seen by students to be useful for fulfilling their "competence needs" (Charles, 2002: 27). Glasser (1998) suggested that teachers can engage their students more actively and increase their concentration span by discussing the subject matter being taught with them and encouraging them to ask questions. Also, including topics which students show a strong desire to learn will clearly increase the likelihood of their being attentive and involved.

(c) *Motivation:* Motivation is often referred to as an inner drive which leads individuals to persist in completing tasks or accomplishing their goals. When pupils are motivated to learn, they will pay more attention and be more actively involved in learning — and therefore be likely to behave well in class. Brophy's (1987) study on motivating pupils to learn contained many insightful suggestions and strategies for teachers:

- *Interest:* There are numerous ways of making a lesson interesting, for example by using multimedia teaching materials, games and simulations, and making the learning meaningful by relating the content to real-life situations.
- *Needs:* Lessons should offer a variety of opportunities for meeting pupils' intellectual and psychological needs. For instance, peer learning can enhance pupils' sense of belonging and acceptance in class, and challenging tasks can fulfil their drive for exploration and increase their sense of satisfaction.
- *Novelty and diversity:* New and creative tasks are likely to engage pupils. Varying the design of activities can enhance interest and helps to cater for pupils' varying needs.
- *Success:* Teachers have to provide opportunities for students to experience success in their learning by preparing tasks which are appropriate and relevant to their level of competence. These tasks must be challenging but manageable, with clear guidelines and support to ensure they can be completed by most students.
- *Tension:* A moderate amount of tension can be beneficial for maintaining students' concentration and effort in learning. Creating a learning atmosphere that is stimulating but not over-tense requires special attention from the teacher.
- *Teacher expectations:* The message of the Pygmalion study by Rosenthal and Jacobson (1968) is well-known to teachers: teacher expectations have a strong impact on student learning and behaviour. However, teachers often overlook the fact that such expectations are usually communicated to the pupils unintentionally, and the effect is cumulative. It is advisable for teachers to communicate high expectations to all learners and, if possible, express this in person in public.

Increasing pupils' motivation is one of the surest ways of helping them to develop their full potential. This is unlikely to be achieved if the instruction and learning activities are boring and unchallenging.

A checklist for effective instruction

√   Are there ample opportunities for your students to engage in meaningful and differentiated activities?

√   Are the activities set manageable and challenging for the students?

√   Are there clear guidelines for completing the activities?

√   Are there ways to let pupils work in groups or collaboratively in the activities?

√   Are there ways to support your pupils in completing the tasks and give them useful feedback?

√   Are there opportunities for students to apply what they have learned in the lesson(s)?

Establishing Classroom Procedures and Rules

According to Eggen and Kauchak (1997), two major goals of classroom management are: (a) to create a learning environment which is conducive to learning; and (b) to develop in students a sense of responsibility and self-regulation in maintaining it. The critical issue in classroom management, therefore, is whether students can be self-disciplined. To accomplish these goals, the teacher needs to establish routines and procedures for daily work and, if necessary, some measures for handling any misbehaviour that disrupts the classroom environment. We now turn to the issue of setting classroom routines and procedures.

The need for classroom guidelines

Classrooms are crowded places with some thirty pupils in a small room packed with tables, chairs, cupboard and shelves. Classroom guidelines are needed for running this small, but complex and sometimes unpredictable, community in which teaching and learning takes place. Clear classroom guidelines can minimize confusion and ensure orderly interaction among pupils, and so minimize the loss of valuable teaching time (Weinstein, 1996: 49). Properly designed classroom guidelines should support teaching and learning by providing pupils with clear expectations and well-defined norms for functioning in a collaborative and cooperative manner to create an orderly environment for learning. The provision of explicitly stated rules and guidelines, and practical experience with them, not only helps pupils to understand the school's expectations but also contributes to their sense of security and academic success (McEwan, 2000: 32).

Classroom procedures

It is useful to distinguish two types of guidelines for effective classroom management: *procedures* and *rules* (Levin and Nolan, 2004: 137). Procedures refer to classroom routines which call for specific behaviour at particular times and on particular tasks. They are necessary not only for the smooth running of instructional activities but also for reducing the frequency with which teachers need to give instructions for daily classroom events. Common examples of such "housekeeping" procedures include entering and leaving the classroom, access to materials, talking and listening in the classroom and passing out exercise books. They are often taught at the beginning of a school year through teacher explanation and peer demonstration. Monitoring of the extent to which these procedures are followed is important to keep the classroom operating smoothly.

A checklist for developing procedures for different situations

The following situations require teachers to specify special procedures for pupils to follow:
- √ Student arrival at and departure from the classroom
- √ Early completion of class work
- √ Proper arrangements for a fire drill
- √ Handing in homework and class work
- √ Lunch-time arrangements
- √ Going for and returning from recess.

Classroom procedures need to make good sense to students; otherwise they are not likely to follow them. For example, it does not make much sense to expect students in reading time to wait silently in the reading corner for others to finish their class work (Gareau and Kennedy, 1991). For students who do not comply with the classroom procedures, the consequences should be logical and natural (Brophy, 1988b) — for example, asking a student who has thrown some scrap paper on the floor to pick it up and put it in the rubbish bin. As with rules and regulations, classroom procedures should be modified and revised if they are found to be inappropriate.

The four pillars of classroom rules

Have you ever considered that there are certain rights which must be protected when teachers try to determine classroom rules for effective teaching and learning? Here are four such basic rights:

1. The teacher's right to teach
2. The students' right to learn
3. The students' psychological and physical safety
4. The protection of the property of schools and individuals.

(Levin and Nolan, 2004: 139)

Classroom rules

If procedures are for "housekeeping" tasks, classroom rules are guidelines for required student behaviour (Levin and Nolan, 2004). Therefore, classroom rules should be designed with the aim of enhancing pupils' positive and on-task behaviour rather than reprimanding disruptive behaviour. Moreover, they should never be employed as a means for controlling pupils in school (Brophy, 1988a). These rules are more wide-ranging and more complex than classroom procedures.

What rules do teachers need?

Rules are necessary to main good discipline in the classroom. Some teachers like to list all the "dos and don'ts" for particular occasions, while others compile a rule book for all occasions. A more practical and civilized way of developing classroom rules is to start thinking about the smallest number of rules which could minimize discipline problems. This set of rules may vary from class to class but the following basic principles for setting them are common to all classrooms. Good rules:

- are fair to everybody, both teachers and pupils;
- make good sense and are not arbitrary;
- can be explained, as necessary;
- have natural and logical consequences when broken;
- are easy to apply when required;
- are positive.

❒ **Activity 3.2**

Designing your own classroom procedures

Working in groups of four, imagine you are the Discipline Masters of a school. You are aware that the new students are not yet accustomed to school life after the first month, and you want to draw their attention to the daily routines. You decide to issue a pamphlet telling them about the school routines. What would the pamphlet look like? What specific school procedures would you include to facilitate the smooth running of the (a) classrooms, and (b) playground?

Communicating classroom rules

It is always a good practice for teachers to develop necessary classroom rules together with the pupils, to exchange views on their rationale, expectations and consequences in an open and democratic atmosphere. An additional advantage of involving pupils in discussing rules is that they are likely to spot any inconsistencies or irrational consequences. In general, this kind of dialogue will increase the chances of pupils accepting the norms and standards conveyed by the rules (Good and Brophy, 1997; Jones and Jones, 2001).

If student involvement in developing classroom rules is impossible, the teacher must communicate the rules clearly to the students so that they fully understand their purposes and rationale; otherwise, they are more likely to be seen as unfair, unreasonable and arbitrary. Also, it is better to express the rules in positive, rather than negative, terms, for example by emphasizing that keeping the classroom clean and tidy provides a better environment for teaching and learning. Finally, all classroom rules should be displayed openly and be subject to constant review.

A checklist for effective classroom rules

√ Keep the number of rules to a minimum.
√ Develop rules with your students.
√ Explain clearly the rationale behind the rules and the consequences of not following them.
√ Phrase the rules positively whenever possible.
√ Ensure that the rules are seen to be fair, realistic and consistent.
√ Apply the rules to all.
√ Display the rules in an appropriate place.
√ Be consistent in getting students to follow the rules.

Managing Discipline Problems

It is often said "prevention is better than cure": it is more desirable to prevent discipline problems from happening than to deal with them in the classroom. As most teachers realize, discipline problems can be contagious. If not monitored frequently and consistently, unacceptable behaviour can gradually become acceptable. The American Federation of Teachers (1995/1996: 24) once warned teachers that "over time, almost imperceptibly, expectations of what constitutes acceptable behaviour get re-defined. We gradually tolerate more and more, until what once was unthinkable becomes the new norm". However, not all discipline problems require direct intervention: in some cases they may be ignored and some student behaviour can be altered by offering appropriate praise. Various ways of managing pupils' behaviour are outlined in the following sections.

Tolerating and understanding behaviour

In broad terms, students, particularly newcomers, may misbehave for reasons such as the following. They may find themselves in a new school environment without support and are unaccustomed to the atmosphere; learning in the classroom and communicating with others in schools could be stressful for them; and they may have trouble in coping with the classroom life, rules and regulations. Although good planning can prevent most of these problems, misbehaviour is likely if they are not handled well. In addition, teachers need to be discerning about difficult behaviour before taking action as it can sometimes be tolerated (e.g. coughing in class because of illness).

When to intervene

When students misbehave despite clear classroom routines and procedures, teacher intervention is needed. Based on the "four pillars of classroom rules", intervention is appropriate for the following behaviours (Grossman, 1995: 274):
- Harmful behaviour (e.g. bullying)
- Distracting behaviour (e.g. playing with toys in the classroom)
- Testing behaviour (e.g. challenging a teacher's authority)
- Antisocial behaviour (e.g. disengagement)
- Contagious behaviour (e.g. talking with a neighbour).

The use of punishment

Punishment in school usually takes two forms: the removal of privileges and the inflicting of physical or other "painful" punishment. Sometimes the removal of privileges can become a logical consequence when appropriately planned and related to the misbehaviour (Levin and Nolan, 2004: 142) — for example, reducing pupils' recess time if they do not form a straight line when going downstairs to the playground. However, in contrast, a teacher's inappropriate planning and aggressive attitude may lead to student hostility, with the logical consequence being perceived as a punishment.

The inflicting of physical and painful punishment also takes several forms. It may involve corporal punishment such as: hitting or shaking; psychological punishment, such as sarcasm or threats; or extra homework or the writing of the school regulations many times. While corporal punishment is forbidden by law, minor psychological punishment or demanding extra work is not uncommon. The use of such punishments is not recommended not only because they are highly controversial but also because they are not based on sound moral and ethical grounds (Jones and Jones, 2001; Kohn, 1999). Research on painful punishments (Clarizio, 1980; Curwin and Mendler, 1988) has shown that they are not effective in the long term and frequent punishment often has the side-effect of teaching the student to find more subtle ways to avoid punishment for misbehaviour in the classroom.

❏ **Activity 3.3**

Ideas about punishment

What is your opinion on the following statements? Share your ideas with your group members.

(a) Punishment is a long-established and effective method that helps students to understand their misbehaviour and develop a sense of personal responsibility.

(b) Without feeling pain, students will not discipline themselves. Punishment involves the inflicting of pain to remind students about their misbehaviour.

(c) "Spare the rod and spoil the child."

Alternatives to punishment

Students often get a teacher's attention either by working well or by misbehaving in class. Docking (2002) suggested that teachers should offer more praise for classroom behaviour, instead of assuming that pupils ought to behave well and that only very good behaviour deserves praise or rewards. While punishment may arouse hostility, praise and rewards create the positive atmosphere needed to maintain good behaviour and promote learning, as well as boosting pupils' self-esteem. Teachers should be generous in giving praise or rewards to both individuals and groups, either publicly or in private.

A checklist for effective use of praise

√   Use praise generously.
√   Give praise early in lessons.
√   "Catch the child being good."
√   Avoid actions which could spoil the effects of praise.
√   Ensure that the praise is informative.
√   Be sensitive to the effects of public versus private praise.
√   Praise for a variety of efforts and achievements.
√   Relay favourable remarks.
√   Be genuine.

(Docking, 2002: 45)

Teacher Authority in Good Management

There are various ways of interpreting what counts as a teacher's authority in the classroom. At one extreme, some teachers may adopt an authoritarian approach and favour controlling the classroom with firm and strict punishments. At the other extreme, some teachers may resort to giving students complete freedom in return for less confrontation with them. In neither case are these teachers exerting their authority appropriately and managing the classroom well.

William Glasser (1998) identified two types of teacher: "boss teachers" and "lead teachers". The former, whom he considers old-fashioned, act in an autocratic way and are unlikely to involve the students in planning their instructional activities, designing the curriculum and developing classroom rules. The latter adopt an open and democratic approach to classroom decision making, inviting student participation in the above activities and respecting their rights as learners.

The way in which teachers exert their authority lies at the heart of successful classroom management. If Glasser's view is correct, a good manager is able to steer the class in an open and democratic manner that gets students to participate in every aspect of school life. Students can share power with the teacher in the processes of planning instructional activities, decision making in classroom affairs, and creating a pleasant atmosphere conducive to effective instruction and learning. In return, teacher authority is reinforced through a more student-centred teaching approach which produces a stimulating classroom environment with better behaviour and learning. Intimidation and autocratic management can never gain students' respect: students respect teachers who understand their needs, share power with them and know how to teach well.

In conclusion, for students, a good classroom manager is a teacher who delivers interesting and creative lessons, generates an engaging atmosphere for learning, and exercises his/her authority in ways which encourage them to be involved in developing classroom routines and rules and, most important, participate fully in all aspects of learning.

Summary

This chapter presents classroom management as a complex task involving the creation of interesting and stimulating lessons, and the development of procedures and rules for establishing a pleasant atmosphere for learning and teaching. In practical terms, classroom management has four major components: management of the physical environment; curriculum management, managing classroom procedures and rules, and discipline management.

Management of the physical environment is concerned with the optimum arrangement of furniture and use of space, for example on the walls, for various purposes — the main one being to produce an environment which will engage pupils in learning.

The management of learning is about planning effective pedagogical strategies which meet pupils' needs and make lessons interesting. Teaching skills are essential for effective instruction.

As classrooms are public and unpredictable places, procedures for good "housekeeping" must be established; and rules are also required to direct student behaviour when necessary. Students should be involved in developing these procedures and rules to make them more relevant and acceptable to them, and teachers need to communicate them to students in a clear and appropriate way.

There are some behaviours which teachers can tolerate, but intervention and punishment are needed when other measures fail. When used effectively, praise can be an alternative to punishment for managing classroom behaviour.

Finally, the proper exercise of teacher authority in managing classrooms is not about autocratic and dominating control. The concept of a "boss teacher" has been replaced by that of a "lead teacher"— a good teacher who gains pupils' respect and stimulates them to participate actively in the learning and teaching process.

Questions for Discussion

1. Define "classroom management". What are the basic elements in managing a pleasant classroom which promotes student learning?
2. Teachers use various kinds of seating arrangements. Discuss among yourselves the instructional strategies which are appropriate when seats are arranged in: (a) rows; (b) horizontal rows; (c) small clusters; and (d) circles. What strategies are inappropriate?

3. Based on your own teaching experience, discuss in pairs what constitutes good teaching and in what ways students can be stimulated to participate fully in classroom learning.

4. Give examples of difficult behaviours which (a) can be permitted; (b) can be tolerated; (c) need teacher intervention; and (d) require punishment.

5. Which kinds of praise are more and less effective for creating a pleasant atmosphere for learning and teaching? Why?

6. In what ways has the concept of a "boss teacher" lost favour and been replaced by a "lead teacher"? How important is being a "lead teacher" for stimulating student participation in classroom activities?

7. How far do you agree with the saying that "a stern teacher produces esteemed students"?

Useful Resources

Websites

1. CAST: Explicit Instruction: http://www.cast.org/publications/ncac/ncac_explicit.html
2. Creating an Effective Physical Classroom Environment: http://www.teachervision.fen.com/page/6506.html
3. Elementary Approach: Classroom Environment: http://content.scholastic.com/browse/article.jsp?id=4134
4. Lesson Presentation: http://www.humboldt.edu/~tha1/hunter-eei.html
5. Routines and Procedures: http://www.educationoasis.com/instruction/CM/routines.htm
6. UKAT– Teacher Authority: http://www.ukat.org.uk/thesaurus/term.php?i=5760

Further Reading

Baker, K. (1985). Research evidence of a school discipline problem. *Phi Delta Kappan*, 66(7): 482–8.

Brophy, J. (1988). Research on teacher effects: Uses and abuses. *The Elementary School Journal*, 89(1): 3–21.

Gordon, T. (1989). *Discipline that works: Promoting self-discipline in children.* New York: Random House.

Kindsvatter, R. (1978). A new view of the dynamics of discipline. *Phi Delta Kappan*, 59 (5): 322–65.

Lepper, M. and Green, D. (1978). *The hidden cost of reward: New perspectives on human motivation.* Hillsdale, NJ: Erlbaum.

Levin, J. and Shanken-Kaye, J. (2002). *From disrupter to achiever: Creating successful learning environments for the self-control classroom.* Dubuque, IA: Kendall/Hunt.

Stipek, D. J. (2001). *Motivation to learn: Integrating theory and practice* (4th edn). Boston: Allyn and Bacon.

References

American Federation of Teachers (1995–96). Elements of an effective discipline strategy. *American Educator*, 19(4): 24–27.

Bredekamp, S. (ed.). (1987). *Developmentally appropriate practice in early childhood programs serving children from birth through age 8* (expanded edn). Washington, DC: National Association for the Education of Young Children.

Brophy, J. (1987). Synthesis of research strategies on motivating students to learn. *Educational Leadership*, 45(2): 40–48.

———. (1988a). Educating teachers about managing classrooms and students. *Teaching and Teacher Education,* 4(1): 1–18.

———. (1988b). Research on teaching effects: Uses and abuses. *The Elementary School Journal*, 89(1): 3–21.

Charles, C. M. (2002). *Essential elements of effective discipline*. Boston: Allyn & Bacon.

Charles, C. M. and Senter, G. W. (2002). *Elementary classroom management* (3rd edn). Boston: Allyn & Bacon.

Clarizio, H. F. (1980). *Toward positive classroom discipline* (3rd edn). New York: Wiley.

Curwin, R. L. and Mendler, A. N. (1999). *Discipline with dignity*. Upper Saddle River, NJ: Merrill Prentice Hall.

Docking, J. (2002). *Managing behaviour in the primary school*. London: David Fulton Publishers.

Eggen, P. and Kauchak, D. (1997). *Educational psychology: Windows on classrooms*. Upper Saddle River, NJ: Prentice Hall.

Evans, G. and Lovell, B. (1979). Design modification in an open-plan school. *Journal of Educational Psychology*, 71: 41–49.

Gareau, M. and Kennedy, C. (1991). Structure time and space to promote pursuit of learning in primary schools. *Young Children*, 47(5): 4–9.

Glasser, W. (1998). *The quality school teacher*. New York: HarperCollins.

Good, T. and Brophy, J. (1997). *Looking in classrooms* (4th edn). New York: Longman.

Gordon, T. (1974). *Teacher effectiveness training*. New York: Wyden.

Grossman, H. (1995). *Classroom behaviour management in a diverse society*. Mountain View, CA: Mayfield Publishing Company.

Jones, V. F. (2000). *Tools for teaching: Discipline instruction motivation*. Santa Cruz, CA: Frederic H. Jones & Associates, Inc.

Jones, V. F. and Jones, L. S. (2001). *Comprehensive classroom management: Creating communities of support and solving problems* (6th edn). Boston: Allyn & Bacon.

Kohn, A. (1999). *Punishment by rewards*. Boston: Houghton Mifflin.

Levin, J. and Nolan, J. F. (2004). *Principles of classroom management* (4th edn). Boston: Pearson.

McEwan, B. (2000). *The art of classroom management*. Upper Saddle River, NJ: Merrill.

Rosenshine, B. and Stevens, R. (1986). Teaching functions. In M. C. Wittrock (ed.) *Handbook of research on teaching* (3rd edn). New York: Macmillan.

Rosenthal, R. and Jacobson, L. (1968). *Pygmalion in the classroom: Teacher expectations and pupils' intellectual development.* New York: Holt, Rinehart & Winston.

Tsui, A. B. M. (2002). *Understanding expertise in teaching.* Cambridge: Cambridge University Press.

Waterhouse, P. (1990). *Classroom management.* Stafford: Network Educational Press.

Weinstein, C. S. (1996). *Secondary classroom management: Lessons from research and practice.* New York: McGraw-Hill.

4

Managing Misbehaviour

Li Wai-shing

Knowing how best to respond to unwanted behaviour is among the most difficult decisions teachers have to make. Should the child just be ignored? reprimanded? punished? counselled? given special treatment?

Docking (2002)

Synopsis

As the above quotation indicates, responding to misbehaviour in the classroom is a very demanding task. This chapter suggests that teachers should formulate their own personal plans for managing student misbehaviour. It also outlines four levels of intervention to stop difficult behaviour, ranging from the least disruptive strategies of non-interference to non-verbal intervention, and from verbal intervention to the use of logical consequences. Practical and effective strategies and measures for each level are introduced to equip teachers for daily classroom practices.

Objectives

After reading this chapter, you should be able to:
- formulate personal plans for managing students' behavioural problems;
- understand the basis for non-intervention and intervention measures;
- understand the continuum for managing students' misbehaviour;
- use intervention strategies to deal with students' misbehaviour;
- employ logical consequences when students choose not to change their undesirable behaviour in the classroom.

Pre-Reading Reflection and Discussion

• Why does a teacher have to take his/her own personality into consideration in formulating a personal plan for classroom management?

• It is often said that the ultimate goal of classroom management is to help pupils to become self-disciplined. Why is this goal so important in managing pupils' behaviour?

• Do you believe in the effectiveness of punishment? If so, in what ways can it be useful for controlling misbehaviour? Why are some forms of punishment not allowed in the classroom?

• Do you think it is practical for a teacher to follow a continuum of strategies in dealing with off-task behaviour? What are the possible drawbacks of doing so?

• In what ways can teachers avoid verbal confrontations with pupils?

• When teachers use logical consequences, how can they avoid pupils perceiving this as punishment?

Introduction

No classroom is completely free from behavioural problems though, of course, some have more than others. Quite often teachers are quick to respond to misbehaviour by verbal intervention and reprimands which can have an adverse effect on student learning and ruin a classroom atmosphere. What is often forgotten is that the goal of classroom management is not to control students but to prepare them to become self-disciplined. Teachers' interventions often provoke negative responses in students and lead to more confrontation, but this can be minimized if teachers adapt their reactions to the seriousness of the misbehaviour: unless serious disruption continues, no verbal intervention or logical consequences should be employed in the first instance. It is sensible, therefore, for teachers to adopt a continuum of intervention strategies from the least intrusive proactive intervention skills to the most intrusive verbal intervention.

   In the following example, at the start of an academic year Ms. Wong faced a class in which she knows there are some students who are very difficult to deal with. She tries to tackle different sorts of behaviour problems using a single approach, which is hardly likely to have any positive impact on the class. It was only later when a colleague, Ms. Leung, suggested that she should analyse the students' misbehaviour and employ different kinds of intervention skills that she became more confident in managing this class. Let us look at Ms. Wong's classroom to see how developing a personal plan and utilizing a variety of intervention strategies would help her.

Classroom scenario

Ms. Wong had been teaching her Primary 6B for about five minutes during which, in general, her pupils were attentive — but then some pupils began to lose interest in her lesson. A boy sitting in the front row near the door seemed to be searching for something inside his desk; at the other side, a girl was combing the hair of a girl sitting in front of her; and a few pupils were talking to each other. When Ms. Wong asked the class a question, a boy started to shout out the answer without raising his hand. While Ms. Wong was trying to decide what to do, another student in the far corner shouted an answer. Ms. Wong immediately yelled, "I can't teach you any more! Would you please behave yourselves! Your behaviour is just shameful!" The atmosphere changed abruptly and the class seemed to be at a standstill. It took five minutes to restart the lesson, with the small number of attentive pupils being puzzled and those who had misbehaved getting more aggressive.

Current Trends in Classroom Management

Traditionally, classroom management was perceived as a way of preventing misbehaviour: as Doyle (1990) asserted, it is the responsibility of teachers to maintain order and discipline and any inappropriate behaviour must be stopped. Managing the classroom can therefore be interpreted narrowly as the establishment of order and keeping control (Hoover and Kindsvatter, 1997). However, in the mid-1970s many teachers found that this approach was ineffective in nurturing an environment conducive to student learning (McEwan, 2000), and began to realize that preventive measures were more likely to enhance self-discipline. As a result, more attention began to be devoted to how to create classrooms which engage students rather than controlling their behaviour (Brophy and Evertson, 1976), with discipline problems being more often seen as resulting from teachers' failure to involve students in interesting and appropriate learning tasks (Kohn, 1996). It is now widely accepted that teachers need personal plans to deal with misbehaviour in order to minimize the disruption to classroom teaching and learning. A continuum of intervention strategies is recommended for dealing with such problems according to their degree of severity.

Personal Plans for Managing Misbehaviour

For handling classroom behavioural problems, it is very valuable for teachers to formulate personal plans which reflect the realities of the classroom situations they encounter and are consistent with their personalities (Charles, 2005: 6). Such plans help teachers to apply classroom management strategies in a constructive manner by providing consistent and non-arbitrary guidelines for decision making when encountering particular kinds of misbehaviour (Lasley, 1989). This is crucial as inconsistency in the ways teachers deal with off-task pupils is often one of the major causes of unnecessary argument and confrontation. Charles (2005: 8) lists twenty useful questions for formulating personal plans, some of which are noted below. Also, any personal plan must provide the basis for creating effective and positive classroom management, an issue which is discussed in the section that follows.

❐ **Activity 4.1**

Developing your personal plan

The following questions are helpful in formulating your own personal plan. Reflect on and discuss them with others. What practical implications can be drawn for organizing your personal plan?

- What do you mean by "good behaviour"?
- Why does misbehaviour occur in the classroom?
- What do you mean by "appropriate" and "inappropriate" behaviour?
- Why do teachers need to intervene when pupils behave badly?
- Who should be responsible for inappropriate behaviour?
- Do teachers have to intervene for all kinds of misbehaviour in the classroom?
- Classroom intervention strategies can be as disturbing and disruptive as the misbehaviour itself. What can teachers do to minimize the potentially negative effects of intervention?
- Intervention strategies have to be perceived by pupils as fair. How can teachers minimize discrepancies in the ways they deal with pupils' behaviour?

The Basis for Intervention

A personal plan helps teachers to clarify their rationales for classroom management, but it has to be supplemented by some intelligent and consistent principles before their intervention plans or strategies can be used effectively in daily practice (Charles, 2005; Levin and Nolan, 2004). This is particularly true for teachers who often face overwhelming behavioural problems as, otherwise, their intervention strategies could appear to students to be unsystematic, arbitrary and irrational. The following guiding principles (Levin and Nolan, 2004) for constructing a basis for intervention in the classroom should be examined critically and reflectively.

Teachers should always:

- ensure that the goal of classroom management is to help pupils to become self-disciplined;
- take a consistent approach to discipline problems;
- approach discipline as an instructional opportunity;
- employ preventive and proactive measures first;
- use the least disturbing intervention measures first;
- ensure that any intervention does not cause more disruption than the misbehaviour it intends to tackle;
- ensure that the measures taken minimize the disruption caused to classroom teaching and learning;
- ensure that the actions adopted protect students from causing harm and being harmed, both physically and psychologically;
- ensure that logical consequences are employed as the last resort in influencing pupils' misbehaviour;
- ensure that punishment has no place in the classroom.

A Continuum of Strategies for Managing Misbehaviour

In line with the argument for developing a personal plan for managing misbehaviour, a continuum consisting of four levels of mediation is now introduced (see Figure 4.1). This can be useful for teachers since it provides a system of graduated responses to different kinds of misbehaviour and thus offers a coherent plan for dealing systematically with such behaviour according to how serious and disruptive it is. The continuum is constructed with reference to the guidelines listed in the previous section.

The four levels of intervention strategies in the continuum

The continuum shown in Figure 4.1 comprises four levels, from the first level of teachers "doing nothing" — that is, permitting or tolerating misbehaviour — to non-verbal intervention (the second level), verbal intervention (the third level) and, finally, the use of logical consequences for influencing student misbehaviour. This continuum therefore has its least disruptive intervention strategies at one end and the most explicit intervention strategies at the other, as shown below in Figure 4.1.

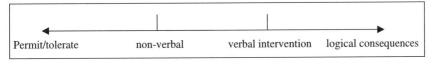

Figure 4.1   A continuum of strategies for managing misbehaviour

Here is a brief outline of what each of the levels involves.

- *Level 1*: The first level of mediation contains all the non-interference strategies and causes least disruption to classroom teaching and learning. These strategies are desirable when the teacher thinks that the off-task behaviour can be tolerated for various good reasons — for example, if it does not cause trouble to the class and is short-lived or, even if it is prolonged, can be resolved by some non-verbal intervention.

- *Level 2*: This level of intervention involves the use of non-verbal skills to stop students behaving inappropriately. These skills range from the least disruptive technique of planned ignoring to the most explicit coping one referred to as "touch interference". The least disruptive non-verbal intervention strategies can be seen as a private communication between the teacher and student.

- *Level 3*: When the misbehaviour remains unchecked, the third level of intervention, the use of verbal interference, can be employed. For instance, using humour is one of the less disruptive ways to change a student's behaviour at this level. For more serious problems, verbal intervention needs to be supplemented by some kind of action to control the situation. For example, when pupils are focusing heavily on some object which is unrelated to the lesson, the teacher has to tell them and take it away; or when pupils starts to harm themselves or others in the class, a loud shout and physical restraint are needed.

- *Level 4*: The last level of intervention, at the right-hand side of the continuum, is the use of logical consequences. This is the most explicit kind of interference in the classroom, which not only conveys the seriousness of the misbehaviour to the student but also sends a message to others that it cannot be tolerated any longer. In this case, the teacher has exhausted all other means of dealing with the misbehaviour, while the student has chosen not to alter his/her behaviour, and now has to take responsibility for this choice.

These four levels of intervention strategies together form a progressive and graduated response to different kinds of misbehaviour in the classroom, although teachers can jump a level of intervention if the situation suddenly becomes worse. It is not meant to be a "cookbook" guide to intervention approaches. The teacher still needs to make informed decisions by taking the classroom situation and pupils' daily performance into account; the guidelines need to be applied intelligently, not in a hasty fashion. The following section gives further details about the four levels of intervention strategies in the continuum.

❒ **Activity 4.2**

Do you have a decision-making hierarchy when dealing with students' misbehaviour? On reflection, you may find that you have worked out a personal system, with some behaviours being considered tolerable, while others need intervention. What kind of decision-making model are you employing at this stage of your professional career? Does your model form a hierarchy which helps you to make consistent decisions in dealing with students' misbehaviour?

Non-Intervention Skills in Managing Students' Misbehaviour

Non-intervention skills are employed when the teacher considers certain off-task behaviour exhibited by pupils to be acceptable as it will not last for long and causes no physical or psychological harm to others. This matches with the principle that any classroom intervention should have the least disruptive effect on teaching and learning. Two common forms of non-intervention are described below.

Permitting

Allowing certain behaviour in the classroom does not mean that the teacher passively accepts misbehaviour or off-task behaviour, but is an indication of what is and is not allowed. For example, Primary 1 pupils who are not accustomed to the routines and environment of a school are likely to make mistakes, as are any new pupils who find the school context stressful. The teacher has to show understanding of the situation; but if the pupils' behaviour begins to affect others in the class, he/she needs to try to redirect it into more appropriate forms by means of non-verbal skills.

Tolerating

There are occasions when mistakes or disruptive behaviour have to be tolerated. For example, students sometimes make logical mistakes; and when a student is coughing in class due to having influenza, a teacher can do little more than ensuring that he/she uses a handkerchief to reduce disturbing others. Such behaviour can be tolerated as long as it does not cause consistent disruption to student learning or harm to students, but when students' emotions get out of control and are harmful to others, immediate verbal intervention and physical restraint may be needed.

Non-Verbal Intervention and Coping Skills

When a problem is getting worse or some more disruptive behaviour takes place, the teacher has to consider employing non-verbal coping strategies. Four common strategies of this kind have been identified by Levin and Nolan (2004), namely, planned ignoring, signal interference, proximity control and touch interference. Sometimes, to cope with disruptive behaviour, the teacher can supplement verbal intervention by taking explicit action, as in the case mentioned earlier where the irrelevant object on which the student was concentrating was removed.

Planned ignoring

Planned ignoring refers to neglecting off-task behaviour in a deliberate manner. It is based on the behaviourist theory (Zirpoli and Melloy, 1997), according to which disruptive behaviour is often reinforced by the attention given to it by the teacher and peers in the classroom, and ignoring it reduces its occurrence. Planned ignoring can be difficult to implement and, to be carried out successfully, needs conscious planning and control. It is important to note that such planned ignoring by the teacher is not likely to produce the desired results in the initial trials; and, even worse, there might be an increase in the disruptive behaviour when the reinforcement is removed (Brophy, 1988). Thus, it is often suggested that planned ignoring should be confined to those off-task behaviours which create little disturbance in the classroom. If this behaviour remains unchecked, other coping skills such as signal interference have to be employed.

❐ **Activity 4.3**

Planned ignoring is best employed for those off-task behaviours which are trivial and cause little disturbance. What examples do you think belong to this category? Why?

Signal interference

Signal interference refers to any kind of body language which communicates to the student not to misbehave. Redl and Wineman (1952) were among the first to note that appropriate use of body language — such as pointing, a wink, a frown, head movement or staring — is helpful in handling minor off-task behaviour. Signal interference could be considered the best technique for teachers when planned ignoring fails. By its nature, signal interference must be expressed clearly and directly, without any extra contradictory messages being conveyed by the gesture, if it is to be effective. If the teacher is unable to get a student's attention in this way, proximity interference may be more appropriate.

Proximity interference

In proximity interference, the teacher closes the distance between him/herself and the student who is misbehaving, usually by moving close to the off-task student while conducting the lesson as usual. This should alert the student and help to redirect him/her to the appropriate task without disturbing the rest of the class. If this is unsuccessful, touch interference may be needed to resolve the problem.

Touch interference

Touch interference involves any kind of non-aggressive physical contact with the student as a way of showing disapproval, and ranges from a slight touch on the shoulder to guiding the student back to his/her seat. Touch interference may sometimes arouse strong feelings in pupils and must be employed with caution, particularly when a male teacher uses it with a student of the opposite sex.

These four intervention skills are valuable for coping with off-task behaviour only when employed appropriately: when they are used in an inappropriate manner, they may well increase the amount of disturbance.

Advantages of non-verbal coping skills
- √ They produce the least disturbance to the classroom.
- √ Off-task behaviour is tackled while the teaching and learning processes continue.
- √ They appear to the off-task student to be "private", without letting others know about the problem.
- √ Since there is no explicit identification of the problem student, they do not embarrass the person involved.
- √ The likelihood of hostile confrontation is greatly minimized because there is no public intervention.
- √ The student is given freedom to discipline him/herself.

Verbal-Intervention Strategies

When non-verbal interventions fail to redirect the students to appropriate tasks, verbal coping skills are needed. Some forms of verbal intervention, for example speaking very loudly, are particularly effective for controlling disruptive behaviour which is harmful to others.

Verbal-intervention strategies or coping techniques refer to the use of verbal messages to influence students and deal with difficult behaviour. Various approaches have been identified (Kerr and Nelson, 2002; Levin and Nolan, 2004), including praising peers, boosting interest, calling on students, using humour, and making requests and demands. All these strategies, which are described below, give students a chance to change their behaviour. As students still have a choice before the teacher employs logical consequences, they are the baseline for all intervention.

Praising peers

Teachers often try to stop disruptive behaviour by not commenting on it and instead praising a student or group of pupils exhibiting the desired behaviour, in the hope that the deviant will notice this and follow their example. This indirect way of attempting to change the behaviour of off-task pupils involves social learning, as advocated by Bandura (1969). It is worth noting that while Bandura's theory (1969, 1977) of social learning often works very well with young pupils, it may not be so effective at secondary school level.

☐ **Activity 4.4**

Reflect upon your own experience as a school student. Can you recall any incident(s) in which your teacher employed "praising peers" successfully to change the behaviour of a misbehaving member of the class? Share this episode with others and discuss why it worked.

Boosting interest

Boosting students' interest is a useful way for a teacher to show care and sensitivity and, indirectly, it helps in building up good relationships. When a student recognizes that a teacher cares, this can change his/her attitude. Showing affection for students is a constructive way of creating a positive classroom atmosphere.

Calling on students

Calling students by name is a powerful means for getting the attention of those who are off-task or inattentive. The idea is simple: it sends the message that the teacher has noticed the problem and the student should now engage again in the lesson (Rinne, 1984). This procedure can be carried out in several ways. For example, the teacher can insert the student's name when discussing a topic, as in "I want to know if Wing Chit knows the answer to . . . ", or alternatively can ask a question first and then call on the student to answer it. The more direct approach of calling on students by name and telling them to pay more attention is not generally recommended as there is a risk of confrontation if they feel they have lost face in front of the class. Overall, verbal intervention fulfils the principle of causing least disturbance to the classroom and gives students the freedom to discipline themselves.

Using humour as a tension-breaker

Humour can be very useful in teaching as it provides a momentary break for the pupils and enhances teacher-pupil relationships. It is particularly effective when pupils are testing the teacher's limits: if he/she rises to the challenge, the atmosphere may become hostile. Instead, the teacher can clear the air with a laugh associated with humour as this helps to depersonalize the challenge (Saphier and Gower, 1982). However, when using humour, the teacher has to be cautious as it must:

* be enjoyed by the class;
* not be sarcastic;
* not be interpreted as a sign of a slack attitude to teaching;
* not get out of control and distract pupils' attention from the major task of learning.

Asking questions

Sending a message in the form of a question to caution off-task students about their disengagement or disruptive behaviour in the classroom will help to redirect them back to learning. For example, a teacher can ask "Chor Ting, have you noticed that there is a long queue behind you? You'll have to be quick in getting back your muppet for the drama show". Levin et al. (1985) found that some students were unaware of the effects of their behaviour on fellow students, so this kind of questioning acts as a timely reminder of the difficulties caused.

◻ **Activity 4.5**

Managing the behaviour of Chor Ting

What would you do in the following situation?

A student always went out to the blackboard to do class work without the teacher's permission. The teacher asked the student: "Chor Ting, do you know that your action has disrupted the class routine and prevented others from participating in class work?" However, Chor Ting didn't understand the teacher's point and answered: "I don't go out when I don't know how to solve the problem!"

Requests and demands

Requests and demands are polite statements and orders made by the teacher explicitly and publicly in class. They are used to show disapproval of disruptive behaviour and an expectation that the student involved will become engaged again in the learning task or activity. Relatively speaking, this is more confrontational than the other verbal intervention techniques described, and is apparently rather teacher-centred. Various types of requests and demands are made daily in the classroom, as can be seen in Table 4.1.

Table 4.1 Teachers' day-to-day requests and demands in the classroom (adapted from Levin and Nolan, 2004)

Request/demand	Description	Example	Remarks
An "I-message"	• A technique often associated with Gordon's (1974) Teacher Effectiveness Training • It makes the student aware that he/she has caused a problem; it is an explicit statement of how the teacher has been affected. • It is useful in helping pupils to become aware of their disruptive behaviour.	"When you shout out answers from your seats, others can't hear them clearly, and I get uncomfortable with the shouting."	• A non-judgmental statement minimizes the chance of confrontation and helps pupils to change their behaviour. There is little feeling of coercion by the teacher.
A direct appeal	• An explicit request from the teacher to correct a disruptive behaviour	"Please be nice. Do not put your shoes on the table."	• This may appear to be confrontational. Teachers should be courteous in making such requests. It is better to avoid making this kind of statement if a teacher lacks confidence in his/her ability to take charge of the classroom.

(continued on p. 75)

(Table 4.1 continued)

Positive phrasing	• Similar to "grandma's law": finish your dinner before you have your dessert. • It emphasizes the positive results of good behaviour.	"You'll have a chance to distribute the books to others if you can sit properly and raise your hand."	• This lets the teacher think positively: it is discouraging for teachers to emphasize the negative outcomes of misbehaviour. • Positive phrasing improves teacher-pupil relationships in the classroom. • It is a good way of training pupils to take responsibility.
Statements involving "Are not for"	• Such statements are used mainly to stop students misusing property or materials.	"Books are not for drawing on; they are for reading."	• This has very limited use. • It sometimes creates confrontations. • It can embarrass students by putting them in an awkward situation publicly.
A reminder of the rules	• Sometimes teachers need to remind pupils of the classroom rules and routines in order to check misbehaviour.	"Leaving the classroom without permission is against our classroom regulations."	• Secondary school pupils may find such reminders annoying, feeling they are not given enough freedom in the classroom. • If a student does not listen to a reminder, logical consequences must be employed. Otherwise, classroom rules would be useless and the teacher's authority questioned.

(continued on p. 76)

(Table 4.1 continued)

Glasser's triplets	• Glasser (1969, 1992) uses three questions to direct students to appropriate behaviour: 1. "What are you doing?" 2. "Is it against the rules?" 3. "What should you be doing?"	"Yat Chui, you were talking to your neighbour while everyone was reading. This is against our classroom regulations. You must focus on your reading task."	• The student can choose not to answer these questions. • It alerts students to behave appropriately. • If a student fails to comply, the teacher can respond assertively to these questions, indicating that the student has done something wrong.
A "broken record"	• A process in which a teacher keeps repeating a demand for appropriate behaviour (Canter and Canter, 1981; 2001). • The repetition sounds like a broken record.	T: "Chi Sang, I want you to get a book and read it now." CS: "I read one a minute ago." T: "That's not the point. I want to you to get a book and read it now." CS: "There are many people in the book corner. I'll do it in a minute." T: "That's not the point. I want you get a book and read it now." CS: "Yes. I am going to."	• In employing this technique, the teacher should maintain eye-contact with the student. • The use of gestures and a suitable tone of voice are helpful. • The technique cannot go on forever. It is often said three repetitions are enough. If the student does not comply, he/she should know what logical consequences will follow.

❏ **Activity 4.6**

Verbal intervention

Reflect on your own experience at school. What comments did you hate most when a teacher was reprimanding you for bad behaviour in the classroom? Suggest alternatives to make these comments less hurtful or provocative.

Sometimes a teacher may be in the difficult position where most pupils in the class are working well, but one or two are off-task. Instead of disrupting the class by demanding that these pupils change their behaviour, the teacher can divert their attention by asking them carry out some other task, such as getting a story book or a pen for him/her.

Checklist for verbal intervention

√ Always start with non-verbal intervention.

√ Try your best to make verbal intervention as private as possible.

√ Avoid prolonged conversations and verbal battles with students.

√ Never make verbal intervention a face-losing experience for students.

√ Be brief, supplementing what you say with appropriate gestures and tone of voice.

√ Never label a student as it is the behaviour that causes trouble, not the person.

√ Never make sarcastic comments.

√ Control your emotions even if you are provoked.

√ Exhaust all possible alternatives for self-discipline before employing logical consequences.

The Uses of Logical Consequences

Logical consequences are sometimes considered to be overt punishment or action taken to reprimand unchecked misbehaviour when the teacher has exhausted alternatives for self-discipline. However, as the name implies, logical consequences should never be viewed as retribution but as the result of a student's decision not to comply. After all, it is the student's reluctance to change misbehaviour that leads to the consequences. This must be distinguished from corporal punishment, which teachers are not permitted to use in the classroom.

Punishment and three kinds of consequences

Teachers should distinguish natural, logical and arbitrary consequences and not confuse them with punishment. Punishment refers to the reliance on power to make something unpleasant happen to a child as a way of trying to alter the child's behaviour (Kohn, 1993: 167). The first distinction between punishment and natural and logical consequences is that punishment is often contrived and coercive, whereas natural and logical consequences are often the outcomes related to the misbehaviour. Also, punishment is commonly seen as a deliberate hurtful action imposed by the teacher (the authority) on the student (viewed as inferior) as a result of wrongdoing, but natural and logical consequences have none of these implications. Arbitrary consequence refers to outcomes seemingly unfair and not based on reason. Other distinctions are listed in Table 4.2.

Table 4.2 Comparison of punishment and logical consequences (Larrivee, 1999: 170)

Logical consequences	Punishment
• are logically related to the behaviour in question; • are deliberately planned and delivered by the teacher; • are emotionally neutral; • are rational and depersonalized; • minimize confrontation.	• is arbitrary and unrelated to the behaviour focused on; • is retributive and reactionary; • is possibly emotionally charged; • is experienced as personal; • often provokes confrontation.

Consequences: Dreikurs and his colleagues (1998) identified three kinds of consequences: natural, logical and arbitrary.

(a) Natural consequences occur automatically as a result of a particular behaviour. They are inevitable and result directly from the student's actions if there is no intervention to prevent it happening.

(b) Logical consequences, in contrast, are deliberately planned and carried out by the teacher. It is often argued that, for the consequences of wrongdoing to be logical, they must be experienced and perceived by the student in this way.

(c) Arbitrary consequences imposed by the teacher on students are not related to the misbehaviour and are often seen by the students as retribution.

❐ **Activity 4.7**

Complete the boxes below. You can discuss the answers with your partners.

Consequences			
Behaviour	Natural	Logical	Arbitrary
A student is late for class.			To do "sit-ups" thirty times in the playground
A student talks in class.	The student misses the information given by the teacher.		
A student shouts out answers from his/her seat.		The student is required to raise his/her hand and answer the question	

Some precautionary remarks

While the use of logical consequences for off-task behaviour is sometimes inevitable, certain precautions need to be taken before employing this approach, e.g.

- The teacher must explain the logical consequences to the student and make sure they are understood.
- The student should be given one last chance to comply.
- The teacher needs to avoid giving any wrong signal that this is punishment or just a way of imposing his/her authority.
- It should be made clear to pupils that every wrongdoing has its consequences and that they should know how to control their behaviour.
- Teachers should prepare various logical consequences in advance in case they are required.

Further considerations

There is no panacea for resolving misbehaviour. In the end, teachers may still find that all their actions are unsuccessful and pupils are sometimes beyond their control. Nevertheless, they should still try to follow their own plans for classroom management, starting with the least intrusive strategies of non-verbal intervention. At the same time, they have to ensure that their lessons are interesting and meet their pupils' needs. It is always good to establish harmonious teacher-pupil relationships, a positive classroom learning atmosphere and a cooperative culture among learners as, if all these aspects are handled well, pupils are much less likely to be disruptive and off-task. In time, they will choose to change their behaviour rather than engage themselves in confrontations with the teacher.

Conclusion

A pleasant and enjoyable environment is the key to successful teaching and learning. As any form of intervention, however minor, is disruptive, teachers should view self-discipline as the ultimate goal in managing behavioural problems. However, intervention is often needed and the best intervention strategies are those which fit the realities of the classroom situation. This requires teachers to formulate personal plans and construct guidelines for making intelligent and informed classroom management decisions.

Intervention should be used as infrequently as possible, and when it is employed, it should be considered the last resort in dealing with misbehavour. In order to avoid arbitrary actions and inconsistency, a system of intervention which guides teachers to make logical and consistent decisions is helpful. A continuum of strategies for dealing with misbehaviour of different kinds is recommended as this helps teachers to deal appropriately with off-task behaviours of differing severity. The continuum ranges from non-intervention to explicit intervention of various kinds and aims to avoid confrontation in any form between the teacher and students.

Summary

This chapter starts with the notion that the aim of all good classroom management is to help students to become self-disciplined, and that students who misbehave should be offered a chance to change their behaviour. If they choose not to do so, logical consequences can be applied to them.

It is pointed out that there are times when behavioural problems require intervention, but every effort should be made to avoid arbitrary decisions and inconsistency in handling them. Teachers have to establish a rationale for their decision making, which can often be aided by developing a personal plan supplemented by practical guidelines as the basis for intervention.

In a similar vein, a continuum of different intervention strategies is suggested in which there is a graduated response to different kinds of behavioural problems which ranges from mediation, which creates the least disruption, to explicit intervention which causes considerable disturbance to the class. Also, four levels of response are proposed for the continuum: ignoring/permitting, non-verbal intervention, verbal intervention and logical consequences.

The first level of these intervention strategies, ignoring/permitting, causes no disturbance to classroom teaching. The behaviour is tolerated simply because it is not under student control and causes very little harm to the student and others in the class. If the problem continues for a time, some intervention may be needed, with non-verbal intervention strategies such as planned ignoring, signal interference, proximity control and touch interference being employed to change the off-task behaviour.

At the third level are verbal intervention strategies which are employed when non-verbal approaches fail and, while they can take various forms, their use always aims to influence pupils and deal with their difficult behaviour.

If pupils persist in misbehaving, logical consequences can be employed as an appropriate last resort. They must be perceived as inevitable and directly related to a student's actions and have to be distinguished from punishment and other arbitrary consequences. When using logical consequences, teachers must take time to plan them, know when they should be employed and ensure that pupils understand when they will be used. Finally, it is advisable for teachers to offer pupils one last chance to change their behaviour before resorting to this strategy.

Questions for Discussion

1. What are the basic principles for employing intervention strategies in the classroom? Do these principles have anything to do with the teacher's beliefs about pedagogy?

2. What are non-intervention strategies? What is the potential danger of non-intervention if the misbehaviour is prolonged in nature?

3. Suggest ways of avoiding arbitrary decision making in influencing students' behaviour.

4. With reference to your own experience in teaching, discuss in pairs what constitute good logical consequences? How can a teacher prepare a good list of logical consequences for daily practice?

5. Discuss some useful ways of minimizing the chance of verbal confrontation between students and teachers.

6. Why should corporal punishment never be employed in the classroom?

7. Working in pairs, one as the teacher and the other as a student, suggest logical consequences for a student who does not line up during a fire-drill assembly. Explain this to the student.

Useful Resources

Websites

1. Aase.edu.au: http://www.aase.edu.au/2004_Conf_papers/aase_harrington_sargeant.pdf

2. Behaviour 4 Learning: http://www.behaviour4learning.ac.uk/browse.aspx?taggingType=1&categoryId=10250&subCategoryId=10326

3. Connections.education.tas.gov.au: http://www.howtobehave.com/manage.html

4. Education.gov.ab.ca: http://www.education.gov.ab.ca/SafeSchools/TimeOut_Oct_2002.pdf

5. Intervention Strategies for Misbehaviour: http://scholar.google.com/scholar?hl=en&lr=&sa=X&oi=scholart&q=intervention+strategies+for+misbehaviour

6. Triple P-The Model-Levels of Intervention: http://www19.triplep.net/?pid=42

Further Reading

Jones, V. F. and Jones, L. S. (2001). *Comprehensive classroom management: Creating communities of support and solving problems* (6th edn). Boston: Allyn & Bacon.

LeCompte, M. (1978). Learning to work: The hidden curriculum of the classroom. *Anthropology and Education Quarterly*, 9: 22–37.

McCord, J. (1991). Questioning the value of punishment. *Social Problems*, 38: 167–79.

Moles, O. C. (ed.). (1990). *Student discipline strategies: Research and practice.* Albany: SUNY.

Raffini, J. P. (1996). *150 ways to increase motivation in the classroom.* Boston: Allyn and Bacon.

Redl, F. and Wineman, D. (1952). *Controls from within.* New York: Free Press.

Rinne, C. (1984). *Attention: The fundamentals of classroom control.* Columbus, OH: Merrill.

Saphier, J. and Gower, R. (1982). *The skilful teacher.* Carlisle, MA: Research for Better Teaching.

References

Bandura, A. (1969). *Principles of behaviour modification.* New York: Holt, Rinehart & Winston.

———. (1977). *Social learning theory.* Upper Saddle River, NJ: Prentice Hall.

Brophy, J. (1988). Educating teachers about managing classrooms and students. *Teaching and Teacher Education,* 4(1): 1–18.

Brophy, J. E. and Evertson, C. M. (1976). *Learning from teaching: A developmental perspective.* Boston: Allyn & Bacon.

Canter, L. and Canter, M. (1981). *Assertive discipline follow-up guidebook.* Los Angeles, CA: Canter and Associates.

———. (2001). *Assertive discipline: Positive behaviour management for today's classroom.* (revised edn). Los Angeles, CA: Canter and Associates.

Charles, C. M. (2005). *Building classroom discipline* (8th edn). Boston: Pearson.

Docking, J. (2002). *Managing behaviour in the primary school.* London: David Fulton Publishers.

Doyle, W. (1990). Classroom management techniques. In O. C. Moles (ed.) *Student discipline strategies: Research and practice.* Albany: State of University of New York Press.

Dreikurs, R., Grunwald, B. and Pepper, F. (1998). *Maintaining sanity in the classroom: Classroom management techniques* (2nd edn). New York: Taylor and Francis.

Glasser, W. (1969). *Schools without failure.* New York: Harper & Row.

———. (1992). *The quality school: Managing students without coercion.* New York: Harper Collins.

Gordon, T. (1974). *Teacher effectiveness training.* New York: Wyden.

Hoover, R. L. and Kindsvatter, R. (1997). *Democratic discipline: Foundation and practice.* Upper Saddle River, NJ: Merrill/Prentice Hall.

Kerr, M. M. and Nelson, C. M. (2002). *Strategies for addressing behavior problems in the classroom* (4th edn). Upper Saddle River, NJ: Merrill Prentice Hall.

Kohn, A. (1993). *Punished by rewards: The trouble with gold stars, incentive plans, A's, praise and other bribes.* Boston: Houghton Mifflin Company.

———. (1996). *Beyond discipline: From compliance to community.* Alexandria, VA: ASCD.

Larrivee, B. (1999). *Authentic classroom management: Creating a community of learners.* Needham Heights, MA: Allyn & Bacon.

Lasley, T. J. (1989). A teacher development model for classroom management. *Phi Delta Kappan,* 71(1): 36–8.

Levin, J. and Nolan, J. F. (2004). *Principles of classroom management: A professional decision-making model,* (4th edn). Boston and Hong Kong: Pearson/Allyn and Bacon.

Levin, J., Nolan, J. F. and Hoffman, N. (1985). A strategy for the classroom resolution of chronic discipline problems. *National Association of Secondary School Principals Bulletins,* 69 (7): 11–8.

McEwan, B. (2000). *The art of classroom management: Effective practices for building equitable learning communities.* Upper saddle River, NJ: Merrill.

Redl, F. and Wineman, D. (1952). *Controls from within.* New York: Free Press.

Rinne, C. (1984). *Attention: The fundamentals of classroom control.* Columbus, OH: Merrill.

Saphier, J. and Gower, R. (1982). *The skilful teacher.* Carlisle, MA: Research for Better Teaching.

Zirpoli, T. J. and Melloy, K. J. (1997). *Behavior management: Applications for teachers and parents* (2nd edn). Upper Saddle River, NJ: Merrill/Prentice Hall.

5

Approaches to Students' Misbehaviour

Li Wai-shing

What is your school of thought regarding how students learn, develop, and grow? What is your school of thought regarding discipline? Teachers are either interventionists, interactionalists, or noninterventionists at heart. Although each school of thought comes complete with classroom management models that get the job done — establishing and maintaining discipline — each represents its own unique set of beliefs.

Tauber (1999)

Synopsis

There are various approaches and models to help teachers manage their classrooms. This chapter first introduces four major kinds of classification networks for classroom management and discipline, and then describes Ramon Lewis's framework which offers teachers a simple and practical strategy for dealing with misbehaviour. Lewis's framework incorporates various models into three simple approaches: teacher-oriented, student-oriented and group-oriented. Well-known models such as Teacher Effectiveness Training, Assertiveness Training and the Social Discipline Model are discussed in simple and practical terms.

Objectives

After reading this chapter, you should be able to:

- identify commonsense models and theoretically-based models in classroom management;
- understand three major approaches for dealing with inappropriate student behaviour, viz. teacher-oriented, student-oriented and group-oriented;
- apply the Teacher Effectiveness Training Model in dealing with student misbehaviour;
- apply the Canter's Assertiveness Model of classroom management;
- apply Dreikurs's Social Discipline Model in managing inappropriate student behaviour;

- use strategies taken from the interventionist, interactionist or non-interventionist approaches to classroom management

Pre-Reading Reflection and Discussion

- Do you advocate a child-centred or teacher-centred style of teaching? Why do you think your chosen style is more effective in dealing with student misbehaviour in today's classrooms?
- Do you think pupils are able to discipline themselves without adult intervention?
- Do you agree with the Chinese saying: "Control and discipline first before you start teaching". Why/why not?
- According to the Canters, there are three kinds of teachers: non-assertive, hostile and assertive. Discuss the drawbacks and advantages of each type.
- Suggest ways to deal with attention-seeking students in the classroom.
- What kinds of strategies would you use in dealing with students who want to challenge your authority, oppose school rules and act in a domineering fashion?

Introduction

Lack of discipline in the classroom is frequently ranked as one of the main concerns in teaching. A large-scale investigation of pupils' misbehaviour carried out by Education Convergence (1999) confirmed that Chinese teachers spent a great deal of teaching time in keeping good classroom discipline. Fortunately, most of these disruptive behaviours are relatively minor — such as talking, shouting without permission, copying homework and sleeping in class — but, overall, it appears that pupils' behaviour is getting worse. For teachers to use coercive methods to regain control of the classroom is ineffective, and so they have to explore other means of maintaining discipline in their classes. Broadly speaking, there are three approaches to managing classrooms: (1) the teacher takes charge and decides how to change a student's misbehaviour; (2) the teacher works with the class to decide how the student's misbehaviour can be corrected; and (3) the teacher helps individual students to decide how to change their own behaviour. Various models and strategies have been generated for these approaches (Wolfgang and Glickman, 1986; Johns et al., 1989; Wolfgang et al., 1999) and they work best when they are in line with the teacher's own philosophy of discipline.

Examine the following Chinese lesson in which the teacher, Ms. Chung, is in her first year of teaching. She learned from her professional training course that a teacher sometimes has to exert his/her authority in dealing with inappropriate behaviour, but at other times can let the pupils tackle problems on their own or work with them to resolve them. What advice would you give Ms. Chung for tackling the case described below? What action should Ms. Chung take if she wants to deal with the problem by (a) exerting her authority, (b) adopting a student-oriented approach and (c) taking a group-oriented approach?

> **Classroom scenario**
>
> Ms. Chung is giving a Chinese lesson on Monday morning. After about ten minutes in her second period, she sees Chi Fai hit his neighbour, Mei Sheung. Mei Sheung cried loudly while other pupils are working in groups of two to create stories. Ms. Chung decides to help Mei Sheung.

Classroom Approaches: An Overview

One can view responsibility for discipline in a school from two perspectives, which are often referred to as administrator-oriented and teacher-oriented approaches (Johns et al., 1989). In the former case, the administrators concentrate on school-based discipline plans, which are often beyond the control of individual teachers; while in the latter, the teachers are responsible for taking care of discipline problems experienced with their pupils. This chapter is concerned with the strategies and approaches teachers can use to deal with their pupils.

In teacher-centred approaches, individual teachers can adopt a commonsense model or choose from a wide range of theoretically-based models. As the name implies, commonsense models include techniques which teachers think are useful but which are not underpinned by psychological, pedagogical or philosophical theories — such as "Control first, teach later", "Stick to the rules", or "Don't smile before Christmas". Theoretically-based models, in contrast, are supported by research or by psychological or social theories, Teacher Effectiveness Training (Gordon, 1987) and the Social Discipline Model (Dreikurs and Cassel, 1972) being two common examples. A good instructional plan together with an appropriate model or set of procedures will ensure maximum student engagement and on-task behaviour.

Teachers should learn and practise using theoretically-based models wherever they find them appropriate. The use of commonsense models in the classroom is not encouraged as they are reactive and lack a well conceptualized base and consistency (Gonzalo, 1977). They can be seen as straightforward "tricks" to solve practical problems. Theoretically-based models, on the other hand, give teachers a greater working knowledge of alternatives at their disposal for dealing with different kinds of classroom situations (Wolfgang and Glickman, 1986). This knowledge also enables them to utilize practices which are consistent with their own beliefs and philosophies when handling student behaviour.

Different Models and Conceptual Frameworks

There is a wide range of theoretically-based models and conceptual frameworks for teachers to choose from for maintaining good discipline in their classes — for example, the classification network of Johns and his colleagues (1989), Weber's (2006) psychological and philosophical classifications and Wolfgang and Glickman's (1986) classification of power relationships between teachers and students. A brief account of these three examples is given below.

Johns et al.'s classification network

The classification network for studying conceptual designs for classroom management and discipline (Johns et al., 1989) identified four different designs — namely classroom management designs, behaviour management designs, socio-emotional designs and group process designs — which are based on different theories and associated with different classroom management models. Table 5.1 summarizes these designs and provides an easy reference for teachers.

Table 5.1 Classification network for classroom management and discipline (adapted from Johns et al., 1989: 6–10)

Design	Theoretical basis	Examples	Remarks
Classroom management	• Effective teacher research	• Kounin's (1971) model	• A primarily non-philosophical design
Behaviour management	• Behavioural psychology	• Canter and Canter's (2002): Assertiveness Model	• Concentrates on determining desired classroom conditions
Socio-emotional	• Theories in counselling, personality and psychotherapy	• Glasser (1969): reality therapy • Gordon (1987): Teacher Effectiveness Training	• Emphasizes a positive learning environment and interpersonal relationships of teachers and pupils
Group process	• Social and developmental psychology	• Schmuck and Schmuck (1979): group processes in the classroom	• Concentrates on establishing and maintaining an effective and productive classroom

Weber's classification

Weber's (2006) classification of different approaches involves a comprehensive introduction of managerial strategies for classroom management. Weber identified eight major approaches (see Table 5.2) which provide easy access to understanding

Table 5.2 Weber's classification of classroom management approaches (adapted from Weber, 2006)

Approach	Major ideas	Teacher's role	Remarks
Authoritarian	• Management as controlling student behaviour	• To establish and maintain order by creating and enforcing humane classroom rules and regulations	• It is characterized by control measures for intimidating pupils.
Permissive	• Management as maximizing student freedom • Allowing students to do what they want	• To promote students' freedom by encouraging them to express themselves, with the least interference	• It fails to recognize that the school or the classroom is a social system.
Cookbook	• Management as performing certain tricks from a "recipe" (for classroom control) when confronting problems	• To react to specific problems by using standard solutions	• It is not derived from a well-conceptualized base and often lacks consistency. • It is reactive rather than proactive.
Group-process	• Management as creating productive groups	• To establish and maintain the conditions which create and sustain productive classroom groups	• It is based on social psychology theories of group dynamics. • Example: Kounin's model
Instructional	• Management as quality design and implementing of lessons	• To plan good lessons and learning tasks that meet the needs and abilities of the learners	• Once a problem surfaces, the model is not productive any more.
Intimidation	• Management of pupils' behaviour by coercion or threat	• To force pupils to behave according to the teacher's desires by intimidation (e.g. sarcasm, ridicule or threats)	• They are inhumane and provocative means of classroom management. • They deal with the problem's symptoms but not the problem itself.
Behaviour modification	• Behaviour is learned and therefore can be appropriated by using positive reinforcement (reward) and negative reinforcement (punishment).	• To master and apply the principles of learning identified by behaviourists for influencing human behaviour	• It is based on principles from behavioural psychology.
Socio-emotional climate	• Management as building positive teacher-student relationships and classroom climate	• To determine and create interpersonal relationships and a positive socio-emotional climate	• It is based on theories in counselling and clinical psychology.

different frameworks for managing our classrooms, namely the authoritarian, behaviour modification, cookbook, group-process, instructional, intimidation, permissive and socio-emotional climate approaches. Weber's classification contains some approaches which are similar to those of the classification network described above.

Wolfgang and Glickman's Teacher Behaviour Continuum

After years of observing teacher behaviour, Wolfgang and Glickman found seven typical techniques teachers use in dealing with inappropriate behaviour. As shown in Figure 5.1, they are: looking on silently, non-directive statements, questions, directive statements, modelling, reinforcement, and physical intervention and isolation. These techniques range from the least teacher control (non-interventionist) to maximum teacher control (interventionist) (Wolfgang and Glickman, 1986: 22–23). (The power relationships of the teacher and students are also depicted in Figure 5.1.) As with the other classifications, Wolfgang and Glickman's model involves a continuum of strategies.

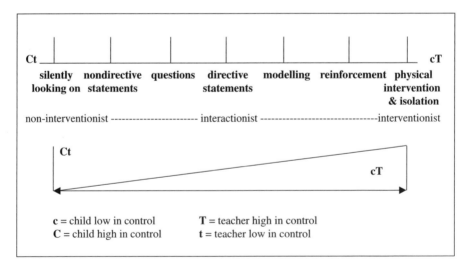

Figure 5.1 A teacher behaviour continuum showing the maximum power of the teacher and the students (adapted from Wolfgang and Glickman, 1986)

❑ **Activity 5.1**

Reflection on the classifications

You have been introduced to three major kinds of classification of approaches for dealing with inappropriate behaviour. With reference to them, discuss the following questions:

1. Which classification specified above do you think is easier to understand as a practitioner? Why?
2. Do you think a teacher would follow a particular model in dealing with pupils' inappropriate behaviour or opt for any strategy that works when facing classroom problems? Why?
3. What sorts of things would teachers want to know when introducing these approaches?

Making It Simple

Although these classifications or approaches provide useful procedures for dealing with students' inappropriate behaviour, teachers may find the various models and the theories that support the frameworks complex. Ramon Lewis (1997) attempted to provide a simple classification built on the idea that when dealing with pupils' inappropriate behaviour, teachers can control, manage or influence pupils to maintain classroom discipline. Lewis's categories — referred as the model of control, the model of management and the model of influence — is introduced in the following sections.

Lewis's framework

According to Lewis, in dealing with student misbehaviour, a teacher can: take charge of how students should behave (*model of control*); join with the students in deciding how they should behave (*model of management*); or let the students to decide how they should behave (*model of influence*). These models (Lewis, 1997: 49) (see Table 5.3) represent three broad styles of discipline known as a teacher-oriented, a group-oriented and a student-oriented approach respectively.

Three models

The three models share the common goal of trying to show teachers how they can deal with pupils' inappropriate behaviour effectively, but they differ as regards who should be in charge of regulating student behaviour and how it should be done. The distinction between the models lies in the balance of power between students and teachers (Wolfgang and Glickman, 1986): the teacher being solely responsible for regulating student behaviour (*the teacher-oriented approach*); students being given freedom to decide on their own behaviour (*the student-oriented approach*); or the teacher and students deciding together on appropriate behaviour (*the group-oriented approach*) (Lewis, 1997: 48).

Table 5.3 Lewis's models (1997)

Control ◄------------- Manage ------------- ► Influence

Tc ◄————————————————————————————► Ct

	Teacher-oriented	Group-oriented	Student-oriented
Model	**model of control**	**model of management**	**model of influence**
Description	teachers decide how students should behave.They use rewards and punishments to control student behaviour	teacher and students decide how they should behave. Together they set pleasant and unpleasant consequences for inappropriate behaviour	students decide on their own behaviour: they modify their behaviour after observing its impact on others

c = child low in control   **T** = teacher high in control
C = child high in control   **t** = teacher low in control

Lewis's (1997: 48) classification can be viewed as a continuum of discipline styles containing two extremes — from the model of control in which the teacher adopts interventionist strategies to the model of influence where pupils have the power to decide on their own behaviour, with teachers adopting non-interventionist strategies. In the middle of the continuum lies the model of management in which all members of the class, including the teacher, are responsible for regulating their own behaviour through interactionist strategies, and set rules and design consequences for misbehaviour.

❏ **Activity 5.2**

How can a siuation be managed?

Form groups and each choose one approach for tackling the situation below. Present your arguments and plans to the class, with other members asking questions and challenging the plans presented.

During a class, the teacher told the pupils to form into groups of three to solve formulas together. The class formed into eight groups, with Pak Sun being the odd man out. When the teacher asked him to join any group, he said: "If I join any one of these groups, I am breaking the rule of trios. I have formed my own group and shall work alone."

Precautions

Before we examine these approaches in detail, teachers should note the following precautionary points:

- No matter how effective these approaches are, it is unlikely that there is no one approach which is capable of dealing with every kind of discipline problem.
- The ultimate goal of classroom management is self-discipline and every effort should be made to enhance pupils' capacity to discipline themselves.
- A clear understanding of the theoretical or psychological assumptions underlying these approaches is necessary before making a choice.
- It is more comfortable to work, select or design an approach which is consistent and compatible with one's personality, philosophy and beliefs about teaching.
- One has to be fully familiar with the different strategies associated with the approach which suits one's needs and preference.
- One's philosophy and beliefs about teaching may vary with different age groups and tasks in a lesson.
- Effective classroom approaches or techniques cannot work for long without good instructional planning and effective teaching.

❏ **Activity 5.3**

Examining your philosophy and beliefs about teaching and learning

Give your honest opinion on the following statements which are useful for exploring your views on teaching and learning.

1. The teacher should have the maximum power to regulate pupils' behaviour in the classroom.

2. The teacher has the sole responsibility for good classroom management.
3. Students have an inner desire to work and to learn in a constructive way.
4. The teacher should use punishments and rewards to reinforce good discipline.
5. The teacher should facilitate pupils' inner drive to do their best in school learning.
6. The teacher should help students to help themselves in keeping good discipline.
7. Students can make rational decisions.
8. Students should be responsible for their own behaviour in school.
9. It is a good practice to work with pupils in regulating classroom discipline.
10. The teacher needs to keep a close watch on pupils at all times in school.

A Student-Oriented Approach

In Lewis's framework, the student-oriented approach is equated to the model of influence. Thomas Gordon's concept of discipline as self-control (Gordon, 1989) and his Teacher Effectiveness Training (TET) (Gordon, 1987) reflect the principles of a student-oriented approach very clearly, as indicated in the box below. Advocates of this approach use non-interventionist strategies believing that individual students are capable of understanding and solving their own problems and that, in general, it is impossible for one person to make appropriate decisions for other people.

Gordon's principles for managing classroom discipline problems

Thomas Gordon is a believer in Rogerian counseling and tries to apply Rogerian theories in the classroom. His Teacher Effectiveness Training is based on teacher-student relationships built upon trust, goodwill and genuine communication. Here are Gordon's principles of teaching and learning:

- Teachers should try to influence pupils, not to control them. By not coercing them, the teacher is more successful in exerting a positive influence over pupils.
- Coercive power results in coping mechanisms or confrontation with students.
- "I-messages" are powerful for influencing students as they lead them to think about and feel the effects of their behaviour on others and realize their responsibility for changing their behaviour to solve problems.
- Trust, goodwill and active listening are essential for building positive relationships between pupils and teachers.
- Good student-teacher relationships and communication are the keys to participative decision making in classroom management.
- Aim for "no-loser" conflict resolution in maintaining discipline where both sides (the teacher and students) are winners.

Defining the problem

The starting point of a student-oriented approach to dealing with misbehaviour is to determine who is responsible for the problem — the students or the teacher. Until one knows who "owns" a problem, teachers cannot decide who should take responsibility for dealing with it. If it is a student's problem, then he/she should define it and decide on a course of action; but if it is a teacher's problem, the teacher should explore ways to resolve it.

Defining the problem often involves letting the student talk with the teacher about it until it is clarified, at which stage the ownership problem can be resolved. The following procedures can be applied to help solve students' problems.

When a student owns a problem

When a student owns the problem, the teacher can help him/her to deal with it. First, the teacher has to make sure that the student keeps calm and explores the issue in a rational manner. At the same time, the teacher listens attentively and demonstrates acceptance of whatever the student wants to say about the problem without offering advice or judgment. However, the teacher can play the role of a consultant whenever necessary by, for example, clarifying issues, summarizing useful facts or helping the student to develop coherent arguments so that he/she can explore the problem in detail. After that, the teacher can encourage the student to make suggestions for solving the problem and give help if needed in evaluating them. Finally, the student should be allowed to select the most appropriate action or plan to resolve the problem. The techniques and ideas in Gordon's TET, which will be discussed in a later section, provide many helpful views and tools for the teacher.

Steps for solving student-owned problems

1. Keep calm and find a comfortable place to sit and talk to the student.
2. Encourage the student to talk through the problem: remember not to intervene, and give the student freedom to explore the problem.
3. Enhance communication and understanding by listening attentively and carefully.
4. Work as a consultant in encouraging the student to identify and clarify issues or questions; offer useful and relevant facts; and summarize ideas and argument for better understanding of the problem and decision making.
5. Be positive and demonstrate acceptance of whatever the student says and encourage rational problem solving.
6. Let the student make informed suggestions and solutions by taking into consideration the issues discussed.
7. Help the student to select the most appropriate action or plan to solve his/her problem.

When the teacher owns a problem

In cases where the teacher owns the problem — for instance, when a student calls out answers when the class is doing sums, cheats in a test or talks during teaching — the teacher clearly needs to handle the problem on his/her own. Following the principles of a student-oriented approach, Lewis (1997: 59–64) introduces a four-step procedure for handling teacher-owned problems.

Four-step procedure

(a)   Let the student understand the problem

It sounds straightforward for a teacher to let pupils know what the problem is, but offering pupils freedom to decide whether or not their behaviour is a problem, rather than directing them, may be difficult in practice. The use of "I-messages" is appropriate here (Gordon, 1989) as they let pupils know how the teacher feels about their behaviour, which can lead to a better understanding between them and allow pupils to make informed decisions about changing their behaviour. In this way, both pupils and the teacher can experience a "no-loser" conflict resolution as described by Gordon (1987).

"I-messages"

Using "I-messages" is the least guilt-inducing way of expressing verbally to students how their behaviour is affecting teaching and learning in the class. With increased awareness of the effects of their behaviour, they can then be more considerate and able to solve the problem by changing the way they behave. The success of an "I-message" depends on good teacher-student relationships; if there is no trust and goodwill between the parties involved, it is unlikely to be fruitful.

Three major elements of "I-messages", which can be presented in any order, are:

*   non-directive statements or descriptions of the behaviour;
*   the expression of feelings and emotions as a result of the behaviour;
*   tangible and concrete effects on the teacher.

(b)   Active listening

In the second step, the teacher tries to listen carefully to and understand the student's analysis of his/her behaviour and suggest solutions to the problem, but the student may need the teacher's help in evaluating the suggestions.

(c)   Finding a solution

There are many ways to find a solution, but it must be acceptable to both parties. It is therefore important to be clear and frank about one's feelings during the discussion and to recognize that it may take some time to reach an agreement with which both parties are comfortable.

(d)   Implementing and evaluating the solution

It is important to examine the suggested solution closely before actually trying it out in the classroom. If anything is inappropriate, it must be revised. Assessing the solution plan is also necessary and must be done in a careful and systematic manner. A good way of rounding up the discussion is to talk about ways of evaluating the effectiveness of the solution.

A Teacher-Oriented Approach

In Lewis's framework, the teacher-oriented approach is equated with the model of control, of which Lee and Marlene Canter's (Canter and Canter, 1976, 2002) Assertiveness Model is an example. This approach views children as being unable to make rational decisions in their best interests, and so gives teachers the responsibility for deciding what is best for them (Lewis, 1997: 68). While this shows teachers' concern for their students, it gives teachers the right to exert their authority and requires the students to adhere to a standard of discipline in the classroom which allows effective instruction to take place.

Needs and rights in the classroom

Both pupils and teachers have the need for and the right to a positive and a supportive classroom environment for effective learning and teaching (Canter and Canter, 2002). Canter and Canter (1976: 2) identified three important teacher rights:

1.   the right to establish a classroom structure and routine that produces the optimal learning environment in the light of their strengths and weaknesses;
2.   the right to determine and request appropriate behaviour from pupils which meets the teacher's needs and encourages positive social and educational development in the pupils;
3.   the right to ask for assistance from parents, principals and other stakeholders to help pupils in need.

It is worth noting that while most models pay attention to pupils' needs, the Canters' model stresses the importance of attending to teachers' needs, at least to those who exert their authority.

Assertive teachers

According to the Canters' description, there are three kinds of teachers, as outlined below. In their view, while all these styles of teaching have an impact on classroom management, only assertive teachers can produce a warm and supportive environment which meets both their needs and those of their pupils.

(a) *Non-assertive teachers* appear to be overly passive and compliant. They often express unclear or inconsistent expectations, and overreact to student misbehaviour when they become irritated. For example, such a teacher may just say in a casual tone, "Wa Man, could you please be more obedient?", which fails to give any clear expectations about how the student should respond.

(b) *Hostile teachers* like to show that they are in charge of the classroom. They are bossy and unfriendly to their students, and they like to issue orders and often adopt a vindictive tone in responding to pupils — for example, "Wa Man, Shut your dirty mouth! When are you going to stop shouting! You are the most inconsiderate student I've ever had!" Such responses provoke confrontation and play no part in developing student self-discipline.

(c) *Assertive teachers* communicate their expectations to their students in a clear, calm and consistent manner. They are serious, but they work hard to build trust with the students and to help them understand the types of behaviour which promote and inhibit learning in school. They have clear guidelines for maintaining discipline and student cooperation. A typical response of an assertive teacher would be: "Wa Man, I want you to get into your seat. I am not going to allow you to run around the class and disturb others. You know the rules. If you get out of your seat again, you will be sent to the reflective corner."

Procedures for assertive teaching

Assertive teaching does not involve the imposition of harsh rules and coercion. Communication, fair treatment and consistency are the keys to successful discipline. It is based on mutual trust and respect and an understanding of each party's needs and rights (Charles, 2005: 41). The following procedures are suggested by Lewis (1997: 74) for assertive teaching.

1. Consider and decide which behaviours are acceptable and unacceptable in the classroom and develop rules to stop inappropriate behaviours.
2. Develop sets of consequences for both acceptable and unacceptable behaviours.
3. Explain the rationale behind these rules as well as the consequences and benefits of appropriate behaviours.
4. Practise, model and reinforce these regularly in class.

❐ **Activity 5.4**

Establishing discipline in the classroom

The four steps outlined above enable a teacher to establish classroom discipline in a systematic way. However, teachers still need to practise them regularly before they pay off. The following questions will help them to enrich their plans.

- How can we determine which behaviours are acceptable and unacceptable?
- What can a teacher do to find out which decisions made are in the best interests of both themselves and their pupils?
- In what ways can teachers show their approval to students who behave appropriately?
- How can we determine what kinds of positive consequences or rewards for pupils are most effective?
- How can we determine what kinds of negative consequences are "logical" or "fit" inappropriate behaviour?

Successful implementation

Successful implementation of these procedures often requires teachers to explain, practise and model the sets of rules in front of the students and involve them in asking questions and demonstrating. Also, these procedures have to be implemented on a fair, consistent, and regular basis in the classroom.

Some advice on dealing with students' behavioural problems may be needed. First, teachers must avoid acting in a hostile way to students who misbehave. All that is required is to inform such students in an assertive and clear voice that they have broken the rules by saying, for example: "Wa Man, I want you to be quiet. I am not going to allow you to talk and disturb your classmates who are reading their books. If you do it again, you will have chosen to be removed from the class for five minutes." If the student persists in breaking the rules, some negative consequences have to be implemented. In contrast, when students behave in an acceptable way, pleasant consequences should follow, including smiling, nodding or winking, clapping hands, making positive verbal statements and giving tangible rewards. It is useful for a teacher to arrange a hierarchy of positive consequences for different kinds of acceptable behaviour (Lovegrove et al., 1991).

A Group-Oriented Approach

In Lewis's framework, the group-oriented approach is equated with the management model, which lies in the middle of the continuum between the teacher-oriented and student-oriented approaches. A good example of this approach is represented by Rudolf Dreikurs's Social Discipline Model (Dreikurs et al., 1998) which asserts that, first and foremost, humans are social animals and that all behaviour, including misbehaviour, is directed purposefully towards achieving social recognition and respect. Dreikurs argues that students' actions are aimed at four major goals, namely, getting attention, seeking power, revenge, and helplessness or inadequacy; and so misbehaviour is seen as a result of using the wrong means to gain social acceptance. Teachers must understand what has gone wrong in order to direct the students to respect them and to regain a sense of belonging among their peers.

The four goals of misbehaviour

When pupils are unable to gain recognition and a sense of belonging in the classroom, they turn to the mistaken goals noted above. Table 5.4 summarizes and gives examples of these misbehaviours and teachers' reactions to them.

(a) Attention-seeking

Everyone constantly tries to seek attention and get recognition from others. Instead of getting recognition through productive work, a student may resort to misbehaviour which demands criticism from the teacher and so gets his/her attention by faulty means. Typical examples of such ways of gaining attention are: making a noise, asking questions or disturbing others while they are working; failing to follow classroom rules; or dressing "cutely" to gain attention from others (Johns et al., 1989: 143). It should be noted that passive-destructive behaviour is relatively more difficult to correct than the active seeking of attention.

(b) Power-seeking

There are two different kinds of power-seekers — those who feel inferior because of their perceived ability and those who have serious difficulties in gaining recognition within their social groups. However, whatever the source of such power-seeking, it manifests itself in the same way: they try to make themselves feel important by, for instance, being bossy, challenging authority or opposing school rules. They want to be in control and force others to comply.

(c) Revenge

Pupils who fail to gain attention and influence in the classroom often feel hurt and rejected and may try to compensate for this lack of social recognition by taking revenge by physically or verbally hurting others. These kinds of violence need to be attended to with particular care because of their harmful nature.

(d) Helplessness or inadequacy

Some pupils feel incompetent and worthless and this may well lead to feelings of complete despair. Such pupils tend to give up hope of doing anything to regain a sense of belonging or status in the class as they think that nobody cares for them any longer. Sometimes teachers fail to notice such desperate pupils in their classes; and even if they do, simply showing pity may not have any beneficial effects.

Table 5.4 The goals of misbehaviour: Students' signs and teachers' feelings and reactions

Goals	Signs and indications of misbehaviour	Teachers' feelings and reactions
Attention-seeking	Being desperate for social recognition and belonging, pupils may exhibit behaviours such as clowning, acting foolishly or bashfully, showing off, always asking questions, performing, and always clinging.	Teachers feel annoyed or see the behaviour as an irritating nuisance and not spend much time on it.
Power-seeking	Feeling inferior and unable to live up to social expectations, pupils may exhibit behaviours such as being stubborn, argumentative, challenging and bossy.	Teachers feel provoked and angry, and sometimes feel threatened or defeated.
Revenge	Being unable to gain attention and power from others and feeling hurt by them, pupils may compensate by bullying and being physically and verbally abusive.	Teachers feel hurt or insulted, and feel sorry for those who are being humiliated or bullied.
Helplessness or inadequacy	Feeling that they are "losers" and having given up any hope of gaining recognition from others, pupils may act dumb, refuse to try, withdraw from the group or wish to be left alone.	Teachers have difficulty in talking to and caring for the pupils and have a feeling of helplessness in trying to support them.

Understanding the Drive Behind the Misbehaviour

According to Dreikurs, it is important to know students' motives for misbehaviour. Dreikurs's model asserts that such misbehaviour reflects their mistaken beliefs and actions aimed at gaining group recognition or social approval. However, these students are basically rational and are able to act appropriately to change their behaviour when given encouragement and guidance (Dreikurs et al., 1998). It is therefore important for the teacher to talk to the students and try to understand their "mistaken goals". This kind of understanding enables students to learn how to discipline themselves and be responsible for their own behaviour. The first step in dealing with student misbehaviour is to identify and clarify the problem and then offer help and explore alternatives for changes in behaviour. The following guidelines and procedures suggested by Johns and his colleagues (1989) are useful.

Control your immediate interventions

Teachers must not reinforce the mistaken behaviour by giving it attention, struggling to impose their power, retaliating or agreeing with the pupils' feelings of inadequacy.

Table 5.5 The "dos and don'ts" in changing student misbehaviour

	Inappropriate responses	Appropriate responses
Attention-seeking	• Paying attention to wrong deeds and attention-seeking actions	• Arrange a time when the student can get full attention and approval from the class • Take opportunities to offer positive recognition of the student
Power-seeking	• Arguing with the student • Using force to make the student change	• Offer choices and alternatives • Offer ways for the student to feel important by assigning tasks or positions to him/her
Revenge	• Retaliating; fighting back • Making sarcastic or insulting comments	• Ask the student to do something helpful and special for you • Show support
Helplessness/inadequacy	• Agreeing with the student that nothing can be done • Showing pity for the student's helplessness	• Offer genuine support by allowing the student to experience success • Show that you have faith that the student can do something well or contribute to the class

Clarify and understand the basis of the problem

The second step is to understand and clarify the problem, which can be a difficult task. To find out as much as you can about it, it is essential to establish communication with the student, be a good listener and show your care for him/her. Teachers can also learn by observing the student's misbehaviour carefully. Table 5.6 offers some hints about clarifying a student's problem.

Table 5.6 Students' misbehaviour and possible mistaken beliefs

	If your students	Possible assessment of misbehaviour
1.	keep repeating a certain misbehaviour after being stopped	Attention-seeking
2.	resist changing misbehaviour or increase it; want to argue; consistently act in a certain inappropriate ways	Power-seeking
3.	become violent and want to hurt people	Revenge
4.	refuse to try anything; isolate themselves from the group; want to be alone	Helplessness/ inadequacy

Disclose the goal of the misbehaviour

It is important for teachers to communicate to pupils that their behaviour is inappropriate and results from a mistaken goal. Talking with pupils about the causes of their behaviour — which is best done privately and with their consent — can be helpful for exploring alternatives. The discussion can begin with the teacher asking why the student has misbehaved in the class; and if an answer is forthcoming, the teacher can go on to discuss the causes of this particular misbehaviour. Sometimes, the student will not explain why he/she acted in this way because of unwillingness to do so or subconscious motivation. In such cases, the teacher has to resort to guesswork and make suggestions based on what he/she already knows and has observed during the conversation (the "recognition reflex" described below may give you some hints); and such guesses/suggestions are best phrased in the form of questions (Johns et al., 1989: 146), e.g.

- "Could it be that you feel this is the only way in which I will notice you, and you want to be noticed?" *(attention-seeking)*
- "Is it possible you want to show me that I can't make you work?" *(power-seeking)*
- "Could it be that you want me to feel as hurt as you do?" *(revenge)*
- "Is it possible you believe you just can't write, and you want to be left alone?" *(helplessness or inadequacy)*

Recognition reflex
• A change in expression
• A body twitch or nervous movement
• A sheepish grin, a smile, or a laugh
• A change in eye-contact
(Johns et al., 1989: 146)

Explore alternative behaviour

Once the goal of the misbehaviour has been recognized, alternatives for changing it can be discussed in a kind, open and warm manner. A good teacher-student relationship is almost a prerequisite for exploring and succeeding in changing behaviour. However, the teacher should be firm in responding to students' answers, and should lead the way by asking questions and making proposals so that the student can consider and make positive suggestions. It must be remembered that the group-oriented approach assumes that students can make rational choices and have the right to determine their own behaviour. Exploring alternatives is a way of respecting this right to choose and of letting them learn how to become self-disciplined.

❐ **Activity 5.5**

Offering alternatives for mistaken behaviour

In groups of four, suggest alternatives for correcting student misbehaviour resulting from (a) attention-seeking, (b) power-seeking, (c) revenge, and (d) helplessness and inadequacy.

Natural and logical consequences

Even when pupils' misbehaviour arises from subconscious reasons, the teacher must deal with it properly. There is no point in punishing the student as the ultimate goal in this approach is to teach self-discipline and give pupils the right to determine their behaviour. Instead of teachers imposing penalties to control them, the students have to experience the unpleasant consequences which their inappropriate behaviour brings.

There are two kinds of negative consequences: natural consequences and logical consequences. The former comprise unpleasant outcomes of inappropriate behaviour, e.g. forgetting one's crayons means that a pupil cannot draw pictures. Logical consequences are unpleasant results which are administered by the teacher in response to the inappropriate behaviour, e.g. a student's forgetting to do homework resulting in staying behind to finish it after school. Obviously, it is helpful if the teacher discusses the consequences of the misbehaviour with the student.

Goodwill and encouragement

As noted before, students who exhibit inappropriate behaviour are being driven by some subconscious and mistaken reasons: they often feel unsafe and helpless, and lack confidence because they have not gained recognition from their peers or the social group to which they belong. It is important, therefore, for teachers to do whatever they can to help these students regain the confidence and respect they have lost, and avoid discouraging them further or making them feel even more ashamed. The whole approach must be geared towards offering opportunities for the students to experience success, achieve something important and know they can do things well. Also, getting more support from their peers and their social groups is of the utmost importance, so the teacher can discuss with other students in the class what they can do to support misbehaving students to regain confidence, social respect and recognition. Both the teacher and the class should be alert and sensitive to situations in which they could offer praise and encouragement for good deeds and behaviour shown by students who have misbehaved.

Summary

This chapter begins by distinguishing between commonsense and theoretically-based models of classroom management, with the latter being well supported by psychological, pedagogical or philosophical perspectives. Different types of classification systems are identified according to their designs and theoretical bases. Broadly speaking, the various models or approaches can be distinguished by the way in which they assign power to the teachers and the pupils. Some common models — Johns et al.'s framework, Weber's classification, and Wolfgang and Glickman's Teacher Behaviour Continuum are introduced and explained.

Ramon Lewis's framework of teacher-oriented, student-oriented and group-oriented approaches offers teachers simple and practical strategies for dealing with inappropriate behaviour by students. These approaches are also referred to as the models of control, influence and management. The control model allows teachers to decide how students should behave; the influence model lets students decide on how to change their behaviour; and the management model values joint effort in dealing with misbehaviour in the classroom.

The teacher-oriented approach is equated with the Canter's Assertiveness Model. The Canters' assumption is that pupils are unable to make rational decisions in their own best interests, and so the teacher has the responsibility to decide what is best for them. In implementing this approach, teachers have to be assertive in communicating clearly their expectations and the consequences of unacceptable behaviour to pupils.

The student-oriented approach reflects the ideas in Gordon's Teacher Effectiveness Training (TET). While many models and approaches direct more attention to what students think, the TET model focuses on what and how teachers feel about their students' inappropriate behaviour. "I-messages" can be used to let students know how the teacher feels about the disturbing behaviour. Overall, a student-oriented approach stresses building positive student-teacher relationships and values "no-loser" conflict-resolution in dealing with inappropriate behaviour.

The group-oriented approach asserts that student misbehaviour is due to a lack of social recognition and respect among peers. This approach is illustrated by Dreikurs's Social Discipline Model which argues that student misbehaviour is driven by four mistaken goals: attention-seeking, power-seeking, revenge and helplessness. Despite their differences, however, all these models have the same goal: teachers should work with good will to help pupils become self-disciplined.

Questions for Discussion

1. What are the differences between commonsense and theoretically-based models of classroom management? Name one or two examples of a commonsense approach and explain why they are not effective for daily practice in the classroom.

2. Why are most of the models or approaches for classroom management based on psychological theories?
3. A "recipe-like" approach to controlling classroom behaviour might sound practical but it is often considered unprofessional. Do you agree with this view?
4. Lewis's classification of the three approaches to classroom management should be valued for its simplicity. Do you agree?
5. Discuss the basic needs and rights of a teacher in providing a positive environment for learning.
6. Why is it argued that students who show mistaken goals for misbehaviour must not be reinforced with what they ask for?
7. Suggest a plan to help a student who appears to be in complete despair to regain some status in the group. How are you going to convince his/her classmates that your plan will be successful?

Useful Resources

Websites

1. Ain't Misbehavin': Discipline Tactics That Work!: http://www.familyeducation.com/article/0,1120,20-11718,00.html
2. Positive Discipline: http://www.athealth.com/Consumer/issues/discipline.html
3. Positive Discipline. ERIC Digest: http://www.ericdigests.org/pre-9218/positive.htm
4. Promoting Positive Discipline: Whole school approaches to tackling low level discipline: www.hmie.gov.uk/documents/publication/ppd-12.htm
5. The Misbehaviour of Behaviourists: www.sentex.net/~nexus23/naa_aba.html

Further Reading

Albert, L. (1996). *Cooperative discipline.* Circle Pines, MN: American Guidance Service, Inc.

Anderson-Levitt, K. M. (1984). Teacher interpretation of student behaviour: Cognitive and social process. *Elementary School Journal,* 84(3): 315–337.

Brophy, J. E. and Rohrkemper, M. M. (1980). The influence of problem-ownership on teacher perceptions of and strategies for coping with problem students. *Journal of Educational Psychology,* 73: 295–311.

Doyle, W. (1981). Research on classroom contexts. *Journal of Teacher Education,* 32(6): 3–6.

Jones, F. H. (1997). Discipline alternatives. Did not! Did too! *Learning,* 24(6): 24–6.

Kohn, A. (1996). *Beyond discipline: From compliance to community.* Alexandria, VA: ASCE.

Milhollan, F. and Forisha, B. F. (1972). *From Skinner to Rogers: Contrasting approaches to education.* Lincoln, NE: Professional Educators Pub.

Skinner, B. F. (1986). Reward or punishment: Which works better. *US News & World Report,* 89(18): 79–80.

References

Canter, L. and Canter, M. (1976). *Assertive discipline*: *A take charge approach for today's educator.* Seal Beach, CA: Canter & Associates.

———. (2002). *Assertive discipline: Positive behaviour management for today's classroom.* Santa Monica, CA: Canter & Associates.

Charles, C. M. (2005). *Building classroom discipline.* Boston: Pearson.

Dreikurs, R. and Cassel, P. (1972). *Discipline without tears.* New York: Hawthorne.

Dreikurs, R., Grunwald, B. and Pepper, F. (1998). *Maintaining sanity in the classroom: Classroom management techniques* (2nd edn). New York: Taylor & Francis.

Education Convergence (1999). *Perspectives on students' misbehaviour* (in Chinese). Longman: Hong Kong.

Glasser, W. (1969). *Schools without failure.* New York: Harper and Row.

Gonzalo, G. (1977). *Classroom management: Implications for supervision.* ERIC Document. ED 141879

Gordon, T. (1987). *T.E.T: Teacher effective training.* New York: David McKay.

———. (1989). *Discipline that works: Promoting self-discipline in children.* New York: Random House.

Johns, F. A., MacNaughton, R. H. and Marabinus, N. G. (1989). *School discipline guidebook: Theory into practice.* Boston: Allyn and Bacon.

Kounin, J. (1971). *Discipline and group management in classrooms.* New York: Holt, Rinehart & Winston.

Lewis, R. (1997). *The discipline dilemma: Control, management, influence* (2nd edn). Camberwell, Victoria: Australian Council for Educational Research.

Lovegrove, M. N., Lewis, R. and Burman, E. (1991). *You can't make me* (2nd edn). Melbourne: La Trobe University Press.

Schmuck, R. A. and Schmuck, P. A. (1979). *Group processes in the classroom* (3rd edn). Dubuque: Willliam C. Brown.

Tauber, R. T. (1999). *Classroom management: Sound theory and effective practice* (3rd edn). Westport, CT: Bergin & Garvey.

Weber, W. A. (2006). Classroom management. In J. M. Cooper (ed.) *Classroom teaching skills.* Boston: Houghton Mifflin Co.

Wolfgang, C. H. and Glickman, C. D. (1986). *Solving discipline problems* (2nd edn). Boston: Allyn and Bacon.

Wolfgang, C. H., Bennett, B. J. and Irvin, J. L. (1999). *Strategies for teaching self-discipline in the middle grades.* Boston: Allyn and Bacon.

6

Enhancing Communication and Strengthening Teacher-Student Relationships

Li Wai-shing

> What conditions make possible constructive change in personality and behaviour? Operational definitions are given of such conditions. These are: that the troubled client is in relationship with a therapist who is genuine, real; is experiencing an unconditional caring for, and a sensitive empathy for the client. When these conditions are experienced by the client, constructive change occurs.
>
> Rogers (1957)

Synopsis

Communication is crucial for good teacher-pupil relationships. This chapter examines ways of inviting communication which is productive for teacher-pupil relationships, and of inhibiting communication, which is not. It goes on to discuss barriers to communication, such as the use of labelling, preaching and interrogating. The use of "I-messages" is suggested and steps for constructing them are introduced, and the chapter also discusses techniques for active listening. By combining good communication and listening skills, teachers can establish rapport and positive teacher-pupil relationships in schools. Strategies for maintaining relationships are analysed so that teachers can learn how to apply them in their own classrooms.

Objectives

After reading this chapter, you should be able to:
- understand the importance of communication in the classroom;
- identify major factors that facilitate communication;
- identify major barriers that hamper communication;
- understand the nature of "I-messages";
- know how to construct "I-messages";

- understand why active listening is useful in establishing good teacher-pupil relationships;
- build and maintain good teacher-pupil relationships in the classroom.

Pre-Reading Reflection and Discussion

- How important are communication skills to teachers?
- What are the factors that facilitate interaction in the classroom?
- List all the possible barriers to communication.
- Do you think teachers are good listeners? Why/why not?
- What do you mean by good teacher-pupil relationships? Give some examples.
- What should a teacher *not* do if he/she wants to establish good relationships in class?

Introduction

The way teachers talk and communicate with students affects greatly the behaviour of students and interaction in the classroom. Good communication generates a climate conducive to quality learning as students are willing to cooperate and demonstrate positive discipline. However, when teachers find their students are being boisterous, destructive and even revengeful, they may become frustrated and annoyed. They tend to be judgmental and use warnings, orders or advice to change the students' behaviour; and even worse, they may use labels to stereotype them. These statements of blame are provocative, causing further disturbance or embarrassment, and may lead students to withdraw or, sometimes, respond aggressively — they are roadblocks to communication, inhibiting it rather than inviting dialogue from the students. The use of "I-messages" is effective in showing teachers' feelings about students' misbehaviour without making judgments and criticisms. Teachers should not only invite students to talk and share but also need to be good listeners. They have to show acceptance of students' strong emotions and feelings and be patient in listening to them, and need to trust that their students can solve their own problems. Establishing and maintaining good teacher-pupil relationships is crucial for student cooperation and effective teaching and learning.

In the example below, Ms. Chung is clearly experiencing difficulties with her class and has acted in ways which show her frustration and hostility. How do you think Ms. Chung is inhibiting communication with her class? Can you spot any roadblocks to communication? In what ways might she change her behaviour to help build up better teacher-pupil relationships?

Classroom scenario

Ms. Chung is the form mistress of a P5B class. She likes to give her pupils funny names and uses unfriendly labels to identify them. Although the pupils may not always know how they are being labelled, they are used to Ms. Chung's evaluative and judgmental remarks in class. Though one of the pupils, Wing Yee, is mediocre overall in her academic work, she is good at mathematics. Ms. Chung notices that Wing Yee likes to talk to her neighbour in mathematics lessons and she usually shouts at her to stop talking and pay attention. Ms. Chung always says: "Wing Yee, if you want to talk, you can talk to me after school for the whole evening. I don't want to hear your ugly voice now". Wing Yee feels irritated by Ms. Chung's criticisms and she is not alone — many of the pupils have very little respect for Ms. Chung because they feel she does not have enough respect for them. The classroom climate is tense and hostile. To make matters worse, Wing Yee has lost interest in learning mathematics and has stopped handing in her homework. Some other pupils are likely to follow her example.

Communication in the Classroom

Communication in the classroom can be defined as the interchange of thoughts, feelings and information between the teacher and the pupils. Through good communication, the teacher motivates, guides and encourages student learning; and without such interaction, good relationships cannot be established and maintained nor can the teacher meets pupils' needs (Charles and Senter, 2002).

Communication is commonly viewed as referring to verbal means of exchange but non-verbal means of communicating, such as facial expression and eye-contact, are very often more powerful (Jones, 2000).

Good teachers must be able to communicate with students, colleagues, administrators, parents and many others. Teaching is not simply the delivering of knowledge, but requires a blending of competent teaching techniques and communication skills that motivate and encourage students to learn; and through their effective use of communication skills teachers convey respect, care and concern for students. Good teachers are good managers of communication.

Inviting and Inhibiting Communication

In communicating their feelings, teachers should express themselves in ways that do not hurt the pupils and encourage them to converse. Expressing your personal needs without inviting your pupils to participate in communicating often closes the door to further exchange. Blaming students is even worse as this often inhibits communication (e.g. *"I feel that it is your fault and you have to change now."*). The difference between inviting and inhibiting communication is that the former is reciprocal and opens a channel for further communication while the latter blocks later opportunities for dialogue.

Avoiding frustrating and negative statements

1. Keep calm when you see misbehaviour in the classroom.
2. Do not rush into commenting. Pause before communicating your feelings to the student.
3. Express how you feel in a positive way, not blaming or criticizing the student.
4. Indicate why the behaviour causes a problem in a non-provocative way.
5. Invite the student or the class to solve the problem.

What is "inhibiting communication"?

Inhibiting communication involves shutting down channels for two-way communication, with one party having taken over. It fails to promote understanding and has detrimental effects on relationships as it is often characterized by the use of language that shows lack of acceptance, invokes defensiveness, and provokes hostility and resistance (Larrivee, 1999: 13). This kind of language is often called *You-language* or *the language of disrespect* and it creates barriers to communication, as seen below.

Characteristics of inhibiting communication

1. It invalidates others' feelings, thoughts, wants and needs.
2. It tells others what the speaker wants, feels, thinks or does.
3. It advocates the speaker's own position without acknowledging others' positions.

(Larrivee, 1999: 113)

- **The language of disrespect**: Communication is strengthened when it is carried out on an equal basis — no one should feel superior to others. Giving orders and criticism is a sign of lack of respect while using "moralizing" language is a sign of a sense of superiority. Such communication fosters distrust and defensiveness.
- **"You-language"**: Fault-finding statements destroy reciprocal communication. Such messages tend to be accusatory by pointing to what one has done wrongly and *should not* be doing. Remarks such as *"You always . . . "* and *"You should never try this . . . "* put students on the defensive and fail to show understanding or empathy for them. When the "You-language" is full of "shoulds", this is often felt by the listener to be humiliating.

Barriers to communication

Barriers are roadblocks on the highway of communication. They inhibit reciprocity and make further communication difficult and sometimes impossible. These roadblocks are confrontational and indicate that pupils' misbehaviour or attitudes are unacceptable. However, they are unlikely to bring about the desired results as, at best, they seek submissive compliance from the pupils which often has negative effects on them.

Gordon (1974) identifies twelve roadblocks to communication as shown in Table 6.1 (see p. 113). These barriers contain information on what the teacher thinks about the students, but show hardly any consideration of the students' points of view. As a result, they will have little success in changing pupils' behaviour, but instead motivate them to be defensive or fight back.

Checklist for roadblocks to communication

√   Giving orders: "Come on. Don't talk anymore, write you poem now!"

√   Warning: "If you fail again, I am going to talk to your parents."

√   Preaching: "You have to complete this and learn it. It's for your own good. All pupils should know this before leaving school."

√   Advising: "Let me tell you, you must follow this rule — otherwise you will find yourself wasting time."

√   Criticizing: "I feel very disappointed to find you fooling around the room without doing anything constructive."

√   Questioning: "What's happening? Why can't you start your project in the right way?"

Overcoming communication roadblocks

To guard against blockages in communication, teachers first need to unlearn all the practices mentioned in this chapter which make communicating difficult. They should then project an attitude which facilitates genuine and open communication with the pupils. This often requires them to change their mindsets, not just learn the skills for enhancing communication. Rogers (1959: 210–211) reminds us of the importance of empathy which involves perceiving "the internal frame of reference of another with accuracy and with the emotional components and meanings which pertain thereto as if one were the person but without ever losing the 'as if' condition. Thus, it means to sense the hurt or the pleasure of another as he senses it and to perceive the causes thereof as he perceives them, but without ever losing the recognition that it is as if I were hurt or pleased and so forth." This is the basis for genuine understanding, sharing and communication, without which active listening is impossible. Empathy also generates a sense of acceptance, sincerity and a non-judgmental attitude which dissolves resistance and avoidance in communication. Adopting an empathetic attitude produces a caring atmosphere which further strengthens the relationship between the parties involved.

What is "inviting communication"?

Inviting communication is reciprocal communication, involving pupils and their teacher, which opens opportunities for further exchange. It is characterized by the use of language of respect and consideration for others' feelings. It does not create enemies or defensiveness but allies and friends. The purpose of inviting communication is to strengthen relationships, and provide mutual understanding and support, and this can be achieved by using, for example, congruent communication and "I-messages" (which were mentioned in Chapters 4 and 5, and will be discussed in the following section).

Confronting Messages and Their Consequences

It is not easy for teachers to respond to pupils' behaviour with positive and non-judgmental statements under great pressure, especially when pupils appear to be non-cooperative and hostile. Quite often, the teacher will resort to punishment or deliver warnings that provoke anger and reduce student self-esteem. This is so common that, in a Teacher Effectiveness Training course, Gordon (1974) found that over 90 percent of the teachers were using messages that encoded negative feelings and frustration. He regards warnings, orders, preaching, criticism, stereotyping, praise and interrogating as examples of confrontational messages that convey feelings of disappointment and exasperation. Here are some illustrations:

- "You know what the classroom will turn into if you keep on doing this!" **(analysing)**
- "Shut your mouth!" **(order)**
- "You are an idiot. You don't use your brain at all!" **(labelling)**
- "If you don't do that you'll have to stay after class with the low achievers!" **(embarrassing)**
- "Do you think you can really challenge me?" **(provocative)**
- "You are stubborn. Stop doing that." **(criticizing)**

Gordon (1974: 126–41) asserts that all these messages are destructive because they result in:

- student resistance;
- the belief that the students are stupid and incompetent;

- the belief that the teacher is thoughtless and irresponsible;
- the generation of guilt feelings among students;
- the lowering of students' self-esteem;
- student defensiveness;
- hostility and challenges to the teacher;
- feelings of helplessness and withdrawal.

Table 6.1 Gordon's roadblocks to communication (adapted from Larrivee, 1999)

Roadblock	Description	Message to students and their reactions
Ordering and commanding	"You must …" "You will …"	• Your feelings are not important. • Feelings of resentment, fear or resistance
Warning	"If you don't do that, …" "Either you do … or … "	• I have no respect for your needs and wants. • Feelings of fear, submission, hostility
Preaching and moralizing	"You shouldn't do … " "Everybody in this school should … "	• Your judgement cannot be trusted. • Guilt feelings, resistance
Advising	"What I would do is …" "If I were you, I would …"	• You are incompetent and incapable. • Feeling of dependency
Providing logical arguments	"You may think like that but the fact is …" "You have to learn …"	• You are being ignorant and not good enough. • Feeling inadequacy, resentment, rejection of the argument
Criticizing and blaming	"You are wrong because …" "You are not listening to …"	• You are no good. • Feeling incompetent, retaliation
Labelling and stereotyping	"You are a slow learner …" "You are immature …"	• You are unworthy of … • Feeling helpless, retaliation, acting as labelled
Interpreting and analysing	"What you really want to do is … " "You do that because …"	• You have to follow my way of thinking. • Feeling threatened, frustrated, embarrassed
Praising and evaluating	"You are smart and I think you can do it…." "I don't think you can solve the sum because …"	• You don't have a problem. • Feeling dependency, patronized
Reassuring and sympathizing	"I know how you feel …" "You will feel better tomorrow …"	• Stop feeling the way you do. • Feeling misunderstood
Interrogating and probing	"Why do you have to do this … ?" "Are you sure you are going to …?"	• I don't trust you. • Feeling defensive, reacting with avoidance
Withdrawal and sarcasm	"Don't talk about it any more, …" "Forget about this …"	• I am not really interested. • Feeling dismissed

It is important for teachers to be cautious when communicating their feelings to pupils. Messages which are confrontational should be avoided as they contribute to poor pupil-teacher relationships in the classroom.

Using Congruent Communication

Instead of using confronting messages, teachers are encouraged to use congruent communication. Congruent messages are statements by teachers that are helpful to pupils while being in line with their feelings about the situation and themselves (Charles, 2000: 79). According to Ginott (1972) who developed this concept, it has the power to address pupils' misbehaviour without embarrassing them. Instead of saying *"You are naughty. You have scattered the books all around the floor"*, a teacher can say *"Can you tidy up the floor during recess"*. Instead of constructing communication roadblocks, the teacher respects the pupils and treats them as social equals who are able to make reasonable choices. Constructive and positive statements made to pupils will avoid angering them and are more likely to get their cooperation in class. In addition, the teacher is unlikely to lose his/her temper or self-control by treating pupils as people with self-worth. Congruent communication holds that the best way to correct misbehaviour is to remind pupils to behave properly; any blaming, preaching, or criticizing is unhelpful and will generate more excuses and frustration (Charles, 2002).

"I-messages" in Communication

An "I-message" is a concept for inviting communication as well as a particular format which conveys a non-blameful message and positive evaluation in communication (Gordon, 1974). One major advantage of "I-messages" is that they allow teachers to speak from their perspectives in a non-evaluative way while at the same time respecting students' self-esteem. The idea in expressing "I-messages" is not to find fault with or blame others, but rather to express why the behaviour is a problem and what can be done to solve it in a mutually agreed way. "I-messages" are often constructed using the language of respect which brings about mutual understanding. Since it takes others' feelings and perspectives into consideration, students' self-esteem is not at stake. It is very likely that students will be cooperative, not defensive or hostile in this mode of exchange; and it allows them to make appropriate changes or adjustments in their behaviour in a voluntary way.

❐ **Activity 6.2**

Use of "I-messages"

Work in small groups. Discuss the advantages of "I-messages" and the disadvantages of "You-messages". By comparing them, write a statement appealing to all teachers to use "I-messages" to express their feelings about students' behaviour in the classroom.

Constructing "I-messages"

"I-messages", in which teachers use non-judgmental language to maintain a positive learning environment in the classroom, generally consist of three parts (Williams et al., 1999: 66) which are described below in detail.

(a) Part I (describing the situation)

It is important for teachers to let students know the specific situations, events or behaviours that are troubling them. Begin "I-messages" with "when" and give an account of the specific event:

- When the books were . . . [describing a situation] (*Compare this with: "Nancy, you are naughty!"*)

(b) Part II (expressing the associated feeling)

The account, which is non-judgmental and evaluative, tells the pupils exactly what is the cause of the problem. It is an expression of the feelings associated with the situation or event described.

- When your books were scattered around the floor [describing], I had a difficult time when I walked in the aisle [feelings]. (*Compare this with: "Nancy, you are naughty. I will punish you if you don't pick up those books."*)

(c) Part III (describing the effect)

Here the teacher expresses the effect of the event or situation in concrete terms:

- When your books were scattered around the floor [describing], I am afraid it caused a lot of inconvenience to classmates [feelings] and we'll spend time tidying them up [effect]. Can we think of a solution? (*Compare this with: "Nancy, you are naughty. I will punish you if you don't pick up your books. I won't allow you to come to my class."*)

When teachers expresses their feelings with "I-messages", students are able to understand how they feel and what problems are. They will recognize what caused the feelings and can work with the teacher for a solution or a change of behaviour (Larrivee, 1999: 121).

This analysis suggests that "I-messages" have five key elements as they: (1) are expressed from the teacher's perspective; (2) aim to clarify what has happened and why the behaviour or event is a problem; (3) give information to pupils about their behaviour; (4) communicate respect to the pupils as their purpose is to describe what has happened without blaming anyone; and (5) invite pupils to communicate and to solve the problem together with the teacher. However, all teachers should be cautioned that when using "I-messages", they are vulnerable to self-disclosure and there is always a chance that they will go unheard.

Why use "I-messages"?

Gordon (1974) argues that "I-messages" are an effective means of communication for changing students' behaviour and strengthening teacher-pupil relationships, e.g.

1. These non-judgmental statements only convey teachers' feelings on the specific behaviour or event. They clarify the cause of the problem without blaming students and so should not lead to hostility, guilt feelings and retaliation but rather increase the chances of students being willing to change their behaviour.
2. While conveying teachers' feelings, they respect students' sense of self-worth and enhance mutual understanding and reciprocal communication.
3. The statements harm no one and encourage students and teachers to solve the problem together.

Once a problem has been identified and defined, teachers and students can work together to generate possible solutions. They can both evaluate the merits of each solution and, once a decision is made, can then cooperate in assessing to what extent the problem has been successfully solved.

Essential Attitudes and Conditions for Communication

Rogers (1982) argues that everything teachers do is a form of communication and that good communication promotes learning and personal growth. Teachers understand that by means of good communication (using "I-questions" or some other effective approach) they are nurturing educational experiences which enable pupils to (Rogers, 1982: 1):

- become critical learners who are able to evaluate information;
- make intelligent choices and be self-directed;

- acquire knowledge relevant to real life;
- use this knowledge in meeting new and difficult situations;
- take self-initiated and responsible action to resolve problems;
- find learning enjoyable, thus becoming life-long learners.

Rogers (1957: 95–103) identifies three qualities or attitudes for making progress in the goals listed above:

(a) Congruency (or genuineness)

The teacher must be a real person when communicating with students. In Rogers's words, "he is what he actually is, in this moment of time". There is no pretence and there is "transparency" in the relationship.

(b) Unconditional positive regard

In interacting with students, the teacher must show positive, caring and non-judgmental attitudes which are unconditional. As Rogers says: "[the teacher] finds himself experiencing a warm acceptance of each aspect of the client's experiences as being a part of that client . . . ".

(c) Empathetic understanding

The teacher must show an ability to understand the inner world of pupils and to express this understanding to them as they perceive it — once again, in Rogers's words, "to sense the client's private world as it were your own, but without ever losing the 'as if' quality . . . ".

In short, teachers must be good listeners who readily understand the world as perceived by pupils. They should have a caring and respectful attitude to all pupils so that they feel secure and are willing to talk openly about their feelings.

Reflection: The potential perils of praise

It is often said that the purpose of communication is to enhance students' personal growth, self-discipline and self-evaluation. However, teachers must be aware of the possible dangers of praise. Praise conditions students to be dependent on outside evaluation and extrinsic motivation. In this regard, it is arguable that the quality of praise is more important than its quantity. It is best if it encourages or enhances pupils' powers of self-evaluation and self-assessment. Encouragement conveys teacher respect and belief in students' capabilities (Dreikurs et al., 1982) and is useful for building students' self-efficacy.

Be a Good and Active Listener

Communication consists of sending and receiving messages, with listening lying at the receiving end of the process. The ability to be an active and effective listener is integral to good communication

Listening is one of the most important elements in developing good rapport with students as it shows respect for them. It also makes genuine dialogue possible as students are more articulate with the support of a good listener, perhaps in particular timid students who may have difficulty in finding words to express themselves and talk things out. It is hardly surprising that students' expression is often vague and indirect when there is no good listener to assist them in reconstructing their experience by encouraging them to express their needs and concerns clearly and in a confident manner. It may be argued that teachers are not counsellors and their class time is too precious to be spent on listening. While this may contain an element of truth, without genuine listening it is impossible to establish meaningful relationships between pupils and teachers which lead to understanding pupils' problems and provide a constructive environment to resolve their strong feelings and emotional difficulties (Williams et al., 1999: 69). It is often said that good listening can be therapeutic and can heal people who are deeply troubled by negative emotions and feelings.

Useful techniques for listening

1. Use verbal cues such as "Ah-ha", "I see" and "That's true" to show you are listening and attentive.
2. Use body language such as a nod, smile or frown to show your responses and feelings.
3. Body language and verbal messages should be congruent.
4. Use "door-openers', such as "Would you like to say something more about this to me?" or "It sounds that this is something important. Would you like to talk more about it?", to promote better communication and probe problems which are bothering the students.
5. State clearly your interpretation of students' messages and make sure your interpretation represents their true meaning.
6. Ask for feedback and ask questions if you are not sure about students' messages.
7. Paraphrase students' feelings to convey acceptance and understanding.
8. Avoid making judgments and giving approving or disapproving feedback during the process.
9. Try to understand students' messages with your heart and let them know that having feelings and emotions is not "bad";
10. Let your students talk things out, analyse the issues and solve the problems.

Active listening

You can prepare yourself for listening by stopping talking and paying attention to the speaker. However, this in itself is just passive listening and a more active approach requires accepting and respecting pupils' opinions and, at times, probing problems by showing eagerness to learn more. When a student comes to a teacher, the teacher often feels compelled to suggest solutions and ideas to tackle the problems and so deprives pupils of opportunities to express themselves fully. It is not suggested that teachers should remain silent in such situations — they should engage in active listening.

As argued by Gordon (1989), active listening is more productive by reflecting to pupils what has been heard and assuring them that it has been heard correctly. It is a mutual effort to ensure that the communication is carried out genuinely, with trust and acceptance (Fields and Boesser, 1994) and the exchange of true feelings. During active listening, pupils are confident that what they say is not only heard but also fully understood, which makes them feel secure enough to reveal their deep emotions and feelings to the teacher. It helps the student to fully express and explore the underlying problems and issues, and releases the emotions of individuals who are deeply troubled.

Checklist for active listening:

√   Avoid being manipulative or patronizing when meeting with students.
√   Show active listening to establish a trusting relationship.
√   Respect students' privacy and confidentiality in whatever they reveal.
√   Show care and concern for students.
√   Have a deep sense of trust and confidence in students' ability to understand their own problems and find solutions to them.
√   Accept students and their true feelings by letting them express themselves freely and openly.
√   Show empathy to students and yet remain separate from their feelings.
√   Show eagerness and willingness to help students and assist them in solving their problems.

(adapted from Gordon, 1974: 75–76)

Why some teachers are not good listeners

It should be recognized that some teachers are not good listeners. It is often said that pupils do not like to listen to teachers because they are always talking, appraising and giving advice. This is not a trivial comment as advice-giving or commenting is a sign of not listening and indicates a serious roadblock in the communication process as it obstructs the exchange of genuine feelings and emotions. One of the most obvious reasons why some teachers are poor listeners is that they often do not like listening to pupils, an attitude which can be attributed to the following factors. Teachers:

- like to make comments and judgments on what students say and that makes genuine communication impossible.
- often think that students' problems are insignificant.
- are busy and pay lip-service to pupils' feelings.
- are more interested in solving students' problems rather than in taking the time to listen to them.
- like to show they are competent and so rush to give advice whenever they hear about any problem.
- do not like to help students and tend to brush them off with some light comments or distract them by raising other issues without listening to them.
- sometimes do not know how to deal with pupils' real feelings.

These approaches or attitudes fail to lead to genuine listening and real understanding and show no respect for students' ability to tackle their problems. To be effective, teachers need to be good listeners (Fields and Boesser, 1994: 127) as positive relationships can only be built when students perceive that adults are willing to listen to them actively. With the support of a good listener, pupils can embrace their strong feelings and work out solutions to their problems.

❒ **Activity 6.3**

The use of active listening

What can teachers do when they see pupils who have strong feelings and want to talk to them? What are the "dos and don'ts" for promoting genuine listening and understanding? What can a teacher do to show respect and acceptance to a student? Discuss and share your experience with the members of your group, and then report to the whole class.

Reflection: Good communication and teacher-pupil relationships

In a sharing session for building rapport among students, a veteran teacher said that it is all about caring for your students. If you are caring, your language will not be inhibiting and you will be willing to listen to students. When you care, you will be punctual, respect your students and plan motivating lessons, all of which are helpful in building good rapport as students will notice your positive attitude and commitment. Good rapport is not merely a skill but must involve the heart and mind, and by adopting this approach good communication and teacher-pupil relationships will come naturally.

Building and Maintaining Relationships

Good communication and relationships are the foundation for transforming a classroom into a learning community where pupils embrace a spirit of acceptance, respect and security. The quality of teacher-pupil relationships often determines whether or not pupils' needs are met and affects their attitudes to classroom behaviour.

Why care about teacher-pupil relationships?

Good teacher-pupil relationships go beyond controlling students and fostering compliance in the classroom: they aim to create a classroom climate that represents an affective blend of warmth, care, tolerance, respect, acceptance and competent teaching (Connolly et al., 1995). It is commonly understood that students like teachers who are warm and friendly. Studies have shown that a positive classroom climate supported by high quality teacher-pupil relationships is able to meet pupils' needs and enhance their classroom learning (Shores et al., 1993; Nichols, 1992; Steinberg, 1992). The quality of the process is directly related to the extent of cooperation between pupils and the teacher in an interactive process which mutually reinforces each party's behaviour in the classroom. How students perceive themselves as learners affects the way they behave in school, and good teacher-pupil relationships built on trust, care and respect not only enhance students' self-esteem but also meet their personal and psychological needs (Jones and Jones, 2001) and develop group cohesion in the classroom. At the same time, teachers serve as role models for their pupils (Bandura, 1969, 1977) and students are more likely to identify with them if they feel positive about their relationship. Teaching must go beyond the delivery of knowledge to develop a classroom climate which is conducive to the development of affection and positive attitudes in pupils.

> ### Assessing teachers' attitudes
>
> One of the first things teachers can do to improve relationships with their students is to assess their own attitudes and behaviour towards them. They should ask themselves questions such as:
>
> - Am I courteous towards my students?
> - Do I listen carefully to students' questions and requests?
> - Do I listen to students and respect their opinions?
> - Do I control my temper when students behave inappropriately?
> - Do I like to be with students?
> - Do I treat students fairly?

It is also helpful for teachers to discover the attitudes of students towards them and the subjects they teach. Teachers can ask students such questions as:

- How relevant are the topics covered in this class?
- What topics do you like most?
- What topics do you like least?
- Do you think that I like you?
- Do I take the time necessary to help you understand difficult concepts?
- Do I treat you courteously?
- Do I have any distracting habits?
- Do I listen to suggestions you make?
- Do your needs and interests receive my attention?

(Edwards, 1997: 343)

Improving teacher-pupil relationships

Teacher-pupil relationships develop continuously: while it may be difficult to measure this precisely over time, they change and evolve significantly with particular events or issues. Connolly et al. (1995) suggested that there are two major variables which influence how relationships between teachers develop. They are (a) personal or affective quality of the relationships, and (b) how the teacher communicates or relates to the pupils. Some ways of strengthening human relationships are outlined below:

(a) *Socially acceptable skills*

Socially acceptable skills refer to a set of behaviours or attitudes — such as sensitivity, respect, caring, trust, willingness to listen and helpfulness — that are valued by members of society. While teachers have to demonstrate that these skills and attitudes are productive for communication in the classroom, they also have the responsibility to teach them to their pupils. This enables teachers to not only exercise quality interaction in the classroom but also help their pupils to develop positive relationships among themselves.

(b) *Quality verbal and non-verbal behaviours*

High quality verbal and non-verbal behaviours are useful means to convey acceptance, warmth and positive interpersonal interactions. Common examples include eye contact, talking to students pleasantly, having a cheerful facial expression, using humour, expressing empathy and concern, using physical contact appropriately and sharing common experiences. Students appreciate teachers who attend their activities or have meals with them. By using such verbal and non-verbal behaviours, teachers can enhance teacher-pupil relationships.

❐ **Activity 6.5**

Promoting positive teacher-pupil relationships

Reflect on your own experiences in schools. What did your teacher do for you and your class that you specially appreciated? What actions should teachers avoid as they are the counterproductive to improving teacher-pupil relationships? Classify your answers into three categories: (1) verbal statements, (2) non-verbal behaviour, and (3) behaviour.

(c) *Making a good impression*

It is important for teachers to make a good impression, especially when they are meeting pupils for the first time, as this has a major effect on the way pupils perceive them. For example, you can smile, memorize and use names, and say something courteous and interesting.

(d) *Reacting positively to others*

It is also important to react positively to others when you are sharing information or talking to them. Even when you disagree, you should do it gently and politely so that there is less defensiveness in the exchange and the door for communication remains open.

(e) *Not reacting in a negative way*

If you want to talk to others, try to give them your full attention and do not show dissatisfaction as these are roadblocks to good human relationships.

In conclusion, building and maintaining good teacher-pupil relationships is an important part of being a professional teacher. If teachers fail to establish a good rapport with students, they cannot expect students to cooperate with them. Good communication is crucial for conveying positive messages that contribute to good relationships, and it requires teachers to display appropriate verbal and non-verbal behaviour to promote understanding and respect for others. Human relationships develop continuously and they are a powerful means for developing a school environment in which effective teaching and learning take place.

Summary

This chapter distinguishes two forms of communication: inhibiting and inviting communication, with the former making communication difficult and the latter facilitating interaction. Teachers are advised to pay attention to barriers that adversely affect the communication process and to avoid at all costs messages which confront pupils as they are detrimental to student-teacher relationships.

"I-messages" are presented as an effective and positive means for inviting communication and establishing good rapport with students. It is proposed that teachers should learn how to construct such messages, following the suggestions by Gordon (1974). They should know that "I-messages" are characterized by non-judgmental statements and clear and concrete expression of the effects of the event or situation that is troubling the teacher, and that they encourage teachers and pupils to work together to solve problems.

Essential attitudes and conditions for communication are discussed, including Rogers's identification of three qualities which are useful indicators, namely congruency or genuineness, unconditional positive regard and empathetic understanding. In this respect, the potential perils of praising pupils should be considered carefully.

It is argued that good listening is essential for establishing effective communication with students. It is often said that teachers are not good listeners because, on the one hand, they regard students' problems as trivial and do not pay enough attention to them and, on the other, they often like to give advice instead of listening to students' problems in a genuine way. Without trust, regard and care, students will not talk about their problems honestly, and so they remain unheard and unsolved. Students must perceive that full attention is given to what they say and that their ability to solve their problems is respected.

Finally, the chapter focuses on teacher-pupil relationships which are crucial for generating a positive and encouraging classroom climate that can meet students' needs and enhances their learning. Good teacher-pupil relationships can be seen as an affective blend of warmth, care, respect, acceptance and competent teaching. Teachers must always reflect on their own attitudes towards their students. Without positive human relationships in the classroom, effective teaching and learning is impossible.

Questions for Discussion

1. Make a comparison between "inhibiting communication" and "inviting communication".
2. List the barriers to communication which are often found in classrooms.
3. Why is it argued that confrontational messages are detrimental to teacher-pupil relationships?
4. What are the three essential elements for constructing "I-messages"?
5. According to Carl Rogers, what are the three key qualities for positive communication?

6. Develop a reminder for local teachers to enable them to be good and active listeners?
7. What can a teacher do to establish and maintain good teacher-pupil relationships?

Useful Resources

Websites

1. Active Listening: http://www.studygs.net/listening.htm
2. Active Listening for the Classroom: http://712educators.about.com/cs/activelistening/a/activelistening.htm
3. Asian Journal of Counselling: http://www.fed.cuhk.edu.hk/en/ajc/0201/0201053c.htm
4. Questia.com: http://www.questia.com/search/teacher-pupil-relationship
5. Teacher-pupil Relationships: http://nzplc.massey.ac.nz/legal/default.asp?page=docs/personnel/relation.htm; http://www.infed.org.uk/biblio/relationship.htm
6. TIP: Theories: http://tip.psychology.org/rogers.html

Further Reading

Carkhuff, R. R. (1993). *The art of helping* (7th edn). Amherst, MA: Human Resource Development Press.

Cooper, P. J. and Simonds, C. J. (2003). *Communication for the classroom teacher.* Boston: Allyn and Bacon.

Huang, G. (1993). *Beyond culture: Communicating with Asian American children and families.* ERIC/CUE Digest Number 94. New York: ERIC.

Kottler, J. A. and Kottler, E. (2000). *Teacher as counselor: Developing the helping skills you need* (2nd edn). Thousand Oaks, CA: Corwin Press.

Lewis, C., Schaps, E. and Watson, M. (1996). The caring classroom's academic edge. *Educational Leadership*, 54: 16–21.

Rogers, C. (1962, Fall). The interpersonal relationship: The core of guidance. *Harvard Education Review*, 32: 46.

Woolfolk, A. and Brooks, D. (1983). Nonverbal communication in teaching. In E. W. Gordon (ed.). *Review of Research in Education.* 10. Washington, DC: American Educational Research Association.

References

Bandura, A. (1969). *Principles of behavior modification.* New York: Holt, Rinehart & Winston.
———. (1977). *Social learning theory.* Englewood Cliffs, NJ: Prentice Hall.

Charles, C.M. (2000). *The synergetic classroom: Joyful teaching and gentle discipline.* New York: Longman.

Charles, C. M. and Senter, G. W. (2002). *Elementary classroom management* (3rd edn). Boston: Allyn & Bacon.

Charles, C. M. (2002). *Essential elements of effective discipline.* Boston: Allyn & Bacon.

Connolly, T., Dowd, T., Criste, A., Nelson, C. and Tobias, L. (1995). *The well-managed classroom: Promoting student success through social skill instruction.* Boys Town: NE: Boys Town Press.

Dreikurs, R., Grunwald, B. and Pepper. F. (1982). *Maintaining sanity in the classroom: Classroom management techniques* (2nd edn). New York: Harper & Row.

Edwards, C. H. (1997). *Classroom discipline and management* (2nd edn). Upper Saddle River, NJ: Merrill.

Fields, M. V. and Boesser, C. (1994). *Constructive guidance and discipline: Preschool and primary school.* New York: Merrill.

Ginott, H. (1972). *Teacher and the child.* New York: Macmillan.

Gordon, T. (with N. Burch) (1974). *Teacher effectiveness training.* New York: Wyden.

———. (1989). *Teaching children self-discipline at home and in school.* New York: Harper/Collins.

Jones, V. F. (2000). *Tools for teaching: Discipline instruction motivation.* Santa Cruz, CA: Frederic H. Jones and Associates, Inc.

Jones, V. F. and Jones, L. S. (2001). *Comprehensive classroom management: Creating communities of support and solving problems* (6th edn). Boston: Allyn & Bacon.

Larrivee, B. (1999). *Authentic classroom management: Creating a community of learners.* Boston: Allyn & Bacon.

Nichols, P. (1992). The curriculum of control: Twelve reasons for it, some arguments against it. *Beyond Behaviour*, Winter: 5–11.

Rogers, C. (1957). The necessary and sufficient conditions of therapeutic personality change. *Journal of Consulting Psychology*, 21(2): 95–103.

———. (1982). Education — A personal activity. In E. Elliott-Kemp and C. Rogers, *The effective teacher: A person-centered development guide.* Sheffield: Sheffield Hallam University.

Rogers, F. R. (1959). A theory of therapy, personality and interpersonal relationships, as developed in the client-centered framework. In S. Koch, *Psychology: A study of science* (vol. 3). New York: McGraw Hill.

Shores, R. E., Gunter, P. L. and Jack, S. L. (1993). Classroom management strategies: Are they setting event for coercion? *Behaviour Disorders*, 18: 92 –102.

Steinberg, Z. (1992). Pandora's children. *Beyond Behaviour*, Spring: 5–13.

Williams, P. A., Alley, R. D. and Henson, K. T. (1999). *Managing secondary classrooms.* Boston: Allyn & Bacon.

7

Promoting Positive Peer Relationships

Hue Ming-tak

A gentleman makes friends through literature and that friendship ennobles benevolence.

Confucius (551– 479 BC)

Synopsis

This chapter highlights the importance of good peer relationships in students' personal growth and academic success. It also describes how students' conceptions of friendship change from primary to secondary education and outlines the characteristics of popular students. Some basic practices for promoting students' popularity are given, with a practical framework for helping students with peer problems to take a new perspective and develop new patterns of behaviour for improving their relationships. Lastly, teachers are recommended to take a proactive approach to promoting positive peer relationships among students in the classroom by developing strategies in the following areas: teaching social-emotional skills, conflict-resolution skills and problem-solving skills; getting students to learn in groups; and creating a classroom climate of positive peer relationships.

Objectives

After reading this chapter, you should be able to:
- understand the significance of good peer relationships for personal growth and academic achievement;
- identify practices and classroom cultures which are detrimental to promoting positive peer relationships;
- provide some basic principles for enhancing peer relationships;
- outline a framework for supporting students with peer problems;
- introduce some strategies for promoting good peer relationships.

Pre-Reading Reflection and Discussion

- What kinds of peer relationships among students encourage effective learning?
- How can you make sense of positive peer relationships?
- If a student in your class had a very bad relationship with his/her peers, what could you do to help him/her change?
- A student comes to you and complains about being given a horrible nickname by three other students in the same class. How would you handle this?
- You are a form tutor of a class, and intend to do something to promote a culture of positive peer relationships in the classroom. What difficulties do you foresee in doing this?

Introduction

The classroom is a social setting in which students engage not just in learning but also in interacting with their peers and teachers. Some of these activities are educational in nature and planned by teachers, for example group discussion and playing games. However, in the course of learning, students simultaneously engage in many other social activities, such as negotiating and competing with others, saving face, asking for help and working in a team; and sometimes these activities involve disruptive behaviour. Peer relationships clearly constitute a crucial part of the classroom climate and have a direct impact on students' personal development and the quality of teaching and learning. Peer influence is so powerful that teachers need to take it into account when examining students' behaviour and evaluating their learning outcomes. In the case below, Miss Ng intended to help one of her students, Shan Shan, who had had some bad experiences of name-calling. Should Miss Ng react to this incident immediately? How should the emotional needs of Shan Shan be addressed? How should the act of name-calling be managed? What should Miss Ng say to the class?

> **Classroom scenario**
>
> A girl in Miss Ng's class, Lee Shan Shan, was tall and very skinny. In the course of a lesson, Miss Ng heard two boys sitting near her repeatedly call her "Monkey Shan (mountain)". Shan-Shan was silent but looked very upset by the incident.

The Importance of Positive Peer Relationships

The benefits of good peer relationships

Many teachers recognize that students can enjoy school life and learn better if they have good relationships with their peers as this provides them with friendship and stimulating recreational activities. For example, when adolescents face difficulties at school or home, they can get sympathy and understanding from their peers and this supportive setting helps them to achieve the primary developmental tasks of adolescence.

Research has shown that students who have good relationships with their peers are able to establish a sense of togetherness, belongingness, self-worth and self-acceptance (Baloche, 1998; Kauffman et al., 2002), and these feelings promote purposeful and responsible behaviour and lead to effective learning. In contrast, those who relate poorly to their peers tend to experience more tension, stress and depression, and they have difficulty in learning, even when teaching is effective and student-centred. More alarmingly, as suggested by many studies, such students misbehave more frequently and are more likely to engage in bullying, violence and dropping out of school (Parker and Asher, 1987).

Students' conceptions of friendship

If students are asked about how important friendship is for them, they will respond very positively, telling you many stories about how they get along with their peers both inside and outside the classroom. By examining their responses in detail, it can be seen that students have different conceptions of friendship at different stages of their personal growth. Some of the features can be summarized as follows (Selman, 1981):

- **From the perspectives of students in primary school**: At this stage, friends tend to be selected from others of the same age, sex and ethnic group. They tend to share interests, attitudes, social orientations and values, but it is not necessary for them to resemble each other in intelligence or personality characteristics. The predominant type of group is the informal "gang", with few formal rules and a rapid turnover in membership.

- **From the perspectives of students in secondary school**: These students recognize that friendships form more gradually, and are deeper and more stable. Friends are judged in terms of mutual understanding, and sharing of their thoughts and feelings. They are more likely to be similar in their educational aspirations. Groups are more formal, highly structured and cohesive. They have special membership requirements and elaborate rules.

❏ **Activity 7.1**

What's a friend for?

1. Imagine asking a student who his or her friends are or what a friend is for. What do you think the answer would be? If you ask a Primary 3 student and a teenager the same question, in what ways do you think their answers might differ?
2. What are the implications of students' conceptions of friendship for the effective management of peer relationships in the classroom?

Helping Students to Become Popular

Some basic practices

If you leave peer relationships to develop on their own, students are likely to get along with those who are popular and put an effort into building close relationships with them; and groups will then form, with in-group members who belong to them and others excluded. What are the characteristics of popular students? Mussen et al.'s (1990) summary of the research findings suggest that popularity may be associated with the following features:

- being friendly and outgoing, and adopting a sympathetic orientation towards others;
- being considered by others to be kind and helpful;
- being deeply involved in activities and groups rather than remaining on the periphery;
- being healthy, physically attractive and with good personal hygiene;
- actively offering solutions to problems;
- having greater social knowledge and awareness of effective ways of interacting.

❏ **Activity 7.2**

Teaching friendship in the classroom

1. To what extent do you think unpopular students can be helped to become more popular?
2. Rewrite the characteristics listed above as some aims of classroom management and suggest strategies for promoting the popularity of students among their peers?

If the positive effect of peer influence is to be enhanced, classroom teachers, the school, parents and students must come together to develop strategies, both proactive and reactive, to guide students' behaviour and support their transition to becoming mature adults and responsible members of society. Here are some proactive practices to consider:

- Use the dynamics of peer groups to create a positive classroom climate and promote good behaviour.
- Help students to pursue and maintain positive peer relationships and make this part of the curriculum.
- Nurture students' social abilities, such as active listening, recognizing their feelings and those of others, and showing empathy, so that they can forge good peer relationships.
- Develop students' self-concepts and sense of self-worth so that they recognize themselves as valued persons.
- Provide students with opportunities to succeed in constructive ways which are valued by their peers, parents and the community.
- Encourage peer interactions and guide students to deal positively with individual differences in background, personality and ability.
- Establish intervention programmes for students with poor social skills or aggressive tendencies.

Practices and aspects of classroom culture which discourage good peer relationships

Some practices currently adopted by teachers for managing students' behaviour may actually hinder the promotion of good peer relationships. For example, in the belief that it will illustrate that misbehaviour is unacceptable and stop it spreading, teachers may isolate students who misbehave in the classroom, both physically and socially. Common ways of doing this are:

- marginalizing the misbehaving students and punishing other students who interact with them during lessons;
- arranging for the misbehaving students to sit in isolation or to stand, normally in a corner at the back of the classroom;
- depriving such students of their right to have playtime or recess.

(Hue, 2005)

However, instead of excluding students who behave badly from the social network of the classroom, teachers should try to help them to relate better to others and regain a sense of acceptance and belongingness so that they can improve their behaviour by learning from others.

Some aspects of a classroom culture certainly discourage the development of good peer relationships. For instance, bullying behaviour — that is, aggression in various forms, intimidation and harassment, including spreading rumours, gossiping, and excluding others from a group (Vitto, 2003) — damages interpersonal relationships in the classroom. When such negative actions are taken repeatedly against a person, the physical, social, intellectual and psychological power of the two parties involved are out of balance (Olweus, 1999), with the victim in general being regarded as inferior and the bully as superior.

The adverse impact of bullying on the personal growth and school life of students are immense (Bonds and Stoker, 2000). This is particularly the case for the students who are targeted as they normally feel helpless, powerless, passive, anxious and insecure. In contrast, the bullies are characterized by an inability to show empathy and experience feelings of guilt. They have a small group of friends who admire them or secretly fear their behaviour.

The most common forms of bullying are isolation and rejection (Asher et al., 1984). Research has suggested that when classmates reject or isolate a student in one school year, they are likely to continue to do so in subsequent years. Rejected students report more feelings of loneliness and a higher level of depression than other students. In general, they display high levels of verbal and physical aggression towards their peers, and most of them are disruptive and off-task in the classroom. These characteristics increase the likelihood of students being rejected by peers not only during the period of schooling, but also throughout their lives.

⊐ **Activity 7.3**

Managing a classroom with negative peer relationships

1. Apart from those identified above, can you identify any other classroom practices and aspects of classroom culture which discourage the promotion of good peer relationships? If so, how could you change them? What difficulties might you face in trying to do so?
2. Think again about the classroom scenario mentioned earlier in which Miss Ng, a form tutor of a class, heard a student, Shan Shan, being called "Monkey Shan (mountain)" by two classmates. What should Miss Ng do to meet the emotional needs of Shan Shan who was very upset?

Stages in Helping Students with Peer Problems

To manage the classroom in a positive and effective manner, teachers have an important role in supporting students who experience problems with their peers. The support is given on the assumption that difficulties students have in social relationships are related to lack of understanding by others and lack of skill in social problem solving (Mussen et al., 1990). Therefore, teacher intervention aims to enhance such students' social skills and support them in building a network of friends in the class. This involves training students in different forms of problem solving, which may include finding alternatives, anticipating consequences and understanding cause and effect (Mussen et al., 1990). This can be implemented in four stages as illustrated in Table 7.1.

Table 7.1 A four-stage framework for helping students with peer problems

Stages	Strategies
1. Understanding and identification	• Talk to the students involved as a mediator. • Identify the problems by using the "ten important questions" introduced in Chapter 1. • Find out in which social skills the students are deficient. • Identify appropriate practices to help the students change, such as problem solving, mediation and negotiation.
2. Learning	• Get the students to exchange their views on the issues concerned. • Look for alternatives and identify new behaviour to be performed. • Anticipate consequences. • Teach new skills, such as social-emotional skills. • Substitute pro-social behaviours for negative social behaviours. • Do role-plays in contexts in which the students feel safe to practise the skills to be learned.
3. Action	• The students use the skills to participate, cooperate, communicate and validate, for example by smiling at, looking at, or encouraging other students. • Choose two or three students who are willing to form a support network for these students.
4. Reflection	• Help these students to review what they have done and to learn from their experience. • Understand the causes and effects of old and new behaviours. • Identify new problems and go back to Stage 1.

When helping students to change their behaviour by putting them through an individual educational plan, teachers have to take into account the potentially strong effects of "reputation bias". Once students have developed a reputation for being socially isolated or rejected, it is difficult for their classmates to abandon this negative perception of them within a short period of time (Hymel et al., 1990). Hence, for the students you intend to help, it is crucial to establish a network of three or four appropriate students from the same class to offer support when they are practising skills to deal with their rejection and isolation.

❐ **Activity 7.4**

Helping a girl, Mei Ling, who is being teased by classmates

In the scenario given below, a girl, Mei Ling, was teased in a very nasty way by Siu Chong and Dai Keung in the classroom. If you were the teacher, Mr. Lee, how you would help these students to resolve the problem? The questions listed in the table which follows are based on the four stages introduced above and the "ten important questions" discussed in Chapter 1. There is no need for you to find answers for all the questions, as the purpose is to get you to think and develop strategies.

Just before Mr. Lee started a Chinese lesson in 2E, he found that Mei Ling was upset because two boys, Siu Chong and Dai Keung, sitting behind her kept saying something to her in a very low voice. In frustration, Mei Ling raised her hand and complained to Mr. Lee that the two boys were saying some nasty things about her. The two boys felt slightly threatened and appeared to be afraid of getting into trouble. Mr. Lee calmed down Mei Ling and promised that her complaint would be dealt with after the class. Having talked to Mei Ling, Mr. Lee realized that she was disturbed by a widespread rumour that she had had sex with Dai Keung. She felt humiliated and could hardly function properly in school because of this defamatory remark. Mr. Lee then talked to the two boys. Siu Chong admitted that he had harassed Mei Ling verbally, but argued that it was the fault of other students in the class who started spreading the rumour. Also, he disclosed that Mei Ling and Dai Keung did have an intimate relationship, but Dai Keung denied this and insisted that he had not spread the rumour or said anything bad about Mei Ling. Mr. Lee then checked with some 2E students and confirmed that the rumour had passed around the class.

Stages	Questions for reflection
Understanding and identification	• Which parties are involved? • What do they intend to achieve? • What is the role of other students who passed around the rumour? • What is your concern? • What skills do you think the different parties are proficient and deficient in?
Learning	• How could you bring Mei Lan, Siu Chong and Dai Keung together and make them feel the need to resolve the problem? • How could you teach the skills identified? • What are you going to do with the 2E students? • What message are you going to give to class 2E? • What skills are you going to teach them? And how could this be done?

Action	• How could you know if the different parties have tried out the skills? • What support network would you establish for them, especially for Mei Ling (e.g. peer mediators and peer support)?
Reflection	• How could you get the different parties to talk and express their feelings?

Developing Strategies for Promoting Positive Peer Relationships

Teachers can help to create good peer relationships in the classroom. The exercise above may have got you thinking about how to deal with problems of relationships among students and, more proactively, about how to promote positive relationships. This section introduces other practical strategies of value to teachers under five headings:

1. Teaching social-emotional skills
2. Teaching conflict-resolution skills
3. Teaching problem-solving skills
4. Getting students to learn in groups
5. Creating a classroom climate of positive peer relationships

Teaching social-emotional skills

Social-emotional skills — including self-awareness, empathy, and communication and conflict-resolution skills (Vitto, 2003) — are critical factors in learning, work and life success (Goleman, 1998). They enable students to establish and maintain friendships and a sense of belonging; and when students feel accepted and respected, they learn well. Otherwise, they can be distracted from learning by spending much of their time and energy trying to fit in and managing social conflict and teasing, and may eventually end up misbehaving.

Limitations in these social skills play a large part in causing classroom behaviour problems (Brophy and Good, 2000), while those who have learned such skills are able to collaborate better with their peers, which has a positive effect on their learning. It has also been confirmed in studies that in the schools where students are explicitly taught social-emotional skills, their academic performance increases and their behaviour problems decrease. Also the quality of peer relationships among students improves (Graczyk, et al., 2000; Zins et al., 2000).

To promote good peer relationships among students in a class, teachers may build these social-emotional skills into the general curriculum and classroom management system. For instance, they can consider integrating themes such as friendships and interpersonal relationships into their classroom teaching. Examples of relevant learning activities are given in Table 7.2.

Table 7.2 Learning activities for enhancing students' social-emotional skills

Subject	Activities
Science	• Students can explore their physical reactions to experiencing feelings, such as loneliness, happiness, anger and feeling threatened.
Music	• Students can listen to a piece of music to determine which emotions it is meant to convey, and what features of the music bring out such emotions. They can then learn how to communicate with others and convey feelings through, for example, loudness and tempo in music.
Writing	• Students can write a journal as if they were characters in history or in a novel they have studied, discussing how they feel, why they feel as they do, and how they relate themselves to other characters.
Reading	• Students can discuss how they think the characters feel and review their interpersonal relationships, especially friendships.
Art	• Students can study masterpieces of art and examine how one can use aspects of art, such as colour, shape and shading, to convey emotions and communicate with others.

❒ **Activity 7.5**

Devising a programme for promoting students' social-emotional skills

The case below offers an example of a programme, "The Stop and Think Social Skills", which was developed by Knoff (2001) to promote good relationships among students. Study the programme carefully. Then identify social-emotional skills and devise a similar kind of programme for a class where some students have problems in relating to their peers.

"The Stop and Think Social Skills" has had remarkable results, including: decreased student discipline referrals, suspension and expulsions; improvements in social interaction; increased on-task behaviour; and improved academic performance.

The programme aims to promote four skill areas in the classroom.

1. *Survival skills*, which are the basic communication skills, such active listening, talking politely, following directions and rewarding oneself.

2. *Interpersonal skills* for developing and maintaining rapport and friendship with others by, for instance, sharing things, asking for permission in polite ways, joining an activity, and waiting for your turn.

3. *Problem-solving skills*, which help students deal with interpersonal problems, such as asking for help, making an apology, accepting the natural consequence of one's behaviour and deciding what to do.

4 . *Conflict-resolution skills*, which help students to resolve conflicts with their peers, over, for example, teasing, losing, accusations, being left out and peer pressure.

A cognitive-behavioural model of instruction was used to deliver the programme. The stages in this model are outlined in the table below. In the classroom, the learning activities for teaching the social skills were typically offered in the following order: demonstrating the skills with a script provided, role-playing the script, giving feedback to students on their performance, and practising the skills in natural settings during the school day.

Stages	Aims
1. Instruction and demonstration	• Explain the skill. • Explain clearly when and how to use it. • Give a demonstration.
2. Role-play or rehearsal	• Make up a scenario and get all students to practise the skill.
3. Feedback and social reinforcement	• Give supportive and constructive feedback about the role-play. • Practise areas which needs improvement. • Discuss any issues raised in the process. • Give recommendations and provide a plan for further practice.
4. Extended practice	• Discuss students' experience when using the skill in real-life situations. • Identify new problems. • Assign homework to practise the skill.

Teaching conflict-resolution skills

Obviously, students may have conflicts not only with teachers, but also with their peers. Research studies have shown that students who are trained in conflict-resolution skills are more likely to resolve such problems in positive ways, instead of withdrawing or becoming violent; and their academic attainment also improves (Johnson and Johnson, 1995).

These conflict-resolution skills, which clearly have great advantages for both students and teachers, include: helping students to handle conflict effectively, preventing the escalation of conflict into violence; and preserving relationships. Many conflict-resolution programmes are available, varying from individual personal practice to a whole-school approach. A general sequence for conflict-resolution for teachers to follow is given below by summarizing the features of these programmes.

1.   Gather information about the students involved and describe the conflict.
2.   Listen to and state each student's point of view.
3.   Brainstorm possible "win-win" solutions.
4.   Negotiate or compromise.
5.   Think about the consequences of possible solutions.
6.   Try out what appears to be the best solution and review it.

One popular programme for conflict-resolution involves peer mediation. It aims to train students to intervene and mediate as a third party when conflicts arise among their peers. Where conflicts are resolved without involving a mediator, this is referred to as "negotiation". Mediation and negotiation, both of which can be used to promote positive peer relationships, comprise five stages (Johnson and Johnson, 1995).

Table 7.3 The five stages of peer mediation

Stages	Action taken
1. Gathering information and gaining consensus	• The two parties agree to work on conflict-resolution. • If a mediator is involved, his or her roles and some ground rules are clearly explained.
2. Sharing, listening and understanding	• The two parties describe what happened. • They recognize each other's feelings. • They understand each other's point of view with empathy.
3. Identifying common interests	• Each party states what he or she wants and why. • Find commonalities. • Look for ways to make it happen.
4. Looking for "win-win" options	• Brainstorm, without judging, a minimum of three possible solutions to which they agree. • Think about the consequences of each solution. • Decide whether the options can be combined, if the combined option is more fair and practical.
5. Reaching an agreement and trying it out	• A detailed plan of action or agreement is reached. • The agreed-upon plan is drafted, restating what it has been agreed to work on together. • Carry out the plan and review its implementation.

Teaching problem-solving skills

Students who master the skills of problem solving are more able to develop and maintain friendships and are likely to achieve better academically and exhibit a higher level of independent thinking. Problem solving should therefore be promoted as one of the key components of classroom management to foster good peer relationships and improve students' behaviour.

These skills can be taught though a self-instructional approach. One of the key features of this strategy is that students learn to solve problems independently and to take responsibility for their own behaviour and decisions, rather than relying on others' opinions and instructions. In practice, teachers at first approach a problem for which a solution is sought by posing a series of questions such as: "What is the problem?", "Have I encountered it before?", "What is the first step, and then the next one, to solve the problem?", "Does the answer make any sense to me?" The students involved are taught to ask the same questions aloud and write down the answers step-by-step. When teachers are teaching these skills, they too often rush into giving the students explanations and solutions. It is more appropriate just to assist students by asking facilitative questions and helping them to evaluate the consequences of the solutions proposed.

A self-instructional approach is adopted in many programmes of this kind, one of which is "Promoting Alternative Thinking Strategies" or PATHS (Kusche and Greenberg, 1994). This programme recommends that teachers develop students' skills in four stages involving eleven steps (Vitto, 2003: 94) which are outlined in Table 7.4.

Table 7.4 Stages and steps in the self-instructional approach to problem solving

Stages	Action taken
1. Stop.	• Stop and think. • Identify the problem. • Identify the feelings.
2. Get ready — what could I do?	• Decide on a goal. • Generate alternative solutions. • Evaluate the possible consequences of solutions. • Select the best solution. • Plan the solution.
3. Go — try my best plan.	• Try out the plan.
4. Evaluate — how did I do?	• Evaluate the outcome. • Try another solution or re-evaluate the goal.

Getting students to learn in groups

Instructional strategies and forms of classroom organization that are student-centred and encourage interaction have more potential for promoting good peer relationships than traditional methods. Also using groups in learning creates more contexts where students are able to collaborate with others and develop their social selves. In Hong

Kong classrooms, teachers tend to be the centre of teaching and learning while students have a passive role, sitting still and listening. As collaborative work is relatively infrequent, the dynamics of peer interaction are not being fully utilized to facilitate student learning. This is particularly obvious in classes in which students are about to sit public examinations or official assessments.

The benefits of learning in groups have been cited in many studies (e.g. Cowie and Wallace, 2000; Putnam, 1998; Slavin, 1995). When working in this way, students can help each other to make progress in learning by giving one other explanations in ways that make sense to them, not from the teachers' points of view. Working together can also enhance the social skills of problem solving, communication, negotiation, showing empathy, respecting others' opinions and active listening, which are all crucial for promoting an inclusive classroom culture. Here are some practical ideas on how to implement collaboration in the classroom:

- Explain to students the reasons for working together and the expected benefits of cooperation.
- Plan activities which reduce competition and promote cooperation.
- Show students how to share expertise as well as tasks.
- Teach students to ask and answer questions, especially the key question(s) which can resolve problems, so that they do not feel threatened.
- Create opportunities for students to teach each other.
- Use random, mixed, ability-based and friendship groups to balance the spread of skills and abilities for specific learning targets.
- Do not create problems by insisting that pupils who never get on with each other work together. Chip away at the problem.
- Have a contingency plan in case of difficulties.
- Monitor group performance to avoid lurkers.
- Plan time for groups to share their experience.

When a group is used as a way of learning, teachers should consider two main issues: the selection of group members and the management of group behaviour. In the former case, the groups may be homogeneous or heterogeneous — that is involving students with similar or mixed levels of ability or characteristics respectively. Which of these approaches is more suitable depends to some extent on the nature of the learning activities. In general, students in heterogeneous groupings are inclined to work in more dynamic and creative ways because of their diverse backgrounds and abilities, such as their academic achievement, language ability, socio-economic status, gender, race and age (Baloche, 1998). It is also common in heterogeneous groupings for students of lower ability to learn from the more able members. Some studies have even suggested that, in such groups, students can understand subject matter in more complex and deeper ways, and the group interaction enhances the quality of individual work (Cowie and Wallace, 2000; Elias, 2004).

Teachers also need to monitor the progress of group activities and to pay attention to what individual students are doing in their groups. For example, Hong Kong teachers who have used group work in the classroom have reported a variety of common outcomes, such as: students becoming involved in casual talk or doing unrelated tasks; poor time management; poor quality work; tasks being completed by only one or two students; and a lack of concentration due to limited ability or motivation. In this regard, attention has to be given to five areas before getting students to learn in groups (Baloche, 1998: 92–93):

- positive interdependence;
- simultaneous interaction;
- individual responsibility;
- interpersonal and small-group learning skills;
- reflection and planning.

Creating a classroom climate of positive peer relationships

Good peer relationships can be developed as a classroom climate. There are many ways in which teachers can enhance a classroom culture of friendship, belongingness and cohesiveness. The basic principle is to get the class to engage in some whole-class activities which are not necessarily directly relevant to school learning — for example, decorating the classroom for special events and festivals, and creating a song or slogan for the class. Such activities are aimed at promoting students' positive feelings about being group members and helping them to develop a sense of belonging to the class. Through being exposed to such a classroom culture, they learn how to appreciate and care for others, and to share happiness with them, as well as developing positive attitudes towards the school and their learning.

One type of whole-class activity is celebrating special events, such as students' birthdays, Christmas, Easter, the Middle Autumn Festival, and students winning awards in competitions or leaving the school because of moving house or furthering their studies abroad. Let's take students' birthdays as an example. As we get older, we tend to downplay the importance of our birthdays, but for school students they have a special meaning. Some teachers may be hesitant about celebrating them because of the large class sizes of about thirty-five to forty, but there are many ways of celebrating birthdays without involving much time and money, such as those suggested below by Hue (2005).

- Combine birthdays which occur in the same month for a monthly celebration.
- Prepare birthday cards and circulate them round the whole class for signatures.
- Identify a lesson in which birthday cards are presented to the students.
- A little gift, such as a muffin or a box of candies, may be given with the birthday cards.

- Organize a special birthday party for the whole class at the start or end of the year.

Apart from celebrating special events, some "acquaintance" games can be used to help students to become familiar with each other. This is particularly valuable at the beginning of an academic year, as it helps to create a warm and secure atmosphere. For instance, the game "Bingo" is popular, easy to implement and provides students with a lot of fun. For this game, you have to prepare a "worksheet" for everyone, over which boxes are printed, in each of which there is a question such as "What do you like for breakfast?" Students are asked to select someone and ask him/her the questions, and all the answers can be written in the spaces in the worksheet. Having asked all the questions, student names are drawn and announced; and any student who gets one row of the names announced says "Bingo" and wins a small prize. When this activity moves to the stage of name drawing, students normally become very excited, and in the course of the game they get to know more about their classmates.

☐ **Activity 7.6**

Changing a negative classroom climate

Mr. Lee is a form tutor of a class with thirty students. Three subject teachers have come to him to report that: four students in the class have formed a "gang" and like to criticize other students in very harsh and disrespectful ways; a boy and a girl in the class are socially isolated; and three students have become very annoyed by the actions of the "gang". In fact, Mr. Lee has already noticed this, and finds an unfriendly climate has been developing in the classroom. If you were Mr. Lee, what strategies would you use in the following areas?

- helping the student "gang" to use problem-solving skills;
- resolving the conflict between 'the gang' and the three annoyed students;
- supporting the two socially isolated students and establishing a support network for them;
- teaching the whole class some social-emotional skills of empathy and mutual respect;
- getting students to learn in group as a way to teach them how to support each other;
- devising some activities for promoting a caring climate in the classroom.

Summary

This chapter begins with the notion that positive peer relationships create a warm, supportive and secure environment in the classroom which facilitates students' learning and desirable behaviour. Students' conceptions of friendship and the characteristics of popular students are then discussed. It is pointed out that conventional beliefs about classroom management and discipline may hinder the development of good relationships in the classroom, and some basic practices for promoting students' popularity among their classmates are outlined.

For helping students with peer problems, a four-stage practical framework — consisting of understanding and identification, learning, action and reflection — is introduced. By passing through these stages of guidance, teachers can help students to adopt a different perspective on their problems and develop new patterns of behaviour for building some close relationships with their peers.

Lastly, the importance of teachers being proactive in creating positive peer relationships in the classroom is restated and some strategies are suggested for doing so in the following areas: teaching social-emotional, conflict-resolution and problem-solving skills; getting students to learn in groups; and creating a classroom climate of positive peer relationships.

Questions for Discussion

1. Students' ideas about friendship change as they mature. What factors contribute to these changing views, and how may a teacher find out about children's friendships?
2. Are there any reasons for some students becoming popular? Is this related to "nature" or "nurture"?
3. Can you think of any classroom and school cultures which have the potential to discourage the promotion of positive peer relationships among students?
4. What strategies can you use to promote good relationships among students in a class?
5. What difficulties do you think you would encounter when helping students to resolve their interpersonal conflicts?
6. What skills do teachers need for helping students to learn social-emotional skills?
7. What are the barriers to prioritizing the development of positive peer relationships in a school?

Useful Resources

Websites

1. National Centre for Culturally Responsive Educational System:
   http://nccrest.edreform.net/subject/peerrelationship

2. Special Connections:
   http://www.specialconnections.ku.edu/cgi-bin/cgiwrap/specconn/main.php?
   cat=behavior&section=main&subsection=classroom/main

Further Reading

Alderman, M. K. (2000). *School groups and peer motivation.* Retrieved 9 September, 2005, from: http://www3.uakron.edu/education/safeschools/PEER/peer.html.

Brooks, R. (2005). *Friendship and educational choice: Peer influence and planning for the future.* Basingstoke: Palgrave Macmillan.

Cowie, H. and Wallace, P. (2002). *Peer support in action: From bystanding to standing by.* London: SAGE Publications.

Frankel, F. H. (2003). *Children's friendship training.* New York: Brunner-Routledge.

Imai, Y. Y. (2005). *How to teach adolescents social skills and facilitate good peer relationships to the current generation attending high schools.* Retrieved 9 September, 2005, from http://www.battlefieldsports.com/owners/GriffithUniversity_LaserSkirmishResearchRep ort.pdf.

Kang, C. (2005). *Classroom peer effects and academic achievement: Quasi randomization evidence from South Korea.* Retrieved 9 September, 2005, from http://nt2.fas.nus.edu.sg/ ecs/res/seminars/seminar-papers/14042005.pdf.

Kupersmidt, J. B. and Dodge, K. A. (2004). *Children's peer relations: From development to intervention.* Washington, DC: American Psychological Association.

References

Asher, S. R., Hymel, S. and Renshaw, P. (1984). LoneDai Keungess in children. *Child Development,* 55: 1456–1464.

Baloche, L.A. (1998). *The cooperative classroom: Empowering learning.* Upper Saddle River, NJ: Prentice-Hall, Inc.

Bonds, M. and Stoker, S. (2000). *Bully-proofing your school: A comprehensive approach for middle schools.* Longmont, CO: Sopris West.

Brophy, J.E. & Good, T.L. (2000). *Looking in classroom* (8th edn). New York: Longman.

Cowie, H. and Wallace, P. (2000). Peer support in action: From bystanding to standing by. London: SAGE Publications.

Elias, M.J. (2004). Strategies to infuse social and emotional learning. In J. E. Zins, R. P. Weissberg, M.C. Wang, and H. J. Walberg, *Building academic success on social and emotional learning.* New York: Teachers College Press.

Goleman, D. (1998). *Working with emotional intelligence.* New York: Bantam Books.

Graczyk, P. A., Matjasko, J. L., Weissberg, R. P., Greenberg, M. T., Elias, M. J., and Zins, J. E. (2000). The Role of the Collaborative to Advance Social and Emotional Learning (CASEL) in supporting the implementation of quality school-based prevention programs. *Journal of Educational and Psychological Consultation,* 11(1): 3–6.

Hue (2005). *Preliminary findings: The social construction of classroom discipline in Hong Kong secondary schools*. Funded by an Internal Research Grant, the Hong Kong Institute of Education.

Hymel, S., Wagner, E. and Butler, L. (1990). Reputational bias: View from the peer group. In S. Asher and J. Coie (eds.) *Peer rejection in childhood*. New York: Cambridge University Press.

Johnson, D. and Johnson, R. (1995). *Teaching students to be peacemakers*. Minneapolis, MN: Burgess.

Kauffman, J. M., Mostert, M. P., Trent, S. C. and Hallahan, D. P. (2002). *Managing classroom behaviour: A reflective case-based approach*. Boston: Allyn & Bacon.

Kusche, C., & Greenberg, M. (1994). *The PATHS curriculum*. Seattle, WA: Developmental Research and Programs.

Mussen, P. H., Conger, J. J., Kagan, J. and Huston, A. C. (1990). *Child development and personality*. New York: Harper-Collins.

Olweus, D. (1999). *Bully prevention program*. Boulder, CO: Institute of Behaviour Science.

Parker, J. G. and Asher, S.R. (1987). Peer relations and later personal adjustment: Are low accepted children at risk?' *Psychological Bulletin*, 102(3): 357–389.

Putnam, J.W. (ed.) (1998). Cooperative learning and strategies for inclusion: Celebrating diversity in the classroom (2nd edn). Baltimore: P.H. Brookes Publication.

Selman, R. L. (1981). The child as a friendship philosopher. In S. R. Asher and J. M. Gottman (eds.) *The development of friendships*. New York: Cambridge University Press.

Slavin, R.E. (1995). *Cooperative learning: Theory, research, and practice* (2nd edn). Boston: Allyn and Bacon.

Vitto, J. M. (2003). *Relationship-driven classroom management: Strategies that promote student motivation*. California: Corwin Press, Inc.

Zins, J.E, Elias, M.J., Greenberg, M.T., and Pruett, M. K. (2000). The implementation of prevention programs, *Journal of Educational and Psychological Consultation,* 11(1): 1–2.

8

Collaboration with Colleagues
to Improve Classroom Behaviour

Hue Ming-tak

People must help one another: it is nature's law.

Jean de la Fontaine (1621–95)

Synopsis

In this chapter, it is suggested that effective classroom management can be achieved through collegial collaboration, which can be promoted at two levels: school-wide and between individuals. At the school-wide level, it can be established by adopting a whole-school approach to behaviour management in which the school takes the initiative to build up an organizational structure where colleagues are encouraged to collaborate with others. It aims at engaging all school members to work together as a team on the classroom issues with which they are concerned, and so to develop common aims, beliefs, practices and action plans in promoting positive behaviour management (Axworthy et al., 1986; Brown et al., 1984; Rogers, 1995). At the individual level, the collaboration is initiated "bottom up" by colleagues themselves rather than in a "top down" fashion. The social networks of collaborating colleagues may vary in formality and flexibility depending on the patterns of interpersonal relationships among them.

Objectives

After reading this chapter you should be able to:
1. recognize that all teachers have collaborative roles in implementing a whole-school policy on discipline, both inside and beyond the classroom;
2. explain the benefits of developing a whole-school policy on discipline as a way to encourage collegial collaboration;
3. understand the phenomenon of classroom isolation and the advantages of collegial collaboration;

4. provide ideas on ways of working with your colleagues to improve students behaviour;

5. recognize the ineffectiveness of referral systems in schools.

Pre-Reading Reflection and Discussion

1. What kinds of school culture and organizational structure are more favourable for encouraging collegial collaboration?

2. What types of colleagues do you like and dislike working with?

3. If you were the form tutor of a class and found that a teacher who taught your class was completely unable to manage the students' behaviour, in what ways could you give him/her some support?

4. If you found some students' behaviour unmanageable and intended to seek support from other colleagues, what inner feelings would you have?

5. In what ways could you work with the form tutor to improve the behaviour of a difficult student in your class?

6. What do you think are the advantages and disadvantages of referring difficult students to a senior member of staff?

Introduction

The classroom is a setting in which teachers can collaborate with each other to manage student behaviour and promote their learning. Collegial collaboration gives support and professional confidence to teachers, and it reduces their feelings of stress and depression when they face problems in managing their classes. When teachers work together closely on classroom issues, they can exchange information about students on, for example, their classroom behaviour, emotional intelligence and academic ability in different school subjects — and in the process, they come to realize that they face many difficulties in common and can learn from each other's classroom experiences. Overall, working with colleagues as a team can help to promote the learning and growth of all students. In the case below, Miss Lee was teaching a difficult class. When she found that some students' disruptive behaviour became unmanageable, she decided to ask the discipline teachers for some help. What are advantages and disadvantages of making such a referral? If you were Miss Lee, would you ask discipline teachers for assistance? Can you think of any other ways to manage the students' misbehaviour? Also, what advice would you have given Miss Lee to prevent the situation reaching this stage?

Classroom scenario

Class 3E was having a lesson in the music room. After a few minutes, some students started throwing chalk at a student while the teacher, Miss Lee, was writing some notes on the blackboard. She warned the class that they would be punished if they continued to do this. The students involved blamed each other for throwing the chalk and the classroom became very noisy. While Miss Lee was talking to these students, others began to engage in casual talk and other activities not assigned by the teacher. Miss Lee stopped the argument and began to teach, though she realized that this incident had ruined the atmosphere for learning. Having taught for a few more minutes, Miss Lee found more students were throwing small pieces of chalk, some of which hit a boy, Ching Chung, by mistake. The chalk was probably thrown by another boy, Li Fung — or at least, Ching Chung thought so and regarded it as an intentional hostile act. Ching Chung stood up and argued with Li Fung and their quarrel became more and more heated. Miss Lee tried to intervene, in vain, and Li Fung rushed to Ching Chung and pushed him to the floor. Miss Lee found that the class was completely out of control and contacted discipline teachers for help. The two students involved were then referred to the discipline teachers.

At a School-Wide Level: Whole-School Policy on Classroom Management

While the classroom is the context in which students learn and spend most of their time in school, it is closely connected to other contexts of schooling, such as the playground, changing rooms, toilets, snack bar and canteen. Often, how students behave in one of these settings affects their behaviour in other contexts. For example, if some students are aggressive towards each other in the toilets, they will also tend to be hostile to each other in class; and, similarly, when two groups of students have a fiery argument in a basketball match during recess, their quarrel is very likely to continue when they come back to the classroom. Such situations may be transformed into other forms of conflict which make collaborative learning impossible. Therefore, the orderly and positive environment necessary for effective teaching and learning can only be created and maintained when all school members are involved in enforcing the discipline policy and work willingly together as a team inside and outside the classroom. In practice, of course, some schools have a more collaborative culture than others.

In schools where there is no whole-school policy on discipline and student behaviour and a collaborative culture has not been established, teachers may react differently to the same types of behaviour in the classroom. In most cases, students know the personalities of their teachers very well and can easily identify inconsistencies in the ways teachers enforce classroom rules (or in the rules themselves). Accordingly, the same class may conform in one teacher's lessons and break the rules with other teachers.

On the other hand, in schools which have adopted a whole-school policy on discipline, teachers work in the same ethos and are consistent in their application of both classroom rules and disciplinary practices across all classes in different forms. In these schools, the rationale behind policies is spelled out to all members, including students, teachers and non-teaching staff, parents and related professional groups. The teachers see the benefits of the policies and are more willing to implement them consistently; and they are more likely to feel they are being supported in improving classroom behaviour and learn how to accept responsibility for the consequences of their actions.

In addition to enhancing the consistency of classroom rules, disciplinary practices and policies on behaviour management, a whole-school policy on classroom behaviour helps to unite teachers in promoting students' good behaviour (Clarke, 1996). It is suggested that such a common ethos can be developed by:

- creating a positive and orderly climate where teaching and learning can take place;
- creating a safe environment for students and teachers through the clarification of expectations, roles, rights and responsibilities;
- reducing teachers' stress through identifying effective systems and practices;
- addressing the demands of changing conditions and approaches.

(Clarke, 1996)

The whole-school approach also has other benefits, as summarized below:

- There is an increase in effective strategies as teachers begin to share good practice and see the results.
- Teachers are generally seen by students as supportive, understanding and caring for their problems and needs.
- Teachers begin to act more consistently when the whole-school policy is the outcome of genuine and wide collaboration.
- Teachers are more confident when appropriate corrective action is spelled out.
- A shared knowledge base provides a stronger support for classroom management.
- Teachers and students have a better appreciation and understanding of why "the classroom is managed this way".
- Parents begin to appreciate, and support, the values underpinning the school's policies. Any school-wide process needs to gain parent understanding, support and, where possible, involvement.

(Rogers, 1995)

☐ **Activity 8.1**

Reflection on some research findings

Study the findings of Hamilton's studies (1986, 1989, cited in Axworthy et al., 1989) as summarized below and then answer the questions which follow:

> Hamilton found that in the schools where a whole-school policy had been adopted, the teachers were used to supporting each other more often and their relative stress levels were lower than those from the control schools where there was no such policy. Also, in the schools which embarked on a process of whole-school review, teachers took school factors into account when explaining students' misbehaviour, their ratings for disruptive behaviour were lower, and the rates for both suspension and referral for misbehaviour were diminishing.

- To what extent do you think these findings are applicable to Hong Kong schools?
- Can you think of any disadvantages in the introduction of a whole-school policy on classroom management?
- What difficulties might there be if a school intends to introduce a whole-school policy on classroom management?
- What problems can you foresee if you taught in a school with no whole-school policy and teachers managed classroom behaviour in very different ways? How could such an organizational culture affect you, in terms of the classroom rules you establish for the class, the procedures you adopt for behaviour management and the measures you take when students behave in a disruptive manner?

At the Individual Level: Working with Colleagues

In schools where a collaborative culture is established by introducing a whole-school policy on effective classroom management, the teachers are never alone when something goes wrong, as support is always available from other colleagues and the school organization. But does this mean that you won't get colleagues' support in a school without such a policy? Obviously, this is not necessarily the case as collegial collaboration can be created by teachers at an individual level. There are nine steps for building collegial collaboration to support your classroom management.

1. Specify issues which you are concerned about and problems you intend to resolve.
2. Collect information about the issues or problems, so that it can be shared with your colleagues.
3. Be explicit about what you want to get from your colleagues, such as emotional support, the sharing of ideas, resources or professional reassurance.
4. Define the forms of collegial collaboration in which you want to work with them — for instance, whether you want to collaborate with them as "a loose team" or have them play a consultancy role.

5. Find appropriate parties you want to work with and then keep them informed of any activities or needs for which you expect their support in your classroom. They may include fellow teachers, clerical staff, librarians, educational psychologists, social workers and even gardeners.
6. Share your concerns with them, and invite them to collaborate with you.
7. Find a time when you and your colleagues are free to meet as a way of maintaining the forms and functions of collaboration.
8. Pose specific problems and initiate discussion on them, and show that you value the time and effort each person is putting into collaborating with you.
9. Evaluate the effectiveness of the forms of collaboration.

❐ **Activity 8.2**

Devising a plan for collaboration

In a class you teach, three students present serious difficulties. They refuse to engage in learning activities, and do not conform to the classroom rules you have set. Devise a plan for collaborating with a colleague(s) by following the steps suggested above. Write down your thoughts and explain them where necessary.

Classroom isolation

Many teachers are hesitant about asking for help when things go wrong in their classes, perhaps in part because they consider this shows their weakness and inability to cope. In fact, as many studies have reported, it is quite common for teachers to be reluctant to seek colleagues' support, even though they know they would benefit from a close working rapport with them (Elton Report, 1989; Fullan and Hargreaves, 1991; Leiberman, 1990; Rudduck, 1991). The Elton Report (1989: 69) pinpointed this issue in stating that:

> Teachers have tended to stay out of each others' classrooms and not talk about their own discipline problems. Too often teachers do not seek help because it feels like an admission of incompetence and they do not offer it because it feels like accusing a colleague of incompetence. As a result, the tradition of classroom isolation persists in many schools.

When a school is dominated by a culture of "classroom isolation", teachers may feel that they are "psychologically alone in the crowded environment" (Watkins and Wagner, 2000: 34). In such cases, teaching may become an isolating experience, with the classroom as the teacher's private territory: its door is closed, and in-depth discussion of classroom behaviour is rarely carried out with colleagues. More important, in a professional sense, by working in such an "isolated" setting, teachers' learning and professional growth are limited. In an emotional sense, they receive less support, recognition and encouragement from others and so they are more likely to feel stress and experience burnout.

Given these outcomes, it is crucial for teachers to examine their own situations by using questions such as those below. If teachers give far more "No" than "Yes" responses, it is likely that they are suffering from the classroom isolation syndrome.

From a cognitive perspective	• Do you think most of your colleagues are supportive? • Do you think your colleagues help you to improve your skills in classroom management? • Could you learn something new about behaviour management from the experience of your colleagues?
From a social perspective	• Can you name two colleagues who show some empathy with the difficulties you experience in the classroom? • Do you tell your colleagues about things which make you happy in the classroom? • Do you talk to your colleagues when you are frustrated by students' classroom behaviour?
From an emotional/affective perspective	• Do you feel happy with the current relationships with your colleagues? • Do you think what you have been doing in the classroom with your students is recognized by your colleagues? • Do you feel that you are accepted when other colleagues know you are unable to maintain order in a difficult class?

Since these questions have not been standardized, they should just be used to give an indication of whether you are likely to be suffering from "classroom isolation". Teachers who think they may have this syndrome can try to take the following six steps to seek help from their colleagues.

1. Analyse the various classroom situations you participate in, and identify any common characteristics.

2. Find out what makes you feel most threatened about disclosing your classroom experience to colleagues. Is it related to a previous bad experience, the school culture, your way of thinking or your acknowledged lack of certain social and communication skills?

3. Build up some positive thoughts about collegial collaboration — for example, by reinforcing the belief that asking colleagues for help does not necessarily mean you are weak, and that it is a professional way of resolving the problems you have encountered.

4. Visualize the staff member(s) you would most like to work with and what form of collegial collaboration, or support network, you would like to establish with him/her.

5. Spare at least five minutes every school day to talk to a particular colleague(s) about what has happened in your classroom. You may start from something which you feel happy about and then introduce aspects which have frustrated you.
6. Maintain this form of collaboration and try to disclose more classroom experience to him or her.

As classroom isolation has a negative impact on teachers' professional lives, it is crucial for them to have some colleagues who play the roles of partners, supporters, counsellors and consultants. In this way, their classroom stories of frustration are listened to, their concerns are empathized with and their struggles are understood. It is unreasonable to impose unrealistic demands on oneself and keep your classroom isolated when you are, for instance, being verbally abused by several students in a class, or when half the class is out of control. On such occasions it is particularly necessary to ask colleagues for support.

❐ **Activity 8.3**
Reflection on classroom isolation

The following questions will help you to think more about the syndrome of classroom isolation, and make you aware of some school, social and cultural factors which may promote it.

*   What kind of school culture may cause a sense of classroom isolation?
*   What do you feel when you tell a senior teacher that you are being teased by your students? Would you feel any differently if you told a junior teacher?
*   Why are you worried about disclosing to your colleagues your inability to manage students' disruptive behaviour in class?
*   To what extent are your concerns about disclosing your experience related to the issue of "face"?

The benefits of collaboration

As can be seen from the points made above, collegial collaboration functions in the form of "reliable alliances" (Rogers, 2000: 141), formal and informal, which are established with one's colleagues. These "alliances", which are dynamic, organic, ongoing, flexible, changeable and transitional, can:

*   reduce the feelings of isolation;
*   offer fundamental moral support;
*   empower staff through the spirit of teamwork;
*   promote committed and caring relationships among staff;

- increase confidence in managing the classroom;
- lessen negative feelings of inadequacy;
- provide a context for problem sharing, problem analysis and problem solving;
- Reduce the possibility of burn out.

(Rogers, 1995)

Apart from the forming of "reliable alliances", collaboration can be understood as a kind of helping relationship which has some therapeutic value. When teachers help each other, the emotional support, listening, trust and demonstration of concern displayed can relieve stress and strengthen teachers' competence in dealing with problems they encounter. The value of this form of collaboration has been confirmed by Bernard's 1990 study, which highlighted the following features:

- Peer groups of teachers provide the most support, followed by family and friends outside school.
- The types of support teachers receive are active listening, getting constructive feedback and the provision of information.
- Female teachers generally tend to give and receive more support than male teachers.
- The more support provided, the lower the levels of teacher burnout.
- Peer support among teachers is related to higher levels of personal accomplishment.

(Bernard, 1990: 291–95, cited in Rogers, 2002)

In brief, in the schools where colleagues work together, classroom teachers are more willing to share information about particular students, and they tend to sympathize with one another and feel committed to helping students improve their classroom behaviour (Rosenholtz, 1989). They are also more ready to assist each other, without making negative judgments about teachers failing to control their classes or perform their roles effectively.

Building collaboration

Before looking for ways to build up a collaborative rapport with colleagues, three important steps are needed. First, you have to get to know your colleagues, particularly when you are new to a school. To do so, apart from using formal settings such as meetings, you may consider taking advantage of social opportunities, such as having lunch with colleagues, to enjoy their company outside the school context.

Second, you need to be honest with yourself. Whenever you don't know something or feel unable to manage any difficult classes, you should admit it and seek help and suggestions from other staff, even if you feel you can ultimately resolve the problems yourself. In the process, you should make your colleagues feel valued and respected for their help. Your honesty and enthusiasm can convince others that you are developing your expertise by communicating your professional experience to them.

Third, keep learning from your colleagues. For example, you can invite them to observe your classroom and comment on your classroom management or other aspects of teaching. Similarly, respond to any requests to sit in on their lessons, and give them supportive comments when they request them.

Before inviting other colleagues to work with you, it is necessary to recognize that students misbehave in many different ways and for different reasons. Although it is very difficult to find an approach which is always effective, using your own problem-solving skills and inviting others who face the same issues to work with you in a team can help to improve the situation. The next section outlines how problem-solving skills can be adopted for initiating professional discussion among teachers and for replacing inappropriate with appropriate behaviour by following these sequential steps:

1. Analyse the issues you are concerned about and the problems you encounter.
2. State the problem(s). Before thinking about a solution, you have to identify what the problem is and when it does and does not occur. Summarizing the problem in one or two sentences is helpful.
3. Specify the aims of the proposed collaboration.
4. Identify the colleagues you would like most to work with — for example, teachers who share the same concerns and/or you think would support and work well with you. If you are not the form tutor of the class, you may consider getting him/her involved.
5. Clarify with them the forms of collaboration you intend to establish and how you expect them to be involved.
6. Invite them to work with you, and help them to see the need for, and value of, their involvement.
7. Brainstorm ideas in the team, with an emphasis on generating as many ideas as possible before assessing their quality.
8. Select a mutually acceptable way of resolving the problem(s). The key is to find an idea(s) that is acceptable to all those involved and seems likely to solve the problem(s) identified in step 2 above.
9. Try it out in practice and monitor how the students react.
10. Exchange information about the results and evaluate its effectiveness as a team. Redefine your concerns and return to step 2 if the problem persists.

Classroom scenario

Helping a difficult student by using problem-solving skills

The scenario which follows illustrates how a teacher can work with colleagues to improve a student's behaviour by using the problem-solving skills introduced above.

You have found recently that Ming Ming, a student in your class, is constantly refusing to conform to the classroom rules you established. For example, although you have told him repeatedly to sit still, he has continued to get up and walk about the room, sometimes even bumping into other students. It appears that the goal of his misbehaviour is to seek your attention.

In this case, you may manage Ming Ming's behaviour by following the steps introduced above.

1. Analyse his behaviour. You may first talk about Ming Ming's behaviour to the form tutor of the class, and try to collect more information about the student. Then contact other teachers who teach Ming Ming to learn more about his behaviour in other lessons.
2. State the problem. After talking with others, the behaviour of Ming Ming which you are all concerned about is his persistent moving around and disturbing other students in the middle of lessons.
3. Specify the aims of the collaboration. You may want to have two teachers helping you to monitor the frequency and intensity of the misbehaviour identified, and to maintain proper behaviour in different lessons.
4. Identify working partners. Invite the teachers you would like to collaborate with you in improving the situation. Eventually you get three teachers to work with, you, Miss Lee, who is the form tutor of the class, Mr. Hung and Miss Fung.
5. Clarify the form of collaboration. For example, you might invite them all to a thirty-minute informal meeting every Friday, to review Ming Ming's behaviour and develop strategies for helping him.
6. In asking them to work with you, express your concern about Ming Ming's behaviour.
7. Brainstorm ideas in the group, thinking of as many possible explanations as you can, e.g. "He is trying to seek teachers' attention when he finds the lesson boring"; "He's not a good listener when his needs are not met"; "He demonstrates poor social skills when his peers refuse to get along with him"; "He is spoiled and is used to doing whatever he wants"; "He can't sit still for a long time as he is physically immature".
8. The team can then go through the ideas to see which seems to be the best explanation of Ming Ming's behaviour. In discussing them, the following observations were made:
   — "Ming Ming is usually a very sweet student. He is polite. I don't think he is behaving badly deliberately to gain attention." (Miss Lee)
   — "He is able to repeat stories we read word for word, so I know he listens." (Mr. Fung)

— "Ming Ming is very active in class and outside. He always likes to keep moving, especially when he feels he has nothing to do. I think he is physically immature and is capable of sitting still only occasionally." (Miss Hung)

— "I try to keep things moving so students don't get bored. Ming Ming can then engage in the learning activities as instructed."

9. Select an idea. The teachers decide that Ming Ming's problem is that he just can't sit still for very long and he begins to misbehave when the lessons bore him. The team agrees to manage Ming Ming in the following ways:

— Let Ming Ming know that we would like to help him become a good learner, and get his consent to work with us.

— Reduce the time spent on lecturing.

— Design learning activities which allow students to move around the classroom.

— Assign Ming Ming to be a teachers' helper.

— Initiate a brief talk with Ming Ming after class.

10. Try out the idea and evaluate its effectiveness. The team notices that Ming Ming does not disturb other students. Occasionally he gets out of his seat, but this is becoming less frequent; and even when it happens, he goes back to his seat when the teacher tells him to do so and engages in the learning activities.

Making a Referral

So far, we have discussed collegial collaboration at both the school-wide and individual levels and considered its benefits. In this section, we examine the common practice of referring a student with behaviour problems to senior teachers or other teams of teachers. Many schools have a well established referral system as a support mechanism, with the departments of school guidance or school discipline normally being responsible for "teaching these students a lesson"; and such students may also be sent to see the year teacher or form tutor. After speaking to the relevant staff, the students return to their classrooms.

Although making referrals of difficult students is a common practice, it must be acknowledged that it is not always effective in improving the students' behaviour and in resolving the real problems. This is because referrals are related more to when a teacher disapproves of students' social behaviour, rather than being directly linked to observed disruptive behaviour (Stage, 1997). Moreover, as reflected in the classroom discourse of teachers and students, it is often used as a threat to get students to conform to a teacher's instructions; in other words, in practice, referral can be seen as a kind of controlling, rather than supporting, mechanism.

Whenever possible, it is more effective to avoid the referral system and help students to improve their behaviour at the individual rather than the institutional level.

From a classroom teacher's perspective, the problem may seem to be resolved when the students are moved away from the context in which they misbehaved to another team of teachers who have taken up responsibility for managing their behaviour. However, these teachers did not take part in the incident and interact with the students involved: they can only deal with the issue at a surface level and manage the students' behaviour according to official guidelines on school discipline.

Of course, there are special cases in which such referrals are justified — for example, classroom violence and sexual harassment — but even then you have to be ready to work with other teachers or senior staff. Also, before you take any action, you need to ensure that you are very clear about all the organizational procedures involved and what roles you have to play in them. In addition, it is very likely that you will become involved in a process of negotiation, especially when there are different views on how to manage the case you have reported. Even if you find these other teachers difficult to deal with, you have to think positively and try to work with them.

As Packard and Race (2000) have advised, in coping with such situations care must be taken to distinguish between conflicts of ideas and conflict of personalities, and to find out what sorts of conflict are involved in the particular case. You can then reflect on your inner feelings and examine the possibility that the current situation has been coloured by previous differences of opinion — and remind yourself that disagreements in the past need not prevent agreement on present issues. If the situation allows, you may talk about the problem with senior staff on a professional level, to help them to understand your situation. Having done all this, try to view the issues from other people's perspectives and value their opinions even when they differ from your own. Finally, you may have to act in the ways determined by others. If necessary, make a note of what you have been asked to do and check this with a senior teacher before and after you have taken action.

Summary

This chapter suggests that teacher collaboration can enhance both classroom behaviour and teachers' professional development; and it recommends that such collegial support can be achieved at both the whole-school and individual levels.

It is indicated that at the whole-school level, all staff can play a collaborative role in implementing a discipline policy inside and outside the classroom. By developing a whole-school policy on behaviour management, teachers can be encouraged to collaborate with other colleagues in more productive ways. Research evidence has shown that in schools which adopt such a policy, teaching staff tend to work together more in helping students to improve their classroom behaviour and fewer discipline problems are reported.

At the individual level, the problems of classroom isolation have been highlighted to make teachers more aware of its negative effects on the quality of teaching and learning and their professional development in classroom management. Six steps are suggested to help teachers to rid themselves of such feelings of isolation and feel comfortable about seeking help from colleagues: (1) analyse the classroom situations; (2) discover the reasons for these feelings of isolation; (3) build up positive thoughts about collegial collaboration; (4) identify a working partner(s); (5) spare a few minutes to talk to this partner(s); and (6) maintain this form of collaboration.

The chapter then discusses a team approach to improving classroom behaviour, involving ten problem-solving steps: (1) analyse the issues concerned; (2) identify the problems clearly; (3) specify the aims of the collaboration; (4) identify a working partner(s); (5) Clarify the ideal form of collaboration; (6) Invite specific colleagues to work together with you; (7) brainstorm ideas; (8) try to reach an agreed view on action to be taken; (9) try to implement it; and (10) evaluate its effectiveness.

Lastly, based on research evidence, it is argued that referring a difficult student to another senior staff member or team of teachers is not an effective way to improve classroom behaviour as the students involved are removed from the context in which the misbehaviour arose; and that, even when students are referred to others, classroom teachers need to play a role in collaborating with them to help the students involved improve their behaviour.

Questions for Discussion

1. What can you do to contribute to a school culture of collegial collaboration?
2. Why should you collaborate with other colleagues to improve classroom behaviour?
3. What difficulties can you foresee when collaborating with other colleagues?
4. How would you support other colleagues who experience difficulties in managing some students' misbehaviour in the classroom?
5. What would you do if there is no referral system available in the school?
6. In which ways could you modify a referral system to make it more effective in supporting students in need?

Useful Resources

Websites

1. Department for Education and Skills:
   http://www.schoolsweb.gov.uk/locate/curriculum/teaching/classteach/cb/

2. Developing a School Wide Behavior Management System:
    http://maxweber.hunter.cuny.edu/pub/eres/EDSPC715_MCINTYRE/SchoolWideSystem.
    html.

Further Reading

Barbour, C. and Barbour N. H. (2001). *Families, schools, and communities: Building partnerships for educating children.* Upper Saddle River, NJ: Prentice Hall.

Carolina International School (2005). *Classroom management and student behavior policies.* Available at the Carolina International School Website, http://carolinainternationalschool. org/academic/classroom.html

Fitzsimmons, M. (1998). *School-wide behavioral management systems.* Reston, VA: ERIC Clearinghouse on Disabilities and Gifted Education. Available at http://chiron.valdosta. edu/whuitt/files/schooldiscp.html

Roffey, S. (2004). *The new teacher's survival guide to behaviour.* London: Paul Chapman. Publication.

Rogers, B. (2002). *Classroom behaviour: A practical guide to effective teaching, behavior management and colleague support.* London: Paul Chapman.

———. (2003). *Effective supply teaching: Behaviour management, classroom discipline and colleague support.* London: Paul Chapman.

References

Axworthy, D., Olney, H. and Hamilton, P. (1989). Managing students' behaviour: A whole school approach. In C. Szaday, *Addressing behaviour problems in Australian schools.* Camberwell, Victoria: Australian Council for Educational Research.

Brown, S., Finlay-Jones, R. and McHale, (1984). Measuring teacher stress in Western Australia. *Western Australian Institute of Educational Administrators,* 14: 28–40.

Clarke, D. (1996). Why have a behaviour policy? In D. Clarke and A. Murray (eds.) *Developing and implementing a whole-school behaviour policy: A practical approach.* London: David Fulton Publishers.

Elton Report (1989). *Discipline in schools: Report of the Committee of Inquiry.* London: The Falmer Press.

Fullan, M. and Hargreaves, A. (1991). *What's worth fighting for? Working together for your school.* Toronto: Ontario Public School Teachers' Federation.

Jones, F. H. (1987). *Positive classroom discipline.* New York: McGraw-Hill Book Company.

Leiberman, M. (ed.) (1990). *Schools as collaborative cultures: Creating the future now.* Basingstoke: Falmer Press.

Packard, N. and Race, R. (2000). *2000 tips for teachers.* London: Kogan Page.

Rogers, B. (1995). *A whole school approach: Behaviour management.* London: Paul Chapman Publishing Ltd.

————. (2002). *I get by with a little help: Colleagues support in schools.* Melbourne: Australian Council for Educational Research Press.

Rudduck, J. (1991). *Innovation and Change.* Milton Keynes: Open University.

Stage, S. A. (1997). A preliminary investigation of the relationship between in-school suspension and the disruptive classroom behaviour of students with behavioural disorders. *Behavioral Disorders,* 23(1): 57–76.

Watkins, C. and Wagner, P. (2000). *Improving school behaviour.* London: Paul Chapman Publishing Ltd.

9

Working with Parents to Create a Positive Classroom Environment

Hue Ming-tak

The way schools care about children is reflected in the way schools care about the children's families.

Epstein (1995)

Synopsis

This chapter suggests ideas on how teachers can establish positive partnerships with parents. It proposes some specific contexts where teachers may take the initiative in inviting parents to work with them to promote their children's learning and growth. In all these contexts of collaboration, parents' contributions are highlighted, and issues which teachers may be concerned about at various stages are raised and suggestions for improvement given. Lastly, teachers' attention is drawn to the confrontation and conflict which may arise in the course of meeting parents and methods for handling such situations are proposed.

Objectives

After reading this chapter, you should be able to:
- recognize the importance of promoting the development, growth and evolution of partnership between teachers and parents;
- establish some forms of partnership with parents to promote students' learning and whole-person development;
- understand how to build a platform for teacher-parent collaboration;
- introduce various approaches to involve parents;
- identify specific contexts where parents can be invited to work with you to enhance the learning and welfare of their children;
- organize meetings with parents in an effective manner;
- develop communication skills for handling any conflicts which may arise in a teacher-parent meetings.

Pre-Reading Reflection and Discussion

*   Why is it beneficial to involve parents in the education of their children?
*   In what ways do you expect parents to work with you to improve the quality of homework assignments produced by their children?
*   How can you gain the trust and support of parents?
*   How can you build up a partnership with parents?
*   If a conflict arises between you and a student's parents in a meeting, what would you do to resolve it?
*   In a teacher-parent conference, a mother is angry because you have given her son an E grade. How would you handle this situation?

Introduction

Parents have a very strong influence on their children's learning and behaviour, and they also have an important role in collaborating with teachers to make the educational process productive, meaningful and fruitful. Although many teachers may find it difficult to build up a partnership with parents, numerous benefits can be derived from interacting with them. For example, teacher-parent partnership leads to positive relationships between teachers and students, and helps to ensure that students and their parents perceive the school in similar ways: for example, when parents make positive remarks about their children's teachers and the school, their children are likely to share their views and feel encouraged to behave well in class. In the case below, Miss Lee found that the behaviour of a student, Siu Ming, had changed slightly and she decided to inform Siu Ming's parents about this, hoping to get them involved in helping the boy. In what way could Miss Lee expect Siu Ming's parents to work with her? What should Miss Lee ask Siu Ming's parents when she calls them? Siu Ming did not want Miss Lee to know what had happened to him. Should Miss Lee tell Siu Ming that she has contacted his parents? Why?

> **Classroom scenario**
>
> Miss Lee is the form tutor of a boy, Siu Ming. He is regarded as a bright and responsible student, but Miss Lee has noticed that lately he has become quiet and has seemingly lost interest in learning. Whenever he is asked about this, Siu Ming does not want to say much, and responds listlessly, "I am fine. Maybe I have spent too much time on computer games at night", but Miss Lee doubts this explanation.

Collaborating with Parents to Improve Classroom Behaviour

All parents care for their children. Even if they have demanding full-time jobs, they have a strong desire to know about their children's lives at school and wish them to be successful (Epstein and Sanders, 1998). Most parents want to work with teachers to improve their children's classroom behaviour, and so there is common ground where teachers can work with parents to maximize students' potential in the classroom. Four ways to create a platform for teacher-parent collaboration are:

- to make parents recognize that they share a responsibility for their children's classroom learning;
- to manage the diversity of parents' needs, behaviours, intentions and feelings;
- to be more proactive in creating contexts where teachers and parents can work together to promote children's good behaviour in the classroom;
- to promote a school culture of teacher-parent collaboration.

❐ **Activity 9.1**

Building a collaborative platform

Miss Cheung and Mr. Wong are friends of yours. Miss Cheung teaches at a school where most of the students come from working-class families and their parents have low educational backgrounds. In contrast, Mr. Wong works in a school where most of the students are from affluent families and have parents who received university education. When parents are informed about their children's classroom misbehaviour, in what ways do you think Miss Cheung and Mr. Wong would differ in the ways they collaborate with parents? You can reflect on this by answering the following questions.

- How do parents perceive their responsibility for their children's classroom behaviour?
- How may the needs of parents from the two schools differ?
- In what ways do you think the parents from the two schools could contribute to improving their children's behaviour in class? Are there any differences? If so, why?
- Will Miss Cheung and Mr. Wong use different ways of communicating with parents? If so, should they use different skills?
- What kinds of school culture would encourage parental involvement in the two schools? Are there any differences?

Shared responsibility

Effective classroom management is characterized by parents and teachers working together towards shared goals as, when such partnerships are established, teachers will be able to manage students' behaviour in a more efficient manner. Teachers have a crucial role in inviting parents to work with them, and offering them opportunities for collaboration so that their partnership can be further developed and sustained. Doing this helps parents to become aware that their children's education is a shared responsibility, not something which should be left entirely to teachers. This process of collaboration guides the development of aims and plans to achieve the goals of education at a wider level.

In practice, a shared responsibility can be promoted through open communication, mutually agreed upon goals, and joint decision making. Together, teachers and parents can discuss their expectations for student performance in all aspects of their school lives — social, personal, academic and emotional. They can also work together to develop strategies for supporting positive academic, behavioural and social competencies in all students, and to increase mutual respect, understanding, caring and flexibility among parents, teachers, students and school managers.

Parents are obviously very familiar with the ways in which their children behave. They know what affects their children's behaviour and in many ways are in a much better position than teachers to use reinforcers — such as privileges related to dining out, watching television and shopping — to improve their behaviour.

Managing diversity

Working with parents from diverse backgrounds and with different needs is a challenge for teachers. Parents may have very different perspectives on issues which concern teachers and the school, and have different expectations and communication styles. Teachers have to recognize that such diversity is a strength which offers explanations and information about students' behaviour.

To manage diversity better, teachers have to find some common ground where they can work together with parents as partners. Efforts should be made to work collaboratively with all parents, including those whose primary language is not Cantonese and those with limited literacy skills. In this process, it is important to ensure that parents are always welcomed by the school and assured that teachers would like to work with them to help their children learn and behave well. This will make it more likely that parents will have positive feelings about the school and perceive themselves as being treated warmly and respectfully by teachers, which will help to build up good personal relationships with them.

Teachers also need to do their best to understand parents' needs, intentions, feelings and behaviour, rather than simply judging them to be right or wrong. For example, when teachers meet the parents of difficult students, they should try to recognize that bringing up children is a complex task irrespective of a family's ethnicity, language ability, socio-economic status and educational background. Empathizing in this way will help to establish good relationships with parents.

Creating more contexts for partnership

Due to the diversity of parents' needs and family backgrounds, it is unrealistic to think that there is only one type of family-school relationships and so take a "one size fits all" approach to collaboration. Instead, teachers should try to create more contexts for parental collaboration and expand their roles in dealing with classroom issues — for example as partners in pastoral care and education, and as volunteers.

From this perspective, teachers need to develop opportunities for parents to participate meaningfully in the classroom life of their children. Such opportunities should be offered in the knowledge that families will differ in what they choose to become involved in, depending on their needs and preferences. Potential avenues for parents' participation in classroom life may include:

- Taking part in classroom activities as volunteers;
- Engaging in learning activities in the classroom;
- Monitoring homework completion;
- Communicating regularly with teachers about their children's progress;
- Communicating frequently with their children about academic and behavioural expectations and progress;
- Participating as decision-making members of behaviour management teams (e.g. IEP teams);
- Supporting form tutors through communication, sharing resources and seeking partnership with educators.

Creating a collaborative culture

The culture of teacher and parent collaboration should be promoted not only at the individual or classroom level, but also at the whole-school level. All teachers have a role in working with other staff to welcome parents' participation in the education of their children, and they should send a consistent message that their contributions in forming effective partnerships are valued.

In summary, parental participation increases when the school encourages collaboration by eliciting and understanding parents' perspectives and expectations. A variety of options for participation, as well as systematic forms of collaboration, should be made available, recognizing that parents from varied backgrounds will support their children in different ways. Schools should foster an open dialogue between home and school and provide opportunities for parents to develop partnership roles in the education of their children. For this purpose, resources must be provided by the school, such a releasing time for teachers to meet parents and providing a parent-support room.

❐ **Activity 9.2**

Conflict behind a quarrel in the classroom

Study the scenario below and answer the questions which follow.

Mr. Wong is the form tutor of Alan and Kevin. One day, Kevin had an argument with Alan in the classroom, and pushed Alan and made him fall from his chair. Mr. Wong intervened, and found out that the quarrel had arisen because Alan was unable to return $500 he owed to Kevin. As Mr. Wong discovered, Alan had borrowed $700 from Kevin but had already returned $200. Mr. Wong decided to inform Alan's parents about this matter, but Alan resisted this strongly, insisting that he would save some of the pocket money from his parents and return the rest of what he owed to Kevin within a month. He said he would be "killed" by his parents if they were told about the situation.

- Should Mr. Wong inform the parents of Alan and Kevin and get them involved in resolving this issue?
- How could Mr. Wong convince Alan that his parents should be informed?
- What suggestions should Mr. Wong make to Alan's parents about talking to their son?
- Should Mr. Wong get Alan's and Kevin's parents to meet? Why/why not?
- If so, what should Mr. Wong recommend that Alan's and Kevin's parents do to help their sons resolve this matter?
- If Alan's parents are angry about what Kevin did to their son, should Mr. Wong tell Kevin's mother? What should Mr. Wong do to resolve the matter?

The four ways of establishing a platform for promoting teacher-parent collaboration outlined above can also be viewed in terms of the following principles of involvement suggested by Charles and Charles (2004) which can be applied in general for involving parents in the education of their children:

- to affirm that parent are concerned about their children's learning;
- to affirm that parents are willing to help;
- to ensure that communication between parents and teachers is clear and effective;
- to value parents' attempts to participate in the process of making decisions which affect the school and students;
- to clarify the roles of parents;
- to teach parents how they can help;
- to show appreciation of the contributions and involvement of parents.

(Charles and Charles, 2004: 67–68)

Maintaining Teacher-Parent Collaboration

So far, four ways of creating a platform for teachers and parents to work as partners have been suggested. We now look more closely at specific ways in which the dynamics of such collaboration can be maintained and evolve. In what follows, Epstein's (1995) six strategies for promoting teacher-parent collaboration are introduced and may be adopted by teachers to encourage parental participation in their children's education. They are as follows:

- Offer parents information about how they can provide better support to their children to become effective classroom learners.
- Communicate regularly with parents about the programmes offered for their children and the learning activities they are engaged in.
- Invite parents to work with you in the classroom as volunteers.
- Assist parents to improve their children's learning and classroom behaviour at home.
- Share the power of decision making with students and parents.
- Pay attention to public concerns and collaborate in community events and activities.

❐ **Activity 9.3**

Developing strategies to support Mrs. Wong and her son Tin Ying

In the scenario below, a form tutor, Miss Lee, intends to work with Mrs. Wong, a student's mother, to improve the classroom behaviour of her son, Tin Ying. Study the case carefully, and consider some specific, manageable and feasible ways Miss Lee could adopt for behaviour improvement. It may be useful to refer to the six strategies given above in answering the questions which follow.

Miss Lee found that Ting Ying liked to perform off-task behaviour to get her attention and that he had serious behavioural problems in other teachers' lessons. When comparing how she managed Tin Ying's behaviour with the other teachers, she noticed that they, unlike herself, had not contacted the student's parents to seek their support. At first, Miss Lee had felt it was enough to send Tin Ying's mother the usual notes and make phone contact. However, after a few contacts, Miss Lee found that Mrs. Wong was a single parent who had to work very hard to support the family. Each day she had to leave home even earlier than her son and, when she got back at night, Tin Ying was often already in bed. When Miss Lee met Mrs. Wong for the first time and expressed concern about his behaviour, Mrs. Wong sighed and did not respond much. She was overwhelmed with a sense of powerlessness, and started sobbing uncontrollably. After a minute or two, she tried to calm herself, saying between sobs, "It is my fault. I just don't know how I've hurt my boy. He is so messed up, but I just don't know what I have done . . ." She said repeatedly how guilty she felt for causing the boy such problems. Miss Lee felt very sorry for her, and tried to comfort Mrs. Wong by showing empathy and a caring attitude. At that time, Miss Lee realized that Tin Ying's mother experienced as many difficulties and pressures as her son did. After this meeting, Miss Lee felt a sense of connection with Mrs. Wong and took an entirely different perspective on Tin Ying's behaviour. Whenever contacting Mrs. Wong, Miss Lee would treat her as a partner and try to act as a bridge between her and Tin Ying. They shared the same goal — looking after the welfare of Tin Ying — and this might be one of the reasons why Tin Ying's behaviour has been improving.

1. What strategies could Miss Lee tell Mrs. Wong for helping Tin Ying to be an effective learner both at home and in the classroom?

2. How could Miss Lee communicate regularly with Mrs. Wong about Tin Yin's progress in learning and changes in classroom behaviour?

3. What learning activities could Miss Lee invite Mrs. Wong to join in and work with her as a volunteer to support Tin Ying in improving his behaviour?

4. What could Miss Lee suggest Mrs. Wong should do at home to enhance Tin Ying's ability in self-control?

5. How could Miss Lee get Mrs. Wong and Tin Ying involved in developing a plan of behaviour modification?

6. How could Miss Lee find out about community services which could support Mrs. Wong in bringing up her son and in managing her personal and emotional difficulties?

Based upon the six approaches introduced earlier, some possible contexts where teachers can keep parents informed about what is going on in the classroom, or get them involved in working with them, are identified below, together with some practical suggestions:

- Write an introductory letter to parents at the beginning of an academic year.
- Organize an informal meeting for special occasions (e.g. a small party).
- Make use of students' daily planners or handbooks.
- Publish a class newsletter.
- Disseminate progress reports.
- Phone parents.

Writing an introductory letter to parents

You may make an initial contact by sending a letter to each student's parents. If you are the form tutor of a class, you can consider including information about the class, including the names of all the other subject teachers. To make it more personalized and informal, you can also introduce yourself, mention your interests and indicate how keen you are to develop positive contacts with them.

Holding an informal meeting at the beginning of new school year

At the start of a new school year, you can set up a situation in which you and the parents can meet and discuss the arrangements for the year, and you can use this occasion to ask parents to work on their children's learning in the classroom and the school more generally. This gathering could take the form of a mini-party with simple refreshments to create a relaxing and comfortable atmosphere for positive communication. Jones and Jones (2001) suggest teachers use such an occasion to:

- describe the curriculum;
- give parents an introductory letter about themselves which includes their personal background and philosophy of education;
- give them the class timetable;
- let them know when you will be available to be contacted during school hours;
- list the projects and homework for which you may require parental assistance;
- explain your classroom management procedures.

(Jones and Jones, 2001: 157)

Making use of students' daily planners or handbooks

In Hong Kong schools, every student has a daily planner. Teachers, especially those in primary schools, may find ways to use them for promoting positive contacts with parents about students' work. For example, on students' records of what they have to do each day, any work not completed or done particularly well can be highlighted, with students expected to show their planners to their parents who may take any action they feel is necessary. Also, the planners can be used to keep parents informed about upcoming school or class events. Here are some guidelines for writing comments in the daily planner:

- Be brief and specific.
- Be positive and try to find something good to say.
- Be honest and, if necessary, make neutral points about the children's behaviour.
- Respond immediately when parents ask for help.
- Be informal and treat parents as partners.
- Use the planner regularly, and expect parents to do the same.
- Avoid jargon or professional terms.
- Avoid projecting one's feelings onto the students or his/her parents.

Publishing a class newsletter

Issuing a newsletter is another useful method for keeping parents informed. It can be produced regularly, for example monthly or every two months, and can consist of just one or two pages which describe student learning, subject knowledge currently being taught, whole-class activities carried out, and so on. Examples of students' work and writing can be included to provide another perspective on their experience of learning. Also, when writing the newsletters, you may invite some students to assist you in data collection, typing and printing.

Disseminating progress reports

Many schools have fixed specific days for collecting students' progress reports, normally twice in an academic year, with parents being notified at the end of each academic term. Given that all the parents will be invited to see you within a day, the meetings need to be very well organized. On average, the sessions should last only about fifteen minutes each, so what you intend to tell the parents about students' progress reports needs to be summarized well and presented positively.

Phoning parents

The most convenient and direct way to communicate with parents is by phoning them. These calls should not be confined to telling parents only about negative aspects of their children's behaviour as this may make them feel frustrated and disempowered, and hesitant about contacting teachers and the school. You may contact parents about any issues related to school life to show your concern and care, and desire to cooperate with them. For example, you may mention:
- good performance in homework or presentations;
- improvement in classroom behaviour and academic performance;
- assisting you in performing certain tasks;
- helping other students;
- doing some volunteer work for the class;
- your concern about their children's poor social skills;
- seeking their help in supporting their children in resolving social difficulties;
- your concern about the decline in their children's academic performance;
- working with parents for special assistance;
- homework arrangements.

❐ **Activity 9.4**

Communicating with parents in various ways

Suggest how parents can be informed about the specific situations noted in the table below. In each case, try to identify the three most appropriate ways of making contact by putting ticks in the boxes.

	Writing a letter	Organizing a party/ gathering	Using daily planner	Publishing a newsletter	Day of disseminating progress report	Making a telephone call	Others
Clarification of classroom rules							
Identification of students' needs							
Explaining the details of project work							
Discussing some aspects of students' classroom behaviour							
Changing the school holidays							
Understanding students' lives at home							
Introducing some strategies for improving students' behaviour							
Commenting on the achievements of the class							

Holding Other Meetings with Parents

Apart from the planned occasions mentioned above, there are many other occasions related to students' special needs when teachers can invite parents to come to the school for a meeting aimed at developing strategies for improving their children's classroom behaviour. In fact, such meetings are a good way to gain parents' support in helping students who experience difficulties. However, to produce any benefits, the meetings need to be well planned and organized so that parents enjoy working with teachers and see the meetings as a positive experience through which they get ideas to allay their children's behavioural problems or resolve other issues of concern. On the other hand, poorly managed meetings may create parental discontent which will probably be reflected in students' behaviour; and, more serious, complaints may be made to senior staff, the principal or even government bodies.

In meetings with parents, there is sequence of stages through which they and teachers can reach consensus (Kauffman et al., 2002):

1. *Laying the foundations*: At this stage, the teachers involved should make themselves very clear about the issues which concern them and collect and organize all the relevant information, data and records which they intend to mention.
2. *Before the meeting*: At this point, teachers need to familiarize themselves with the documentation, make an agenda for the discussion and choose a place where the meeting can be take place without any interruption.
3. *During the meeting*: Teachers have to be good facilitators, ensuring that all communication blockages are removed so that the parents feel free to express their concern and opinions, and have their needs addressed.
4. *At the end of the meeting*: Here, all issues raised and discussed should be followed up and evaluated.

Table 9.1 summarizes some important issues for teachers' attention at the four stages in such meetings. It is also very helpful to prepare some guidelines for the three parties involved — the teachers themselves, the parents and the students — before meetings, as shown in Table 9.2 (see p. 178).

Working Effectively with Parents' Criticisms and Confrontation

It is not uncommon for conflict to arise in the course of meetings with parents. This can be understood at both the psychological and institutional levels. At the former level, parents and teachers may perceive one another in some negative ways. Teachers worry that parents will call their behaviour management practices into question or make unreasonable demands; while parents, especially those whose own school experience was unpleasant, are reluctant to listen to how their children have behaved badly in school. Also, parents may disagree with the teachers' views on managing

Table 9.1 Guidelines for parent-teacher meetings

Stages of the meeting	Targets to be achieved
Laying the foundations	• Review the student's cumulative records. • Familiarize yourself with the student and his/her family culture. • Consult with other professionals about the student. • Establish rapport with the parents and keep them informed. • Collect information to document the students' academic progress and behaviour. • Share positive comments about the student with parents. • Invite the parents to observe or volunteer to work in your classroom.
Before the meeting	• Discuss the goals of the meeting with the parents and solicit their input. • Involve the student, as appropriate. • Schedule a mutually convenient day and time for the meeting. • Provide written notice prior of the meeting.
During the meeting	• Welcome the parents and speak informally with them before beginning. • Reiterate the goals of the meeting. • Begin with a discussion of the student's strengths. • Support your points with specific examples and documentation. • Encourage the parents to share their insights. • Ask open-ended questions. • Avoid jargon. • Practise active listening (e.g. show interest, paraphrase comments, avoid making judgements, etc.) • Review the main points of the meeting and determine a course of action. • Provide additional resources (e.g. support groups, family resources centres, websites.)
After the meeting	• Document the results of the meeting. • Share the results with colleagues who work with the student. • Follow up with the parents as needed to discuss changes.

(Kauffman et al., 2002: 134)

their children's behaviour and may find it hard to accept that their children are as disruptive as the teachers claim as they may not behave in such ways at home. On being told about their children's behaviour, some parents may try to defend it, especially if they feel they are being held responsible for the misbehaviour; and they may also blame the teachers' weak management skills or the unsupportive discipline system.

At the institutional level, the conflict may be related to how parents and teachers work together in school. Although both teachers and parents may acknowledge that they share responsibility for acting in the best interests of children, not many schools have formal mechanisms which allow them to cooperate in doing so. Unless initiated by one or the other party, there is not much opportunity for collaboration. In such situations, it is easy to understand why parent-teacher conflict occurs from time to time.

Table 9.2 Preparing the three parties involved for a parent meeting

Teachers' preparation for the three parties	Something to pay attention to	Action taken
Teachers	• Parent contacts are time-consuming, especially when there are up to forty students in a class. • Most parents have to work and are not contactable during office hours. Teachers can find contacting parents difficult. • The educational level of some parents is low. Teachers may find it hard to get them to understand issues from the school's perspective.	• Make contact as early as possible through different channels, such as email, telephone, sending an SMS message and mail. • Use basic communication skills, such as active listening, and not giving judgmental feedback.
Parents	• Parents can find it difficult to contact teachers. • Working parents have to apply for special leave in order to meet their children's teachers. • Parents feel powerless to change school decisions. • Parents sometimes give up doing anything to improve their children's behaviour. • Parents may consider teachers incapable of helping them to deal with their children's behaviour. • Parents can feel annoyed and frustrated by constantly receiving complaints about their children's behaviour when they meet teachers. • Parents may be unable to manage their emotions and may lose their temper during the meeting.	• Make yourself available and let parents know how they can contact you. • Try to fix a day which suits the schedule of the parents. • Empower parents with the use of some basic counselling skills, such as encouragement, praise, positive feedback and reinforcement. • Keep calm, and avoid provoking parents' discontent and anger.
Students	• Students often feel very uneasy and frustrated when they know their parents are going to meet their teachers. • Students worry about being interrogated and condemned by their parents after going home.	• Contact students and inform them of the details and agenda for the meeting. • Explain to them what you intend to achieve in the meeting, and in what ways you expect their parents to work with you. • Invite students to attend the meeting. • Ensure that students are allowed to voice their views and are listened to and respected throughout the meeting.

There are several strategies for dealing with angry or critical parents and coping with such situations in an effective and professional manner (Jones and Jones, 2001; Kauffman et al., 2002):

- Take a positive perspective in interpreting parents' anger and frustration.
- Find something positive to say about the child and the parents.
- Allow parents to say whatever they want.
- Help parents to become fully aware of the problems described.
- Try to empathize with parents' feelings and view the behaviour of their children from their perspectives.
- Appreciate what parents have contributed to improving their children's behaviour.
- Use active listening to calm down parents' emotional responses.
- Respond to parents in a calm and professional manner.
- Show parents that you are eager to work with them and care for their children.
- Make whatever you say very specific.
- Avoid blaming parents.
- Admit when you are wrong.
- Admit when you don't know the answer to parents' questions
- Accept the parents and their children as they are.
- Recognize any cultural differences between yourself and the parents.

❏ Activity 9.5

Working with a very angry parent

Study the case below and suggest what methods the form tutor Mr. Cheung could adopt to resolve the conflicts which arose in the meeting.

An English teacher, Miss Li, reported that Mei Ling, a girl in her class, bullied another student Sau Lai by calling her "ugly pig" and pushing her to the floor. The form tutor, Mr. Cheung, tried to resolve the matter by inviting Miss Li, the parents of Mei Ling and Sau Lai, and the students involved to meet. In the course of the meeting, they expressed very different views on the event which are given briefly below:

- Miss Li asserted that it was completely wrong for Mei Ling to act in such a disgraceful way to Sau Lai.
- Mei Ling strongly denied responsibility for what happened. She insisted that she had called Sau Lai a name because she had annoyed and irritated her, and refused to confess to pushing Sau Lai to the floor.
- Sau Lai claimed that she had not slipped but had been pushed to the floor by Mei Ling.
- Mei Ling's mother was infuriated by what she was being told by Miss Li. She tended not to believe that her daughter had been as disruptive as was claimed.
- Sau Lai's mother questioned Mei Ling's account of the event and accused her of bullying her daughter.

Summary

This chapter highlights the advantages of teachers and parents collaborating to enhance students' learning and improve classroom behaviour. It is suggested that teachers should make an effort to build some form of partnership with parents by: (1) getting parents to take some responsibility for their children's education; (2) managing the diversity among parents in positive ways; (3) creating more contexts for collaboration; and (4) promoting a culture of teacher-parent collaboration at school level.

It is essential for partnerships between teachers and parents to continue developing and growing. Also, teachers should identify specific ways in which parents can be invited to work with them for their children's benefit — for instance, by writing letters, organizing small informal gatherings, making use of daily planners, publishing a newsletter, sending out student progress reports and telephoning.

Parental meetings are effective and productive if they are well planned and organized in the following four stages: (1) laying the foundations; (2) drafting an agenda before the meeting; (3) conducting the meeting; and (4) reaching a consensus and evaluating the outcomes of the meeting. Teachers need to develop their ability to react appropriately to difficulties which may arise during meetings, such as resolving conflict and handling confrontation.

Questions for Discussion

1. To what extent do you think students' misbehaviour is related to the socio-economic background of their familes and the educational level of their parents?

2. What difficulties could a teacher encounter when she/he intends to collaborate with parents from mainland China? What problems could the teacher face when trying to cooperate with parents who have to work very long hours?

3. Why do some parents feel hesitant about working with teachers to improve their children's classroom behaviour? When a teacher works with such parents, how could she/he encourage them to work together as a team?

4. In a case of disruptive classroom behaviour, the form tutor of the student involved found that the views of the student and his parents had not been included in a discipline meeting chaired by a senior member of staff. What do you think the teacher could do to ensure that students' and parents' views are taken into account in such meetings?

5. What communication strategies would you recommend teachers to adopt when facing parents who blame the school for the disruptive behaviour of their children?

6. In what ways can teachers encourage parents who feel powerless about changing their children's behaviour to work with them?

Useful Resources

Websites

1. Department for Education and Skills:
   http://www.standards.dfes.gov.uk/primary/publications/?
   view=listing&subject=behaviourattendance&audience=parents &publisher=&year=
2. LEARNC:
   http://www.learnnc.org/support/nt-communicating
3. Teaching Today:
   http://www.glencoe.com/sec/teachingtoday/educationupclose.phtml/48

Further Reading

Cavell, T. A. *Working with parents of aggressive children: A practitioner's guide*. Washington, DC: American Psychological Association, 2000. Available at http://www.findarticles.com/p/articles/mi_m2248/is_149_38/ai_103381775.

Diffily, D. (2004). *Teachers and families working together*. Boston, MA and Hong Kong: Pearson.

Porter, L. (2000) *Behaviour in schools, theory and practice for teachers*. Buckingham: Open University Press.

Roffey, S. (2002). *School behaviour and families: Frameworks for working together*. London: David Fulton Publishers.

Shah, M. (2001). *Working with parents*. Oxford: Heinemann.

Working with parents: Advice from teachers. *Education Oasis*. Available at http://www.educationoasis.com/resources/Articles/working_with_parents.htm.

References

Charles, C. M. and Charles, M. G. (2004). *Classroom management for middle grades teachers*. Boston: Pearson Education, Inc.

Epstein, J. (1995). School/family/community partnerships: Caring for the children we share. *Phi Delta Kappan*, 76: 701–712.

Epstein, J. and Sanders, M. (1998). What we learn from international studies of school-family-community partnerships. *Childhood Education*, 74: 392–394.

Jones, V. F. and Jones, L. S. (2001). *Comprehensive classroom management: Creating communities of support and solving problems*. London: Allyn and Bacon.

Kauffman, J. M., Mostert, M. P. Trent, S. C. and Hallahan, D. P. (2002). *Managing classroom behavior: A reflective case-based approach* (3rd edn). Boston: Allyn and Bacon.

10

Learning from Classroom Experience: Reflection and Action Research

Li Wai-shing

Teacher inquiry is an integral part of every lesson or unit taught. Each time we solicit reactions to an idea, activity or speculative question, we are inquiring, attempting to assess perceptions, understandings and beliefs. Sensitive teachers know that no matter how teaching is carried out, learning is always idiosyncratic and personal. The processes of inquiry are simply processes of assessment, i.e. strategies designed for finding out what the state of affairs may be as our students or others perceive them.

Stevenson (1986: 3)

Synopsis

Good teachers are reflective practitioners: they are aware of and reflect on what is happening in the classroom. This chapter introduces the idea of an "inquiring classroom" in which teachers are critical of what they do and observe in class. Three kinds of reflection — technical, practical and critical reflection — are discussed, and action research, a related concept, is introduced. Action research is a tool to help teachers to reflect upon their own experience and construct action plans to tackle any problems or improve situations which they find difficult. It is also a good means for professional development. Other alternatives for dealing with classroom management issues are introduced, namely school action plans and personal management plans. These plans are effective for dealing with students' difficult behaviour at a school and personal level. Throughout the chapter, the use of systematic investigation and reflection upon teachers' experiences to help in solving classroom management problems is emphasized.

Objectives

After reading this chapter, you should be able to:

- understand the importance of an inquiring classroom;

- know why questioning and reflection are important means to better classroom management;
- distinguish three levels of reflectivity;
- distinguish three major practices of reflection;
- identify critical incidents in the classroom and school;
- conduct action research for effective classroom management;
- construct personal management plans;
- write school action plans.

Pre-Reading Reflection and Discussion

- Why do teachers have to be aware of what is happening in the classroom?
- Why do teachers need to ask questions about their own behaviour and decisions in managing their classrooms?
- Do you think that teachers need to guard against practices which have become routine? Why/why not?
- Socrates said that "an unexamined life is not worth living". Does this apply also to unexamined teacher decisions?
- Recall any incidents which had a significant impact on you as a student or a teacher. How significant were they?
- Do you think teachers have to carry out classroom research or investigations to improve their own practices? Why/why not?

Introduction

Misbehaviour in schools often used to be perceived as solely attributable to factors related to the children and their families (Farrington, 1972; Rutter, 1975). However, it can be illuminating to consider the part schools play in contributing to students' behavioural difficulties (Rutter et al., 1979). There is evidence to show that pupil behaviour is largely shaped by the school environment and teachers (Cooper et al., 1994; Galloway and Goodwin, 1987); and teachers should therefore work together to examine school factors that are influencing pupils' behaviour. Classroom management is best viewed and approached as an ongoing activity in which teachers pay more attention to preventive discipline, reflect on their own practices to improve their classroom management, and then take action to handle misbehaviour. No matter which approaches to management teachers adopt, they need to examine their own behaviour and management styles, to provide the best environment for teaching and learning. Increasingly, teachers are becoming reflective practitioners and carrying out action research to deal with discipline problems and critical incidents in schools; and similarly they are becoming more aware that constructing personal management plans can be helpful in changing pupils' misbehaviour. In the scenario below, Mr. Cheung is shocked when told by a student teacher what she had observed in his laboratory. In what ways do you feel Mr. Cheung is a poor classroom manager? Do you think he is insensitive to his pupils? How can he enhance his classroom management skills? What kind of personal management plan can you suggest to Mr. Cheung to alleviate the problems he faced in his lesson? If Ms. Tsang is going to write an action research plan for better management of Mr. Cheung's class, what should her priorities be?

Classroom scenario

This is the first time for ten years that Mr. Cheung has been called upon to be a mentor teacher for the practicum of a local teacher training institution. His student teacher is Ms. Tsang. On the fourth day of the practicum, Mr. Cheung invited Ms. Tsang to observe his lesson. Having taught in the school for eleven years, Mr. Cheung appeared to be carefree and casual on this occasion. It was a General Studies lesson and he was conducting an experiment on the formation of H_2O (water) in the Chemistry laboratory. Ms. Tang was concerned by what she saw early in the lesson: half the class was copying homework at the rear tables and the other half was playing with test-tubes and Bunsen burners while Mr. Cheung was introducing the purpose of the experiment. He never looked at the pupils sitting at the back of the class, nor did he notice pupils doing homework during his lesson: he focused only on a few pupils sitting in the front desks. The experiment was conducted with utmost care and, as long as the students kept their positions and there was no mishap, Mr. Cheung continued to smile. The demonstration went smoothly, though he had not really got the attention of the class. Then he gave his concluding comments and dismissed the class with a reminder to hand in their reports in the next lesson.

After the lesson, Mr. Cheung and Ms. Tsang had a short sharing session. He felt very happy that the class had appeared to behave well in front of a guest teacher. However, Ms. Tsang asked her mentor many questions, such as: "Did the students have any laboratory routines to follow?"; "Did Mr. Cheung notice that many students were copying homework during the experiment?"; "What did Mr. Cheung expect his pupils to do during the experiment?"; "Would the pupils be able to write good reports if they hadn't paid attention to the experiment?"; "What could be done to get the pupils' attention in the lesson?" Mr. Cheung did not expect the student teacher to raise so many questions in such a direct way. After all, he had done this experiment many times and his pupils were not particularly interested in his lesson. This was a good reflection exercise for Mr. Cheung. While he was still rather disturbed by these questions,

Ms. Tsang felt many aspects of the practicum needed to be reflected on and wanted to discuss with her supervisor the drafting of an action research proposal to improve the situation in Mr. Cheung's lesson.

Promoting an Inquiring Classroom

The dynamics of the classroom prevent there being any standard practices which are panaceas for managing student misbehaviour. Even strategies which have proved effective in one class may not be so in another. While teachers have to be familiar with strategies for classroom management, simply applying them does not mean they are successful classroom managers. In order to be effective, teachers need to be aware of what is happening in the classroom and be sensitive to the signals in pupils' behaviour. Without such awareness and a reflective attitude, even skilled teachers cannot deal successfully with the ever-changing classroom environment. Classroom management must be seen as an ongoing activity, not a static one in which teachers apply some ready-made recipes for managing. Promoting an inquiring classroom and becoming reflective practitioners are promising ways for promoting good classroom management and professional development.

What is inquiry?

For teachers, "inquiry" simply means thinking deeply about aspects of the classroom situation. In practical terms, when teachers inquire, they often pose questions about situations which puzzle them or they find problematic (Tripp, 1993). To be a good classroom manager involves questioning your own approaches, strategies or beliefs about classroom management and discipline problems.

All inquiry or questioning is value-laden. Teachers want to know whether or not they have achieved their goals, made the right decisions and acted correctly; and they also want to find out more through inquiry about certain situations they encounter to see if they could handle them in a more intelligent and informed way (Stevenson, 1986).

❒ **Activity 10.1**
What questions would you ask yourself about managing pupil behaviour/misbehaviour in the classroom? Why are these questions useful? Exchange your questions with your partners.

Goals in questioning teachers' practices

Questioning their practices, decision making and behaviour is a practical way for teachers to enhancing their professional thinking, though it is just one of many ways of doing so. Five of the major relevant goals for this professional activity by classroom managers are listed below:

(a) *To understand pupils and their behaviour*, which will facilitate classroom management and pupil cooperation.

(b) *To understand one's practice in classroom management and dealing with pupil misbehaviour*, which will empower teachers by being reflective and critical (Elliott, 1991).

(c) *To understand the social environment and atmosphere of the classroom*, which will enhance the social dynamics and interaction within it.

(d) *To understand one's personal beliefs and values in managing pupil behaviour and misbehaviour*, which will improve teachers' understanding of their own long-held approaches and skills (Bullough and Gitlin, 1995: 226).

(e) *To understand what is happening in the classroom*, which will help to increase teachers' awareness of the factors affecting pupil and teacher behaviour, and the consequences for classroom teaching and learning (Schôn, 1991).

Questioning is central to practice and professional development and should be integrated into every lesson. However, mere questioning without follow-up action is not enough: teachers have to become reflective practitioners by involving themselves in systematic self-reflection and problem solving. We now look at the issue of reflective teaching.

Reflective Teaching

Teachers have to learn how to do reflective teaching and become reflective practitioners (Cruickshank, 1987), as good classroom management is more than an accumulation of skills and strategies. In reflective teaching, teachers develop habits of inquiry and should be self-monitoring, reflective, adaptive, experimenters and action researchers (Zeichner, 1983).

A shared understanding of reflection, however, focuses on the teachers' ability to look back critically, to think about cause and effect and to derive explanatory principles from their practice (McCaleb et al., 1992: 41). It is a commitment to be critical of one's own teaching and to reflect and act on one's behaviour in the classroom (Stenhouse, 1975), which explains why reflective practice often goes hand in hand with action research. Reflection is needed to clarify our thinking and the reasons for our behaviour. Applying skills and strategies without aligning them with beliefs and philosophies often creates conflicting decisions — for good classroom management, teachers' responses to pupil behaviour should be congruent with their management styles and beliefs about teaching and learning.

Three kinds of reflection: technical, practical and critical

Van Manen (1977) has suggested a hierarchical model with three levels of reflectivity: technical reflection, practical reflection and critical reflection. Ideally, fulfilling these three levels should parallel the growth of the individual from novice to expert teacher:

(a) *Technical reflection* is concerned with effectiveness in the application of skills and technical knowledge. This is the kind of thinking that teachers use to design lessons, plan activities and decide on teaching methods and approaches. It is instrumental in finding the best ways of achieving practical goals without considering the underlying moral or ethical issues (Carr and Kemmis, 1986; Sparks-Langer and Colton, 1991).

(b) *Practical reflection* involves reflection about the assumptions underlying specific classroom practices, and also directs attention to the consequences of the strategies, curricula or decisions. It differs from the first level of reflection in applying educational criteria to teaching practice to make individual and independent decisions on pedagogy.

(c) *Critical reflection* is characterized by the questioning of moral, ethical and other types of normative criteria practised by teachers in the classroom or policies affecting schools. It deals with social issues such as justice and equity in education.

> **Reflection**
>
> What criteria does Van Manen use for the three levels of reflectivity? Why do you think these levels of reflection should ideally match the development from novice to expert or master teachers? Justify your arguments.

Many of the discipline problems which teachers encounter are not simply technical issues that can be explained by analytical thinking or tackled using scientific knowledge. Issues in classroom management, such as equality, power and morality, are value-laden. Without critical examination of the underlying values, teachers are highly likely to miss the significant impact such issues have on their teaching practices.

❏ **Activity 10.2**

Questioning your own beliefs and practices

Being a reflective practitioner requires one to be open and honest about one's practices. List any five questions on your personal philosophy, teaching style, disciplinary approaches and attitudes that you want to reflect upon. Give a brief statement on why you think self-reflection can help you to improve.

Against routines and reflexive loops

Critical reflection helps teachers to examine and make sense of practices which may have become routines and be taken for granted, and to guard against reflexive loops. According to Argyris (1990), teachers' beliefs can be self-generated and often untested when they tend to draw conclusion inferred from their selected observations. They select things and add personal meaning to them while ignoring others. Relexive loop is the term coined by Argyris (1990) to describe the circular process by which we select data and make assumptions based on their own interpretation of the selected data and drawn conclusion and take action (Larrivee, 2006: 983). Thus, teachers' long-held beliefs and untested approaches can remain unexposed for years, and mistakes tend to be repeated again and again. This not only hinders the development of better classroom practices but is also detrimental to teachers' professional development.

By becoming reflective, teachers can increase their awareness of the complexity of the classroom environment and interactions within it by:

- taking the initiative to examine class routines and practices;
- paying attention to the impact of teacher behaviour on pupils;
- making sense of what is happening while withholding judgement;
- slowing down the process of reasoning, and enhancing the interpretation of reality;
- exploring diverse ways of interpreting and perceiving things; and
- being critical and open to personal assumptions about teacher behaviour.

Reflective practices can take many forms. For example, keeping a reflective journal is a good activity for teachers to engage themselves in deep thinking; and conducting classroom investigations or tackling particular issues is another approach. These practices can be done on a collegial or school basis, and as an ongoing activity or case-by-case.

Checklist for reflection

Critical reflection can be enhanced with the following activities (Brookfield, 1995):

√   *Writing a reflective journal*: Writing reflective journals enables teachers to clarify and explore the complexities of teaching and gain insights into their professional practices.

√   *Writing an autobiography*: Writing a biography of one's own provides a window through which teachers can review and evaluate their life experiences and their impact on their professional practices.

√   *Writing interactive journals*: Writing interactive journals with a critical friend or colleague provides a promising means of professional dialogue for empowerment and development.

√   *Writing teaching logs*: A teaching log is simply a record of the events happening in school. By focusing on these events, teachers are able to review and evaluate the assumptions underlying their daily practices.

√   *Peer observation*: Peer observation makes use of collegial support to explore teachers' strengths and weaknesses in the classroom. Critiquing one's own practices in the light of the comments of a colleague(s) can result in insights and constructive changes.

√   *Student learning journals*: These journals, which are regularly compiled summaries of students' experiences of learning written in their own terms, can be highly revealing about what they perceive and think about teachers' ideas and practices.

Critical Incidents and Reflection

It is appropriate to introduce the term "critical incidents" here. The term refers to events and situations which mark turning points or changes in the life of a person, an institution or a social phenomenon (Tripp, 1993: 24). In terms of classroom situations, Measor (1985: 66) suggested that critical incidents "provoke the individual into selecting particular kinds of actions", which in turn lead them in particular directions, and end up having implications for identity. These are highly charged moments and episodes that have very significant consequences for personal and professional change: they are flashpoints that illuminate some key problematic aspects of the teacher's role which need very careful attention (Woods, 1993: 357; Sikes et al., 1985: 230). In short, critical incidents are significant because they change teachers' perceptions and philosophies, and offer them problems to solve and puzzles to decipher. While such events can occur every day and are not at all dramatic (Tripp, 1993: 8), they contain critical problems that capture teachers' attention for further exploration and solution. They warrant systematic reflection to capture their full significance or action research to tackle them successfully. Action research and school action plans are discussed in the section that follows.

Action research

Action research is conducted by teachers to improve their own teaching or to test the assumptions of educational theory in practice (Hopkins, 1985). It is characterized by the use of self-reflective inquiry to identify problems in a situation and is very often incorporated into the inquiry process to provide the necessary link between self-evaluation, professional development and change in practice — and so reflection, reflective practice and action research are closely related. Action research is "insider" research carried out by practitioners in their own workplaces to focus on problem-solving at a local level, with the practical results and insights yielded being immediately applicable to specific situations or problems (Noffke, 1997). Undertaking action research enables teachers to improve their decision making and actions.

Teachers who take part in action research are better practitioners, with skills and confidence in problem solving. The process makes them more critical and open to other practices and policies, and develops a positive attitude towards change. Action researchers are active learners through critical thinking and are dedicated to professional development (Peppard, 1997). In brief, action research offers a tool for professional development and empowers teachers by engaging them in considering the perspectives of other practitioners (Li, 2003).

Teachers often ask anxiously: "Do I have to conduct action research whenever I spot a problem in managing my classroom?" As Stenhouse (1975) argued, action research should be promoted among practitioners to foster an action-research orientation towards classroom difficulties and to act and reflect on action in practice. Rather than requiring mere acquaintance with the techniques and methods, it involves an attitude of committing oneself to systematic questioning of one's own teaching and to testing theory in practice. By adopting such an orientation, teachers are able to avoid making unnecessary mistakes and become more aware of the issues related to better classroom management. Moreover, the action research process provides insights which enable them to identify and tackle significant problems.

Questions on possible classroom management problems for action researchers

The following issues or topics can be illuminated or tackled by means of action research:

1. What kinds of activities are best for academically low achievers?

2. What type of instruction is most effective in guiding slow learners in reading lessons?

3. How effective is assertiveness discipline for mainstream classes?
4. How successful would it be to assign misbehaving students to become prefects in school?
5. Are class meetings a good opportunity for enhancing pupil-teacher communication? Why/why not?
6. How effective is a token system for helping pupils to respond positively in the classroom?
7. Is the setting up of "reflective corner" in the classroom useful for reducing pupil misbehaviour?

The process of action research

Kurt Lewin (1952) was among those who pioneered the "spiralling" cyclical process for conducting action research which consists of three major steps: planning, execution and reconnaissance. Following Lewin's conception, Stephen Kemmis (Kemmis and McTaggart, 1988) created a popular and well-known model for action researchers (see Table 10.1) which comprises four major steps: planning, action, observation and reflection.

Kemmis's model is practical and easy to implement. The four major steps, "P–A–O–R" in Table 10.1 show the important phases of the action research cycle. Teachers who are not used to conducting research may need to learn the skills and techniques for conducting simple classroom investigations, but they can use whatever skills are appropriate to help them. If you have never used this model before, you need to pay attention to the details in each of the steps, as seen in Table 10.2.

Table 10.1 The Kemmis model of the major steps in action research

	Major Steps	**Description**
1.	Problem (P)	Define the problem or area for improvement. The starting point may come from a problematic situation, a skill that you want to improve, or a critical incident that puzzles you.
2.	Action (A)	Develop an action plan that helps you to solve the problem or offers you new insights into the issue under consideration.
3.	Observation (O)	Monitor your action plan and observe what happens with the intervention. Data collection and analysis are often done during this stage.
4.	Reflection (R)	Evaluate the whole process in the light of the data collected and see how successful the action plan is. After reflection and review, prepare the second cycle of action research for further improvement.
5.	Second spiral	Revise the plan in the light of reflection.

Table 10.2 Procedures and tasks in implementing an action research plan

Major Steps	Procedures / tasks	Suggestions and remarks
1. Planning	1. Locate the problem or area for improvement. 2. Define specific areas for improvement and/or construct specific action research questions. 3. Consider potential solutions. Construct an action plan that would help to solve the problem. 4. It is an advantage to carry out a literature review on the current problem. 5. Decide on criteria or standards for evaluating the action research. 6. Decide on an action research plan for intervention.	• Action researchers can benefit from the process by empowering themselves and reflecting upon their own teaching practices. • Action research questions should be specific and unique to the particular events or situation: avoid asking "yes/no" questions. • Questions exploring the process and consequences of a certain phenomenon are preferable (e.g. "How effective is my weekly form meeting for enhancing pupil-teacher relationships?"). • Potential solutions should be workable and practicable. • Collegial support is always welcome and suggestions from critical friends are valuable.
2. Action	1. Implement the action plan.	• Keep monitoring the implementation plan. • It is possible to amend the action research plan, for instance if circumstances change.
3. Observation	1. Decide on a proper and systematic plan for data collection. 2. Use alternative strategies for collecting data. 3. Data analysis can be done simultaneously, if necessary.	• Decide on specific strategies and instruments for data collection. • Invite colleagues to be independent observers, if necessary. Writing a reflective journal throughout the process is helpful. • The data analysis process can start whenever appropriate.
4. Reflection	1. Analyse the data collected, and review the whole process in the light of the analysis. 2. Evaluate the solution(s) and the effectiveness of the action research. 3. Ask questions to see if there is anything that does not work well and what could be done to improve it. 4. Decide on the actions to be carried out in the next cycle of action research.	• It is important to reflect upon the personal experience of action research. • Be objective and critical. • Be open to all kinds of comments and data analysis. • Has the problem been solved? If not, what is the follow-up plan? Consider and prepare for what has to be done in the next cycle.
5. Second spiral	1. Consider the objectives for the next spiral. 2. Work out the details of the next cycle's action plan and implement it.	• Successful action research should solve the problem. • Consider the plan to continue the action research. • Focus on other issues that may emerge or areas for improvement in the next cycle.

Action research is widely practised for solving classroom management problems and can be conducted by teachers individually or on a collegial and group basis. The advice of experts can be sought at each stage, but their views must not dominate the process and silence the practitioners' voices. If large-scale action research which demands the participation of all staff is undertaken, it can be done as school-based action research, but this requires more detailed and fuller cooperation among the teaching staff.

❒ **Activity 10.3**

Designing your own action research project

This is the first year in which your school has recruited pupils newly arrived immigrants from Shenzhen. Your headmistress has decided to put all these twenty-eight pupils in one class, and you are their English and form teacher. After a month, teachers who have taught the class hold a meeting. They agree that these pupils are hard-working but are not used to the school's expectations and discipline, which is reflected mainly in their limited participation in group work and unwillingness to share experiences in class activities. You would like to conduct an action research project to improve the situation and a colleague who teaches them Chinese and arithmetic is willing to work with you. Prepare a written action research plan for your headmistress. State clearly the objectives of your project and then present your implementation plan and how you are going to evaluate your action research.

It is not difficult to find illustrative examples of action research on classroom management.[1] The extensive cases published locally, and in Taiwan and mainland China, show that action research is becoming an increasingly more common approach for tackling classroom issues among teachers in Asian countries.

School Action Plans

Despite teachers' best efforts, pupil misbehaviour occurs. If intervention strategies do not work well and this behaviour continues, a more concerted effort is called for. A written school action plan is a powerful tool for this purpose.

A school action plan is designed to set goals and guidelines for teachers to commit themselves to effecting appropriate changes for a particular pupil (Albert, 1996). It is a kind of cooperative discipline in practice. This type of concerted effort requires not only cooperation from staff members but also consistency in their practices.

---

1. Interested readers can read the books by Hui and Ng (2000); Lou et al. (2005); Sin et al. (2003); Wang, (2001); and the National Tai Dong Normal School (2002).

Establishing a school action plan

Designing a school action plan takes time and needs to be prepared well. It aims at changing the misbehaviour of pupils and encouraging certain kinds of appropriate behaviour. (While it includes behaviour which teachers view positively, the focus here is on the issue of misbehaviour.) Albert (1996: 141–148) suggested that there are five major steps to follow:

1. Pinpoint and describe the student's behaviour.
    - Specify three or four examples of misbehaviour which concern teachers most. (Too many specifications will make the plan unworkable.)
    - Observe and gather data that describe the pupil's misbehaviour objectively and systematically.
    - Avoid using subjective terms and support your description with quantitative data.

2. Identify the goal(s) of the misbehaviour.
    - The goal(s) is based on analysis of the objective descriptions of the pupil's misbehaviour.
    - Dreikurs and Cassel's (1972) classification of mistaken purposes for pupil misbehaviour can be helpful.
    - School meetings can be held for this purpose, if necessary.

3. Choose intervention techniques for the misbehaviour.
    - After careful diagnosis and consideration, you can decide on the intervention strategies or plans to encourage positive behaviour.
    - Choose those which make the best sense and are congruent with your personal philosophy and beliefs or the school ethos.
    - The measures or strategies should be practical and easy to implement.

4. Select encouraging techniques to build self-esteem.
    - School action plans should not harm pupils' self-esteem and the overall approach should be positive.
    - Pupils need to feel they are capable and accepted by the school.
    - Interventions must be accompanied by encouragement to ensure the measures taken are effective and constructive in building self-esteem.

5. Involve students, parents, and others as partners.
    - Involve students, parents and others as partners.
    - School action plans are regarded as a kind of cooperative discipline in school.
    - A successful plan provides new ideas and mutual support for all pupils.

The school action plan needs to be reviewed and evaluated from time to time. Unsuccessful strategies should be replaced by more appropriate measures. Overall, the actions planned must be seen as a kind of support and effort to help pupils, not as something negative imposed upon them.

An Alternative: Personal Management Plans

Teachers who are unfamiliar with or prefer not to conduct action research can choose other approaches to improve classroom management practices — such as constructing their own personal management plans.

A personal management plan helps teachers to organize and communicate a disciplinary approach and system that is most effective for them in managing the classroom (Charles, 2005: 273–274). It is about clarifying one's thoughts and philosophy on classroom management and adopting a personal approach to pupil discipline, and it is best to prepare it in written form so that every detail can be examined. Such a plan can also help teachers to communicate their expectations to their pupils and establish effective practices in classroom management.

Establishing personal management plans

Five major steps are suggested by Charles (2005: 288–90) in constructing a personalized discipline system in the classroom:

1. Specify how you will present and conduct yourself in school.
   - Specify the professional, ethical and legal codes or standards that you will follow.

2. Specify the goals and aspirations you have for your students.
   - Specify and explain to your pupils how to conduct themselves in the classroom.
   - Specify your expectations for your pupils when they are attending your lessons and participating in activities.

3. Describe the classroom conditions you want to maintain.
   - Specify and explain the physical, social and psychological conditions that are helpful for improving teaching and learning.

4. Specify how you will work individually or cooperatively with students to help ensure appropriate behaviour.
   - Specify and explain to pupils the atmosphere, routines and expectations that are conducive to individual and group work in lessons.

5. Indicate how you will intervene when misbehaviour occurs or appears imminent.
   - Specify and explain the consequences and interventions when discipline problems occur in the classroom.

A personal management plan is often wrongly perceived as something imposed personally by the teacher on the pupils. It is a formal way of communicating teachers' expectations to the pupils and is successful only when it is seen by them as reasonable and fair. That is why the plan must be thoroughly explained to pupils and get their full consent.

Important questions before developing a personal system of discipline

1. What is the purpose of discipline?
2. What sorts of results do you hope for?
3. What is classroom misbehaviour and why does it require attention?
4. What do you consider to be essential components of a good discipline system?
5. How do those components relate to or influence each other?
6. What makes you believe these components will produce the results you desire?
7. What can teachers do to limit the occurrence of misbehaviour?
8. How can teachers react most effectively when students misbehave?
9. How can teachers help students to actually want to behave more responsibly?

(Charles, 2005: 273–274)

In conclusion, classroom management can be best seen as an ongoing reflective inquiry undertaken by teachers. Teachers have to be critically reflective practitioners to guard against actions and practices that have become routine. They must learn from their own experiences in the classroom to work out effective strategies or plans for influencing pupil behaviour. These techniques of enquiry include action research, personal management plans and school action plans. Teachers can work singly or collaboratively at individual or schools levels. All these practices view classroom management as a change process which begins with self-awareness and self-reflection. Then, teachers go on to define the problem areas or issues and, with a systematic approach to data collection and description, they can work out their action plans and interventions for improvement; and this is followed by evaluation and reflection on the measures taken. This kind of conscious and systematic approach to classroom management also promotes professional development.

Summary

This chapter describes the use of self-reflection and self-awareness to help teachers conduct action research, and develop school action plans and personal management plans as means to effect changes in pupil behaviour. It is argued that classroom management must be seen as an ongoing activity which requires teachers to inquire and reflect continuously on what is happening in school.

The importance of an inquiry classroom is supported by the idea of reflective teaching. Reflective practitioners often ask questions about their own practices and critically assess what they see in the classroom. Reflection is useful for teachers for avoiding routines and reflexive loops. There are three kinds of reflection — technical, practical and critical — and critical reflection aims at understanding social issues and policies affecting classroom practices and making school life a more enjoyable and productive process for all students.

The closely connected concepts of "critical incidents", "reflection" and "action research" are examined. Critical incidents are highly charged moments or events which have very significant consequences for professional development and, as such, they deserve teachers' close attention and analysis. They provide channels for exploring issues in classroom management and clues for improving teaching practices. Conducting action research to explore and solve the problems associated with these incidents is a useful way of understanding what is happening in the classroom. Action researchers are likely to accept change in the light of the data obtained from their inquiries.

The aims and processes of action research, which is conducted by practitioners for improving their own teaching, are explained. Action research is a cyclical process in which teachers plan, take action, observe and evaluate how effective they have been in dealing with problems. It can be done on an individual basis or at a school level. It acknowledges the fact that reflecting on teachers' practical experiences and deciding on actions to solve difficulties are important means for both changing pupils' behaviour and professional development.

School action plans and personal management plans are introduced as alternative approaches. These both emphasize the importance of teachers' and schools' expectations for pupil behaviour. They are often perceived as ways of communicating to enhance teacher-pupil relationships in classroom management. With the support of objective data to define the problem or focus of interventions, constructive and positive measures can then be taken for changing pupils' behaviour.

Questions for Discussion

1. Suggest three action research questions for Ms. Tsang (see classroom scenario) to be included in her action research proposal?

2.   What are the goals in promoting an inquiring classroom?

3.   Distinguish between technical and critical reflection and illustrate this with examples.

4.   Suggest some effective means to help teachers reflect upon their own practices in school. Use practical examples as far as possible.

5.   Who is the best judge of how critical "critical incidents" are? Why is it argued that it is the teacher who construes how critical an incident is, rather than this being determined by the event itself?

6.   Do you think that action research is useful in helping teachers to solve problems and improve their practices? If so, why? If not, why not?

7.   What are the differences between a personal management plan and a school action plan?

Useful Resources

Websites

1.   Inquiry-based Learning: Explanation:
     http://www.thirteen.org/edonline/concept2class/inquiry/

2.   Reflective Teaching Model: http://www.emu.edu/education/model.html

3.   Reflective Teaching: http://www.philseflsupport.com/reflective_teaching.htm

4.   Educating the Reflective Practitioner: http://educ.queensu.ca/~ar/schon87.htm

5.   Action Research Resources: http://www.scu.edu.au/schools/gcm/ar/arhome.html

6.   Bath.ac.uk: http://www.bath.ac.uk/~edsajw/

7.   ARIS: http://ci-lab.ied.edu.hk/aris/

Further Reading

Ashton, P. and Urquhart, C. (1988). *Detrimental effects of mandated models of discipline on the practice of reflective teaching.* Florida. Project Description. ERIC Document Reproduction Service No. ED 307 267.

Cruickshank, D. R., Bainer, D. and Metcalf, K. (1995). *The act of teaching.* New York: McGraw-Hill.

Hopkins, D. (2002). *A teacher's guide to classroom research.* Buckingham, UK, and Bristol, PA: Open University Press.

Hui, L. H. and Ng, Y. M. (2000). *Multiple intelligences in education* (in Chinese). Hong Kong: Galaxy Publisher.

Luo, W., Jiang, P. and Liu, C. H. ((2005). *Case studies of school-based action research* (in Chinese). Beijing: Capital Normal University Press.

Rogers, B. (1989). *Making a discipline plan.* Melbourne: Thomas Nelson.

Sparke, J. and Skoyles, P. (1998). Analysis of critical incidents. *The Cantarnet Journal,* Summer.

References

Argyris, C. (1990). *Overcoming organizational defenses.* Boston: Allyn & Bacon.

Albert, L. (1996). *Cooperative discipline.* Circle Pines, MN: American Guidance Service.

Brookfield, S. D. (1995). *Becoming a critically reflective teacher.* San Francisco: Jossey-Bass.

Bullough, R. V. Jr. and Gitlin, A. D. (1995). *Becoming a student of teaching: Linking knowledge production and practice.* New York: Garland Publishing.

Carr, W. and Kemmis, S. (1986). *Becoming critical.* London: Falmer Press.

Charles, C. M. (2005). *Building classroom discipline* (8th edn). Boston: Pearson.

Cooper, P., Smith, C. and Upton, G. (1994). *Emotional and behavioural difficulties.* London: Routledge.

Cruickshank, D. R. (1987). *Reflective teaching: The preparation of students of teaching.* Reston, VA: Association of Teacher Educators.

Dreikurs, R. and Cassel, P. (1972). *Discipline without tears.* New York: Hawthorn.

Elliott, J. (1991). *Action research for educational change.* Milton Keynes, UK: Open University Press.

Farrington, D. P. (1972). Delinquency begins at home. *New Society,* 21: 495–497.

Galloway, D. and Goodwin, C. (1987). *The education of disturbing children.* Harlow: Longman.

Hopkins, D. (1985). *A teacher's guide to classroom research.* Milton Keynes, UK: Open University Press.

Hui, L.H. and Ng, Y.M. (2000). *Multiple intelligences in education.* Hong Kong: Galaxy Publishers.

Kemmis, S. and McTaggart, R. (eds.) (1988). *The action research planner* (3rd edn). Geelong, Victoria: Deakin University Press.

Larrivee, B. (2006). The convergence of reflective practice and effective classroom management. In Evertson, C.M. and Weinstein, C.S. (eds.) *Handbook of classroom management* (pp. 983–1001). Mahwah, NJ: Lawrence Erlbaum Associates, Publishers.

Lewin, K. (1952). Group decision and social change. In G. E. Swanson, T. M. Newcomb and E. L. Hartley (eds.) *Readings in social psychology.* New York: Holt.

Lou, W., Jiang, P. and Liu, S. H. (2005). *School-based education research.* Beijing: Capital Normal University Press.

Li, W. S. (2003). Understanding action research. In O. S. Leung (ed.), *Conference proceedings of reform and initiatives in teaching and learning.* Macau: University of Macau.

McCaleb, J., Borko, H. and Arends, R. (1992). Reflection, research, and repertoire in the Master's Certification Program at the University of Maryland. In L. Valli (ed.), *Reflective teacher education.* New York: State University of New York Press.

Measor, L. (1985). Critical incidents in the classroom: Identities, choices and careers. In S. J. Ball and I. F. Goodson (eds.), *Teachers' lives and careers.* London: The Falmer Press.

National Tai Dong Normal School (ed.) (2002). *Education action research and innovation in teaching* (in Chinese). Taipei: Yangzhi.

Noffke, S. (1997). Professional, personal, and political dimensions of action research. *Review of Research in Education,* 22, 305–343.

Peppard, J. (1997). *A guide to connected curriculum and action research.* Madison, WI: Wisconsin Department of Public Instruction.

Rutter, M. (1975). *Helping troubled children.* Harmondsworth: Penguin.

Rutter, M., Maugham, B., Mortimore, P. and Ouston, J. (1979). *Fifteen thousand hours.* London: Open Books.

Schôn, D. A. (ed).(1991). *Reflective turn: Case studies in and on education research.* New York: Teachers College Press.

Sikes, P. J., Measor, L. and Woods, P. (1985). *Teacher careers: Crises and continuities.* London: Croom Helm.

Sin, K. F., Ho, F. C. and Hui, L. H. (eds.) (2003). *Information technology in special education: Action research.* Hong Kong: The Hong Kong Institute of Education.

Sparks-Langer, G. and Colton, A. (1991). Synthesis of research on teachers' reflective teaching. *Educational Leadership,* 48(6), 37–44.

Stenhouse, L. (1975). *An introduction to curriculum research and development.* London: Heinemann.

Stevenson, C. (1986). *Teachers as inquirers: Strategies for learning with and about early adolescents.* Columbus, OH: National Middle School Association.

Tripp, D. (1993). *Critical incidents in teaching.* London: Routledge.

Van Manen, J. (1977). Linking ways of knowing with ways of being practical. *Curriculum Inquiry,* 6, 205–208.

Wang, J. J. (ed.) (2001). *Innovative action research in education.* Tianjin: Tianjin People's Publisher.

Woods, P. (1993). Critical events in education. *British Journal of Sociology of Education,* 14(4), 355–371.

Zeichner, K. (1983). Alternative paradigms of teacher education. *Journal of Teacher Education,* 34(4), 3–9.

Index

Authors

Albert, L., 106, 194–195
Alley, R. D., 117, 120
American Federation of Teacher, 45, 56
Ames, C., 5
Anderson-Levine, K. M., 106
Arends, R., 187
Argyris, C., 189
Asher, S. R., 131, 134
Ashton, P., 199
Axworthy, D., 149, 153

Bainer, D., 199
Baker, K., 60
Baloche, L. A., 131, 142–143
Bandura, A., 72, 123
Bennett, B. J., 86
Boesser, C., 121–122
Bond, M. H., 31–35
Bonds, M., 134
Borko, H., 187
Bredekamp, S., 49
Brookfield, S. D., 190
Brooks, D., 127
Brophy, J., 3, 51, 53–55, 60, 65, 70, 106
Brophy, J. E., 137
Brown, S., 149
Bullough, R. V. Jr., 187
Burman, E., 99
Butler, L., 135

Campbell, J., 3
Canter, L., 76, 85–86, 88, 97, 105
Canter, M., 76, 85–86, 88, 97, 105
Carkhuff, R. R., 127
Carr, W., 188
Cassel, P., 87, 195
Charles, C. M., 48–50, 66, 98, 111, 116, 170, 196–197
Charles, M. G., 170
Chu, R. L., 35
Clarizio, H. F., 57
Clarke, D., 152
Colton, A., 188
Conger, J. J., 132, 135
Connolly, T., 123–124
Cooper, P., 127, 184
Corrie, L., 5
Cowie, H., 142, 146
Criste, A., 123–124
Cruikshank, D. R., 187, 199
Curwin, R. L., 57

Docking, J., 57–58, 63
Dolye, W., 12, 65, 106
Dowd, T., 123–124
Dreikurs, R., 78, 85, 87, 100–101, 105, 119, 195

Education Convergence, 86
Edwards, C. H., 124
Eggen, P., 52

Elias, M. J., 137, 142
Elliott, J., 187
Elton Report, 154
Epstein, J., 165, 167, 171
Evans, G., 48
Evertson, C. M., 65

Farrington, D. P., 184
Fields, M. V., 121–122
Finlay-Jones, R., 149
Forisha, B. F., 106
Fullan, M., 154

Gabrenya, W. K., 32
Galloway, D., 184
Gareau, M., 53
Geiger, K. M., 12
Gillborn, D., 5
Ginott, H., 116
Gitlin, A. D., 187
Glasser, W., 50, 58, 76, 88
Glickman, C. D., 86–88, 90, 92, 105
Goleman, D., 137
Gonzalo, G., 87
Good, T., 3, 55
Good, T. L., 137
Goodwin, C., 184
Gordon, T., 48, 60, 74, 87–88, 94–96, 105, 113–116, 118, 121, 126
Gower, R., 73, 82
Graczyk, P. A., 137
Green, D., 60
Greenberg, M., 141
Greenberg, M. T., 137
Grossman, H., 56
Grunwald, B., 78, 100–101, 119
Gunter, P. L., 123

Hallahan, D.P., 131, 176–177, 179
Hamblin, D., 12
Hamilton, P., 149, 153
Hargreaves, A., 154
Hargreaves, D. H., 12
Henson, K. T., 117, 120

Ho, D. Y. F., 33–34
Ho, F. C., 194
Ho, I. T., 31
Hoffman, N., 73
Hofstede, G., 31
Hoover, R. L., 65
Hopkins, D., 191, 199
Hsu, F. L. K., 31
Hu, H. C., 34–35
Huang, G., 127
Hue, M. T., 3, 23–24, 28–30, 33, 36–37, 40, 133, 143
Hui, L. H., 194, 199
Huston, A. C., 132, 135
Hwang, K. K., 31–32, 34–35
Hymel, S., 134–135

Ip, K. C., 31–32
Irvin, J. L., 86

Jack, S. L., 123
Jacobson, L., 51
Jiang, P., 194, 199
Johns, F. A., 86–88, 100–101, 103, 105
Johnson, D., 139–140
Johnson, R., 139–140
Jones, L.S., 3, 55, 57, 81, 123, 173, 179
Jones, V., 3
Jones, V. F., 49, 55, 57, 81, 111, 123, 173, 179

Kagan, J., 132, 135
Kauchak, D., 52
Kauffman, J. M., 131, 176–177, 179
Kemmis, S., 188, 192
Kennedy, C., 53
Kerr, M. M., 72
Kindsvatter, R., 60, 65
King, A. Y. C., 31
Knoff, 138
Kohn, A., 57, 65, 77, 106
Kottler, E., 127
Kottler, J. A., 127
Kounin, J., 88–89
Kusche, C., 141

Larrivee, B., 78, 112, 115, 117, 189
Lasley, T. J., 66
LeCompte, M., 81
Lee, P. W. H., 32
Leiberman, M., 154
Lepper, M., 60
Levin, J., 18, 53–54, 57, 60, 66, 70, 72–74
Lewin, K., 12, 192
Lewis, C., 127
Lewis, R., 85, 91–92, 94, 96, 97–99, 105–106
Li, W. S., 191
Liu, S. H., 194, 199
Lord, E. M., 31
Lou, W., 194, 199
Lovegrove, M. N., 99
Lovell, B., 48

MacNaughton, R. H., 86–88, 100–101, 103, 105
Marabinus, N. G., 86–88, 100–101, 103, 105
Matjasko, J. L., 137
Maugham, B., 184
McCaleb, J., 187
McCaslin, M., 3
McCord, J., 81
McEwan, B., 52, 65
McHale, 163
McTaggart, R., 192
Measor, L., 190
Melloy, K. J., 70
Mendler, A. N., 57
Metcalf, K., 199
Milhollan, F., 106
Moles, O. C., 82
Mortimore, P., 184
Mostert, M. P., 131, 176–177, 179
Mussen, P. H., 132, 135

National Tai Dong Normal School, 194
Nelson, C., 123–124
Nelson, C. M., 72
Ng, Y. M., 194, 199
Nichols, P., 123
Nixon, J., 5

Noffke, S., 191
Nolan, J. F., 18, 53–54, 57, 66, 70, 72, 74

Olney, H., 149, 153
Olweus, D., 134
Ouston, J., 184

Packard, N., 161
Parker, J. G., 131
Peppard, J., 191
Pepper, F., 78, 100–101, 119
Pruett, M. K., 137
Putnam, J. W., 142

Race, R., 161
Raffini, J. P., 82
Redl, F., 70, 82
Renshaw, P., 134
Rinne, C., 73, 82
Ritzer, G., 6
Rogers, B., 149, 152, 156–157, 163, 199
Rogers, C., 109, 113, 118–119, 126–127
Rogers, F. R., 113
Rohrkemper, M. M., 106
Rosenholtz, 157
Rosenshine, B., 50
Rosenthal, R., 51
Rudduck, J., 5, 154
Rutter, M., 184

Sanders, M., 167
Saphier, J., 73, 82
Schaps, E., 127
Schmuck, P. A., 88
Schmuck, R. A., 88
Schon, D. A., 187
Selman, R. L., 131
Senter, G. W., 48–49, 111
Shanken-Kaye, J., 60
Shores, R. E., 123
Sikes, P. J., 190
Simonds, C. J., 127
Sin, K. F., 194
Skinner, B. F., 106

Skoyles, P., 199
Slavin, R. E., 142
Smith, C., 184
Solomon, R. H., 32
Sparke, J., 199
Sparks-Langer, G., 188
Stage, S. A., 160
Steinberg, Z., 123
Stenhouse, L., 187, 191
Stevens, R., 50
Stevenson, C., 183, 186
Stipek, D. J., 61
Stoker, S., 134
Stover, L. E., 34

Tauber, R. T., 85
Tobias, L., 123–124
Trent, S. C., 131, 176–177, 179
Tripp, D., 186, 190
Tsui, A. B. M., 50
Turiel, E., 12

Upton, G., 184
Urquhart, C., 199

Van Manan, J., 188
Vitto, J. M., 134, 137, 141

Wagner, E., 135
Wagner, P., 9, 12, 154
Wallace, P., 142, 146
Wang, J. J., 194
Waterhouse, P., 47
Watkins, C., 9, 12–13, 154
Watrous, B. G., 31
Watson, M., 127
Weber, W. A., 88–90, 105
Weinstein, C. S., 52
Weissberg, R. P., 137
Williams, P. A., 117, 120
Wilson, R. W., 32–34
Wineman, D., 70, 82
Wolfgang, C. H., 86–88, 90, 92, 105
Woods, P., 190

Woolfolk, A., 127
Wright, A. F., 31

Yang, K. S., 31, 33
Yu, A. B., 32
Yuan, G., 32

Zeichner, K., 187
Zins, J. E., 137
Zirpoli, T. J., 70

Subjects

action research, 183–187, 190–192, 194, 196–199
active listening, 27, 94, 96, 109–110, 113, 121–122, 133, 138, 142, 157, 177–179
administrator-oriented approach, 87
advising, 113, 115
alternatives to punishment, 57
appropriate responses, 102
arbitrary consequences, 77–78, 80
asking questions, 73, 93, 99–101, 103
assertive teacher, 97–98
Assertiveness Model, 85, 97, 105
attention-seeking, 86, 100, 102–105
authoritarian approach, 58
authoritarian design, 58, 89–90
autobiography, 190

barriers to communication, 109–110, 112–113, 126
behaviour management design, 88
behaviour modification, 90, 172
behavioural problems, 63–66, 79–80, 99, 171, 176
behaviourist theory, 70
bingo, 144
body language, 10, 70, 120
boosting interest, 72
boss teacher, 58–60
broken record, 76
bullying, 56, 101, 131, 134, 179

calling on students, 72–73
childhood socialization, 21, 29, 33, 35, 40–41
classroom atmosphere, 64, 72
classroom behaviour, 1–2, 4–6, 9–10, 12, 16–17, 21, 28–29, 45, 57, 59, 65, 106, 123, 137, 149–150, 152–155, 157, 161–163, 167, 171–172, 174–176, 180
classroom environment, 3, 39, 46–47, 52, 58, 97, 165, 186, 189
classroom experience, 8–9, 150, 155–156, 183
classroom guidelines, 52
classroom isolation, 149, 154–156, 162
classroom management, 1–7, 10, 16–17, 21, 23–24, 28–30, 33, 36, 38, 41, 45–48, 50, 52–53, 58–59, 64–67, 79–80, 85–86, 88–89, 93–94, 105–106, 132, 138, 141, 145, 149, 151–153, 155, 158, 162, 167, 173, 183–188, 191, 194, 196–198
classroom manager, 21, 45, 58, 185–187
classroom procedures, 45–47, 52–54, 59
classroom rules, 10–11, 30, 37, 40, 45–46, 53–56, 58, 75, 100, 152–154, 159, 175
classroom rules and routines, 45
classroom scenario, 2, 6, 11, 13, 15, 22, 33, 46, 65, 87, 111, 130, 134, 151, 159, 166, 185, 198
classroom situations, 1, 9–11, 17, 25, 65, 87, 155, 162, 190
collectivism, 21, 29, 31–33, 35, 40
collegial collaboration, 149–150, 153, 155–156, 160, 162
commonsense models, 85, 87
communicating classroom rules, 55
communication, 68, 94–95, 98, 102, 109–116, 118–126, 137–138, 142, 155, 165, 168–170, 173, 176, 178, 180, 192
complementary roles, 26
conflict-resolution skills, 129, 137, 139
conformity, 21, 23, 29, 31–35, 37, 40
confronting message, 114, 116
Confucianism, 21–25, 27–30, 35, 37, 40, 41
congruent communication, 114, 116
constructing I-messages, 117
continuum of intervention strategies, 64–65

continuum of strategies, 64, 67, 80, 90
cookbook approach, 89–90
cookbook guide, 68
corporal punishment, 57, 77, 81
countertop space, 48–49
critical incidents, 184–185, 190, 198–199
criticizing, 112–116
culture, 3, 7, 21–22, 25, 29, 35, 40, 79, 129–130, 133–134, 142–143, 145, 150–151, 153–156, 162, 167, 169, 177, 180

Daoism, 23, 25–26, 28, 30, 37–38, 40–41
direct appeal, 74
directive statements, 90, 96
discipline, 1–5, 13, 16, 29, 33–35, 37, 45, 47, 54–57, 59, 65, 67, 71, 73, 85–88, 91–94, 97–101, 105, 110, 138, 145, 149–152, 154, 160–161, 177, 180, 184–186, 188, 192, 194–197
discipline problem, 2–3, 54–56, 65, 67, 87, 93–94, 154, 161, 185–186, 188, 197
disrespect, 112
disruptive behaviour, 49, 54, 69–70, 72–74, 86, 130, 150, 153, 156, 160, 180
diversity, 28, 51, 167–169, 180
door-openers, 120

effective instruction, 50, 52, 58–59, 97
empathy, 27–28, 30, 37, 39, 109, 112–113, 121, 124, 133–134, 137, 140, 142, 144, 155, 172

fa, 24, 25, 30
face, 10, 14, 21, 29, 34–35, 40, 73, 77, 156
facets of the physical environment, 48
floor space, 48
friendship, 129, 131–132, 137–138, 140, 142–143, 145

general ambience, 48–49
good listener, 102, 110, 119–122, 126, 159
Gordon's principles, 94
group-oriented approach, 85, 87, 92, 99, 103, 105

group-orientedness, 32
group process, 88–89

harmony, 27, 32
helplessness/inadequacy, 100–105, 115
hierarchical relationship, 29, 31
hostile teacher, 98
humour, 68, 72–73, 124

I-message, 74, 94, 96, 105, 109–110, 114, 116–118, 126
inappropriate responses, 102
individual differences, 26, 28, 133
in-group members, 132
inquiry, 183, 186–187, 191, 197–199
instructional approach, 89
interactionism, 6–7
interactive journal, 190
interrogating, 109, 114–115
intervention, 56, 59–60, 63–74, 76–81, 90, 102, 133, 135, 192–195, 197–198
intervention strategies, 63–68, 79–81, 194–195
interventionists, 85–86
intimidation, 58, 89–90, 134
intimidation approach, 89–90
inviting communication, 109, 111, 114, 116, 125–126

labelling, 109
lead teacher, 58–60
learning in group, 142
least disruptive strategies, 63
legalism, 21–25, 28, 30, 40–41
lesson planning and design, 45
Lewis's Framework, 85, 91, 94, 97, 99, 105
li, 27–28, 31–32
logical consequence, 54, 56–57, 63–64, 67–68, 72, 75–81, 104

mianzi, 34–35
misbehaviour, 2, 4–5, 14, 16–17, 31–32, 36, 38, 40, 46, 52, 56–57, 63–69, 75, 77–81, 85–86, 91–92, 95, 98, 100–106, 110, 112–113, 116, 133, 150, 153, 159, 162, 167, 177, 180, 184–187, 192, 194–195, 197

model of control/teacher-oriented approach, 87, 91, 92, 97, 105
model of influence/student-oriented approach, 87, 91–92, 94–96, 100, 105
model of management/group-oriented, 85, 87, 91, 92, 99, 103, 105
motivation, 3–5, 24, 51, 103, 119, 143

natural consequences, 78, 104
needs of students, 50
non-assertive teacher, 98
non-directive statements, 90, 96
non-interference, 63, 68
non-interventionist, 86, 90, 92, 94
non-verbal communication, 111
non-verbal coping skills, 71
non-verbal intervention, 63, 67–68, 70–71, 77, 79–80

open and democratic approach, 58
orders, 24, 47, 74, 98, 110, 112–114

parent-teacher meetings, 177
partnership, 165–170, 180
peer influence, 130, 132
peer mediation, 140
peer observation, 190
peer relationships, 129–134, 137–138, 140–141, 143–145
perfect gentlemen, 28, 30
permissive appproach, 89–90
personal action plans, 183
personal management plans, 183–185, 196–198
personal plan, 63–67, 79–80
physical environment, 45, 47–49, 59
physical intervention and isolation, 90
planned ignoring, 68, 70, 80
positive phrasing, 75
power-seeking, 100–105
praise, 37, 46, 56–60, 104, 114, 119, 178
praising peers, 72
preaching, 109, 113–116
preventive measures, 65
proactive measures, 67

problem-solving skills, 129, 137–138, 140, 144, 158–159
process of action research, 192–193
proximity control, 70, 80
punishment, 3, 5, 9, 24–27, 30, 33, 36–37, 40, 45–46, 56–60, 64, 67, 77–81, 89, 92, 94, 114

questioning, 73, 113, 184,186–189, 191

recognition reflex, 103
referral, 138, 150, 153, 160–162
reflection, 2, 5, 22, 46, 49, 64, 69, 86, 91, 110, 119, 122, 130, 135–137, 143, 145, 150, 153, 156, 166, 183–185, 187–193, 197–199
reflective journal, 189–190
reflective practitioners, 183–184, 186–187, 197, 198
reflective teaching, 187, 198
reflexive loops, 189, 198
reinforcement, 25, 70, 89–90, 139, 178
reliable alliances, 156–157
ren, 27–28, 30–32
ren-yi-li systems, 32
reprimands, 64
revenge, 9, 100–105
reward, 24–26, 30, 36–37, 45–46, 49, 57, 89, 92, 94, 99
roadblocks to communication, 110, 113, 115
Rogerian theories, 94
routines, 10–11, 45, 52–54, 56, 59, 69, 75, 185, 189, 196, 198

school action plans, 183–184, 191, 194–195, 197–198
seating arrangement, 45, 48–50, 59
self-awareness, 137, 197–198
self-discipline, 4, 65, 77, 93, 98, 104, 119
self-esteem, 3, 5, 39, 57, 114–116, 123, 195
self-instructional approach, 141
self-reflection, 187, 189, 197–198
shelf, 48–49
shi, 24–25, 30
shu, 24–25, 30

signal interference, 70, 80
social abilities, 133
social behaviour, 13, 22, 27–29, 31–32, 34, 40, 160
Social Discipline Model, 85, 87, 100, 105
social selves, 32, 141
social-emotional skills, 129, 135, 137–138, 144–145
socially isolated, 135, 144
socio-emotional approach, 88
stereotyping, 114–115
student learning journal, 190
student-centred teaching approach, 58
student-oriented approach, 85, 87, 91–92, 94–96, 100, 105
student-owned problems, 95

Taijitu, 38
teacher authority, 58, 59
Teacher Behaviour Continuum, 90, 105
Teacher Effectiveness Training, 85, 87, 94, 105, 114
teacher inquiry, 183
teacher takes charge, 86
teacher-oriented approach, 85, 87, 91–92, 97, 99, 105
teacher-owned problems, 96
teacher-parent collaboration, 165, 167, 170–171, 180
teacher-pupil relationship, 73, 79, 109–110, 118, 122–127, 198
teachers' attitudes, 123–124
teaching log, 190
technical reflection, 183, 188, 198
techniques for listening, 120
ten important questions, 1–2, 13, 17, 135–136
The Stop and Think Social Skills, 138
theoretically-based models, 85, 87, 88, 105
tolerating, 11, 56, 67–69
touch interference, 68, 70–71, 80

verbal exchange, 111
verbal interference, 68
verbal intervention, 63–64, 67–74, 76–77, 80

wall, 48–49
warning, 7, 8, 11, 110, 113–115
Weber's classification, 88–90, 105
Whole-School Policy, 149, 151–153, 161
wu lun, 31–32
wu wei, 26–27

yang, 21, 24–26, 36–41
yi, 27–28, 31–32
yin, 21, 24–26, 36–41
yin-yang symbol, 38
You-language, 112